THE NEW EQUINE SPORTS THERAPY

.... BY ....

MIMI PORTER

.... FOREWORD BY ....

TRACY A. TURNER, DVM

The Blood-Horse, Inc. Lexington, KY

ISBN 1-58150-015-7

Printed in Canada

First Edition: December 1998

1 2 3 4 5 6 7 8 9 10

Other titles offered by
The Horse Health Care Library

Understanding EPM

Understanding Equine First Aid

Understanding The Equine Foot

Understanding Equine Lameness

Understanding Equine Nutrition

Understanding Laminitis

CONTENTS

THE PAST 20 years have seen amazing advances by human athletes. World records fall routinely. In the summer of 1998, not one but two men are shattering the home run record held for 37 years. How can this be? Sure, better nutrition, more scientific training, but just as importantly, these athletes are staying healthier, avoiding injury, and continuing to compete at their highest capacity. It is not unusual for each of these athletes to have their own personal therapists using the latest physical therapy techniques to keep these athletes competing.

The equine athlete is unrivaled in its speed, grace, agility, and competitive spirit. Just like the human athlete, the horse strives to excel. Over the past 20 years, veterinary knowledge has grown exponentially. With this growth, our ability to diagnose and treat injury has also grown. Diagnostic techniques such as digital radiography, computed tomography, ultrasonography, thermography, scintigraphy, and magnetic resonance imaging have each enhanced our ability to detect injury. There are a myriad of new drugs on the market to help treat the injured athlete. But there is one area where we have sorely lagged behind: physical therapy.

Most veterinarians would agree that the ability to prevent injury is much more important than the ability to treat an injury. Only in the past few years has this subject really been addressed in the veterinary field. Trainers have certainly recognized the importance of early detection of injuries and the application of an appropriate therapy. One only has to pick up any horse magazine to find advertisements for neutraceuticals, gizmos, and gadgets each claiming to keep the equine athlete in top condition and prevent injuries from occurring. There is so much information that it is difficult to separate the wheat from the chaff.

In *The New Equine Sports Therapy*, Mimi Porter has used her vast experience and expertise in physical therapy to write an excellent text that discusses the scientific and empirical knowledge that has been amassed to produce an easy to read and very informative book on physical therapy of the horse. The book begins with a review of the principles of equine physical therapy, then delves into each of the major therapeutic modalities. Chapters cover therapeutic electrical stimulation, therapeutic ultrasound, therapeutic laser, magnetic field therapy, heat therapy, cold therapy, massage, trigger point therapy, joint mobilization, acupressure, chiropractic manipulation, and finally stretching. Each chapter discusses the theories behind the modalities, the scientific basis of the modalities, uses of these techniques as well as contraindications. You will find the text fascinating and simply a must read for any horse professional.

Tracy A. Turner, DVM, MS
Diplomate, American College
of Veterinary Surgeons

An Introduction to Equine Therapy

As one part of the body suffers, all members suffer with it...Jesus

EQUINE THERAPY has gained a place of respect in the management of horse injuries over the past decade. As we move into the 21st Century, a medical philosophy based on advice from Hippocrates, a physician who lived in 400 BC, is blossoming. "Honor the healing power of nature," is one of his credos, although he is known best for his admonition to doctors: "First, do no harm." Equine therapy tools, which stimulate the natural healing power of cells in the body, give the veterinarian or horseman a simple, effective, non-pharmacological medical alternative.

Applying the concept of human sports medicine techniques to horses has many benefits. As with humans, externally applied energy can affect tissue metabolic repair, circulation, and pain response in horses. Ultrasound machines, electrical stimulation units, and magnets have been designed specifically for equines, and horsemen have a variety of treatment choices. As this type of therapy has become more prevalent at

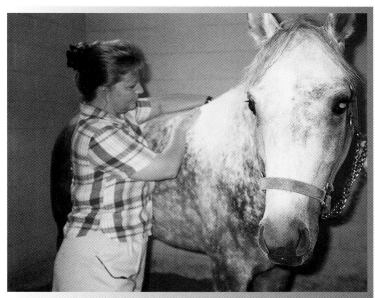

The flexible athlete is less injury prone and more likely to perform optimally than the inflexible one.

barns and racetracks, its acceptance has grown.

Numerous studies using horses support the benefits of equine therapy. The awareness of these benefits among veterinary practitioners, however, remains relatively low.

In a recent study, 150 veterinary surgeons in the United Kingdom were asked about animal physiotherapy. Of those replying, only 37% said they knew this type of therapy existed. The respondents indicated that they thought it would be useful to learn more about animal physiotherapy and that they considered a liaison between physiotherapists and veterinary surgeons important. The veterinarians, however, expressed

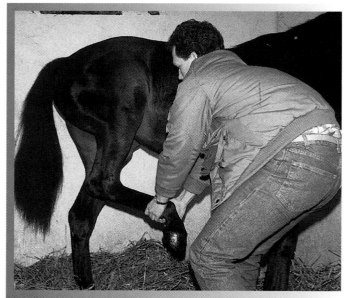

Equine therapy is based on the principles of athletic training and physical therapy as it applies to sports injuries.

concern about physiotherapists who diagnose and treat animals without referrals from veterinarians; some of them said they were reluctant to embrace the field because they had been called in only after a failed course of physiotherapy based on an incorrect diagnosis. There was some concern that "non-professional specialists" were treating animals without knowledge of the full con-

dition. Physiotherapy is often used as a last resort in the United Kingdom, as it often is here in the United States. This is an unfortunate misuse of this professional approach.(1)

Equine therapy is a wide open field for research and development of practice standards. In general, veterinarians are interested in learning more about it, and horse owners certainly have shown an interest.

The equine therapist has many tools and techniques to help ease pain and improve function. These include photon therapy (also called laser therapy), magnetic therapy, electrical stimulation, ultrasound, ice, heat, compression, massage, acupressure, stretching, and controlled exercise. This book will discuss each in terms of physiological effects and treatment techniques. The modalities are described separately here, but they are not often used that way.

Defining Equine Therapy

Equine therapy has been defined by the American Association of Equine Practitioners as the use of non-invasive techniques for the rehabilitation of injuries. The work must be performed in accordance with the state practice acts under the referral of a veterinarian following a veterinary diagnosis. At the time of this writing, there are no degree programs in this area. But brgeoning interest in equine therapy makes it important to establish the boundaries in which the therapist works.

Equine therapy is based on the principles of athletic training and physical therapy as it applies to sports injuries. These sports medicine specialties involve the treatment of diseases and physical injuries using hands-on, or physical, techniques rather than drugs. The Latin "physica" refers to a knowledge of nature or of the natural. As our understanding of the electrical and magnetic fields of the body increases, we realize how appropriate this term is for the application of the equine therapist's tools.

It has been recognized for some time that the word "healing" stands for a process that is prompted by our internal electrical system. Electrical current applied externally encourages skin wounds and bone fractures to heal. These currents, magnetic fields, and light energy can be used to increase blood flow to an injured area, increasing the supply of nutrients and removing the debris accumulated from the injury. Photon stimulation or even finger pressure to acupuncture points will produce measurable changes in the patient's electromagnetic field. That electromagnetic field is the communication medium through which adaptation signals are sent from cell to cell. Cell resonance (vibration of molecules) in specific tissues is affected by vibrations from light therapy, thus affecting their function. Externally applying an electrical or magnetic field can reduce pain perception dramatically. Reducing pain aids the immune system, thus improving the healing potential.

Goals of Equine Therapy

The equine therapist is part of a health care team that includes the horse's trainer, the veterinarian, and the therapist. The trainer works to avoid injury through careful planning of the exercise regimen and appropriate increases in training. The veterinarian evaluates an injury and makes a diagnosis. He or she formulates the plan for recuperation, prescribes medications, and oversees the post-injury care. The equine therapist uses skills and training to aid the horse in the return to full function.

The therapist must set goals and apply tools and techniques to achieve them. The primary goal often is to reduce pain. Another goal is to help the horse regain full joint range of motion of the injured part and to restore or enhance strength to the area. The therapist should be able to communicate to the trainer and the veterinarian what he or she plans to accomplish with treatment. The therapist also can be helpful in formulating a plan, along with the trainer and the veterinarian, to avoid reinjury.

The goals of equine therapy include:
- Reduce pain.
- Regain range of motion in injured part.
- Regain strength.
- Regain full functionality.
- Avoid reinjury.

It is a mistake to make speed of recovery a goal in equine therapy treatments. Although the therapy can eliminate or reduce pain and chase away edema quickly, it is important to allow time for tissue remodeling and maturation. Do not assume that when injury symptoms are gone high-intensity training can resume.

For an example of the value of patience and good care, I'll relate a story of a magnificent race filly with which I had the pleasure to work. Although the filly showed no signs of lameness and was training brilliantly, the trainer observed a subtle change in her walk. Diagnostic ultrasound revealed a small tear proximally in her suspensory ligament. There were no visible or palpable symptoms of swelling and heat. With important races coming up in the spring, a less careful trainer might have continued with her training until the injury symptoms were undeniable. This filly received eight weeks of hand walking, along with ultrasound and photon therapy treatments. She then had an additional five months walking under tack, jogging, and trail riding. Throughout her recovery, regular diagnostic ultrasound exams were done to assess the extent of repair. She enjoyed a full recovery, with no recurrence of injury. She went on to compete in a full year of grade III competition, winning or placing second in every race. It took a bout of pneumonia to slow her down. Giving her the proper care and adequate recovery time made the difference between possible breakdown and a full season of successful competition.

Effects of Equine Therapy

Equine therapy tools often are referred to as modalities. They are used to affect one or more of four target systems:
- the nerve network
- the lymphatic system
- the blood circulatory system
- the inter and intra cell messenger system

Injury results in an imbalance in one or more of these systems. Equine therapy aims to correct the imbalance as rapidly as possible so the horse can get back to normal activities sooner and without pain.

Principles of Equine Therapy

If equine therapy treatments are to be successful, certain physical principles or laws must be observed. The following concepts should be kept in mind when applying equine therapy.

Equine therapy is the application of energy. This energy must reach the target tissue and be absorbed there to trigger a response. Many of the topical medications we apply to horses are absorbed in the hair coat or in the first few millimeters (mm) of skin. Blistering agents cause damage to the outer dermal layer with no direct effect on the supportive structures below the skin —the ligaments, tendons, nerves, and muscles that suffer injury.

Getting to the target tissue involves selecting the correct tool. Consider the difference in depth of penetration and absorption of a heating pad and a therapeutic ultrasound. The heating pad emits infrared energy and is capable of increasing tissue temperature in the top 3 mm of tissue. This would include the outer dermal layers of skin and the capillaries and nerves there. Vasodilation, a reaction to heating, will carry the effects a bit deeper, perhaps into the sub-dermal connective tissue. Ultrasound has penetration depths of 4 to 6 centimeters (cm). (2) This places the ultrasound energy well into muscle, blood, and nerve tissue, even to the depth of bone. The physiologic effects of ultrasound will be available to tissues that lie deeper than those reached with a heating pad.

Equine therapy should be applied as soon after the injury or surgery as possible. The benefits of cold and compression applied immediately after injury are well known. Cold decreases blood flow and tissue metabolism, thus decreasing bleeding and acute inflammation. The application of cold elevates the pain threshold, making the early stages of recovery more comfortable. Photon therapy, electricity, and pulsed ultrasound can be applied within hours of injury. Magnetic fields can be applied as soon as the inflammatory phase is over. Equine therapists often see a case for the first time weeks or even months after the injury first was noticed. Therapy will still help, but treatment will take more time than if it had been started earlier.

Using the correct dosage is also important to success, as stated in the next law: Too low a dose causes no effect, too high a dose causes damage, the correct dose causes the desired effect. For example, ultrasound given at the correct dose stimulates osmotic changes across cell membranes; at high doses it can cause cell destruction. Electrical stimulation at correct doses is comfortable and relieves pain; at high doses it can be uncomfortable. Similarly, massage can be soothing and relaxing, but given too aggressively, it can cause muscle spasm or cell damage.

A principle of equine therapy that will be repeated throughout this book is that it must follow a complete veterinary evaluation. Veterinarians are the only equine health care personnel trained and empowered to diagnose injury. Diagnostic tools from acupuncture diagnosis to xerography were developed to identify the location and extent of injury. Close cooperation with the attending veterinarian will give the therapist valuable information and help the horse.

A final principle of equine therapy is that it makes constant use of specialized points on the body called trigger points. These points are similar in structure and location to acupuncture points, although there is disagreement in the scientific literature as to whether they are the same in all cases. (3) The trigger points, which have been identified by physical therapists since the early 1940s, are local spots of tenderness that can cause a twitch response when stimulated. They consist of motor points, superficial nerves, the muscle spindle, the muscle-tendon junction, and the Golgi tendon organ. You might have felt a trigger point when someone has clapped you on the shoulder, accidentally pressing a point in the trapezius muscle.

When these points are stimulated — it can be done with finger pressure, photon therapy, ice, electricity, magnets, or ultrasound — the nerve arrangement beneath the skin is irritated. Elimination of these sites will relieve pain and elevate endorphin levels in the blood. When a trigger point is active, it is producing a continuous low level of noxious input into the central nervous system.

Deactivating the points eliminates a source of pain. Finding these points and stimulating them is central to equine therapy treatments. All the techniques mentioned are considered non-invasive and are accepted equine therapy techniques. The use of non-invasive techniques would preclude the use of ingested or injected drugs, as well as the use of needles to stimulate acupuncture points or surgery of any type. The equine therapist is not responsible for making a diagnosis or suggesting medications.

Chiropractic

The practice of chiropractic technique falls outside the scope of the equine therapist as well. Chiropractic manipulations of the spine and other joints are gaining increased attention in both human and equine injury care. In human physical therapy, many have become skilled in joint manipulations. Human physical therapists work under the direct supervision of physicians, but equine therapists often do not have the benefit of such guidance from veterinarians. Joint manipulations for the horse, beyond the normal range of movement, should be left to the veterinarian who has been certified by the appropriate association for veterinary chiropractic. Manipulative treatments for the horse fall within the realm of veterinary medicine, rather than equine therapy, because of the need for a complete diagnosis and qualified selection of cases.

Before manipulation, it is imperative to know that the procedure is safe and valuable. The veterinarian is the only one qualified to use the diagnostic tools necessary to make such a decision. The equine therapist should endeavor to understand the potential value and danger of joint manipulations to help the horseman make a sound choice among the growing list of therapeutic options. Equine therapy techniques applied before chiropractic can make the manipulations easier to accomplish by rendering the fascia and connective tissue more mobile and elastic.

When equine therapy is applied after chiropractic manipulations, the effects of the manipulation will last longer. Muscle spasm and contracture are relaxed so the "adjustment" will be maintained. Many chiropractors advocate the use of therapeutic modalities to supplement manipulation. Local heat will enhance the muscle relaxation necessary for successful adjustment. After manipulation, stretching exercises or electrical stimulation may be used to prolong the effects.

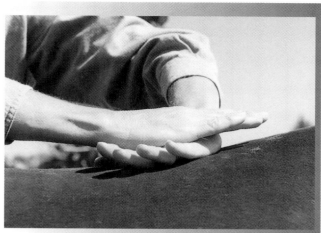

Chiropractic treatments fall within the realm of veterinary medicine.

Acupuncture

The use of needles to stimulate acupuncture points is considered outside the realm of the equine therapist because the needles penetrate the skin. The International Veterinary Acupuncture Society offers training and certification to veterinarians. Only those who have graduated from both veterinary and acupuncture schools are recognized as qualified to practice needle acupuncture on horses.

Acupuncture points, however, can be effectively stimulated with finger pressure or any of the tools of the equine therapist. Electrical stimulation and photon therapy have been found to be effective in stimulating the points to prolong the effects of needle acupuncture treatment. Magnetic beads can be taped on active points to treat pain.

Medications

Recommending or administering medications is considered the practice of veterinary medicine. This has come to include the

Acupuncture should be practiced only by veterinarians certified in the specialty.

use of herbs and homeopathic remedies, according to the American Association of Equine Practitioners' guidelines. The equine therapist can contribute much to the care of the horse by understanding the proper use and effects of medications and remedies but cannot prescribe or administer them.

Equine therapy techniques can be used in a complementary or adjunctive manner with many veterinary procedures. Physical therapy techniques have long been recognized as vital in the rapid recovery from a surgical procedure. Pain relief and accelerated wound closure are expected outcomes of physical therapy. Research in the field of human medicine has shown that post-surgical hospitalization is shortened and the return to full function is more rapid when therapy techniques are used.

Equine therapy has much to offer to extend the effects of veterinary treatments. Any horse facing rehabilitation from surgery or injury can benefit from its application.

Educational Requirements

Standardizing the educational requirements of the equine therapist presents a challenge. Many people of varying backgrounds pursue equine therapy as a career. Unfortunately, without college-level courses specifically on this topic, appropriate and adequate educational preparation is sometimes lacking. Health-care specialists must have extensive specialized training in a particular field to be considered specialists. Short courses in a specialty such as massage or the newer approaches such as Cranial-sacral therapy or Feldencrist offer only an introduction to that area; they do not make one a qualified practitioner of equine therapy. Indeed, it often is someone with a lot of enthusiasm and a little knowledge who endangers the patient and misleads the client.

Until college-level courses in equine therapy are offered, athletic training and human physical therapy courses are the best sources for education. Either of these curricula offers a background that will provide skills in injury recognition and rehabilitation. Anyone who applies therapeutic techniques to a horse must possess certain skills, knowledge, and experience. This experience cannot be acquired in a few weeks or less.

Education is not the only important factor in the success of the equine therapist. Personal qualities determine the success of treatment to a great extent.

Personal Qualities

The therapist's own health is an important quality because the work requires energy and vitality. The therapist must be prepared to give full attention to each horse and must be alert to the horse's movements and body language during treatment. Each horse should be approached with the same enthusiasm and interest.

Having personal experience as an athlete or being involved in sports or fitness activities will give the equine therapist insight into such concepts as over-use injury and the process of rehabilitation. This is not to suggest that the potential equine therapist needs to experience injury before he or she can properly address injury in the horse. But engaging in athletic pursuits deepens appreciation for the experiences of another athlete.

The equine athlete must go through the rigors of training daily. Those who plan a horse's training program will have a unique insight if they, too, are engaged in fitness pursuits.

The treatments of the equine therapist — electrical stimulation, therapeutic ultrasound, therapeutic laser, magnetic fields, heat and cold, stretching, and massage — have been studied in controlled laboratory tests and in many clinical trials to assess their effectiveness. It is up to the therapist to apply them correctly and under the appropriate circumstances and to communicate their values. A skilled therapist is a good communicator. It is essential that the therapist be able to communicate the treatment goals to the veterinarian as well as the owner or trainer.

The equine therapist must possess good horsemanship skills. He or she must be able to detect a subtle lameness or discomfort in the horse. Reading the horse's body language can be more telling than verbal information once the therapist is skilled in recognizing it.

The therapist also should be aware of hazards around the barn and how to correct them. Knowledge of horse safety is essential to avoid creating a dangerous situation.

Questions a therapist could ask before starting a treatment session include:

• Is my vehicle in the way of horses moving in and out of the barn?

• Will extension cords be stepped on or tripped over?

• Is the electric outlet properly grounded?

• Is the treatment environment clean, dry, and well lighted?

• Is the horse relaxed and ready to accept treatment?

• Does my therapeutic equipment present a hazard to the horse if he should move suddenly?

• Do I have a full understanding of the nature and extent of the injury I am treating?

Besides good personal health and horsemanship skills, an equine therapist must possess compassion and patience. Those who truly care about the horses they treat will have the patience to behave calmly and in a gentle manner. Remember that, for the most part, a horse's behavior is either a reaction or is based on a biological urge. When people become impatient with a horse, they must remember that they are smarter than the horse and show more control. An equine therapist must have the intellectual capacity to deal with the problems of life and separate them from work.

Being a fight-or-flight animal, a horse will be on edge when he feels he is not physically capable of doing either. If you approach the horse slowly, talking to him in soothing tones, and touch him reassuringly, his fear will subside.

Horses that are irritated because of restricted activity or pain can be calmed with patience and compassion. Surprisingly, veterinarians only recently have recognized the importance of easing an animal's pain. Although anesthesia is used to eliminate pain during surgery, little has been done afterward to help the animal. In 1982, when I began my equine therapy practice, I offered post-surgical care for the horses in a major veterinary clinic. The offer was turned down, and I was told that they wanted the horses to be a bit uncomfortable to keep movement to a minimum. The idea was that this would allow the tissues a chance to heal and keep stitches intact.

We now know that pain can erode the animal's well-being to the point of slowing recovery. A depressed horse has a much lower chance for recovery. Medical doctors recognize that pain causes the body to mount a metabolic, neurologic, and hormonal stress response. This stress response has a depressor effect and can significantly reduce the energy level. Signs of depression in the horse include decreased appetite, fatigue, and a constant state of distress from being unable to fight or flee.

It might be helpful to begin each therapy session by practicing a relaxation technique such as meditation. This will allow your mind to release tension and stress and put your body in a relaxed posture. This promotes relaxation in the horse and clears your mind to receive communication from him. The meditation can take only a minute, just long enough for you to put yourself in a receptive mode and to bring to the fore your healing energies.

A lively intellectual curiosity is truly an asset for the equine therapist. Because there is no college degree program in this area, potential therapists must be dedicated to reading scientific journals and books in several fields. A working knowledge of equine anatomy and physiology, as well as exercise physiology and sports medicine, are necessary. Certainly it would be helpful to be knowledgeable about nutrition and pharmacology.

Equine therapists must have a complete knowledge of the modalities and their effect. They must have an understanding of the modalities available and their therapeutic indications and contraindications. There is much research to be done concerning the horse and his response to therapeutic techniques. The equine therapist is in the ideal position to carry out these investigations. Encouraging clients to have diagnostic ultrasound scans done before and after treatment of tendon injuries will add to the body of knowledge on tendon rehabilitation. Scintigraphy can help evaluate the effectiveness of a course of treatment for joint or muscle injury. And systematic X-ray evaluation will aid in the assessment of a course of treatment for laminitis or an exostosis (bone injury).

Finally, equine therapists must have a sound philosophy or attitude toward the profession. They must believe that what they are doing is worthwhile and have confidence that they can offer helpful techniques and information. Therapists cannot claim to be diagnosticians unless they have a veterinary license. One who is competent, however, can make a vital contribution working within the profession's limits and in conjunction with a veterinarian.

Getting to Know Your Patient

Knowledge of horses is vital to the equine therapist. Before beginning any treatment, they must thoroughly evaluate each horse. The first step is to obtain a veterinarian's diagnosis of the problem and discuss the proposed treatment.

When the therapist sees the horse, he or she should look around the stall or paddock for clues about the horse's behavior. Observe the state of the hay bed. Has the horse been lying down more or less than usual? Does he walk the stall? How does he stand when at rest in the stall? What is his eating or grazing stance? What changes in his way of going are evident as he moves around the stall or paddock? Make note of his facial expression and body tension. Observe the buckets, walls, fences, and gates. Is there evidence of chewing or kicking? Are nails sticking out or boards broken? Do not rely solely on what you are told by the barn personnel. They may have overlooked some detail that could be important to your understanding of the situation.

As you look at the horse, note the expression and clarity in the eyes. Note the posture of the head and neck and observe the nostrils and mouth. Observe the horse's stance. Is he camped under? Is he shifting his weight from foot to foot? As your eyes scan over the horse, look for muscle wasting or lack of symmetry. Note the horse's confor-

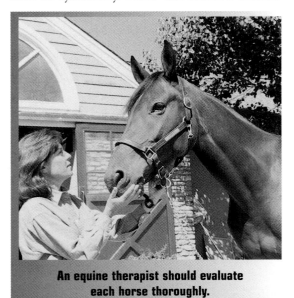

An equine therapist should evaluate each horse thoroughly.

mation. Poor conformation can be the cause of or a contributing factor in lameness. This topic has been authoritatively addressed in the first chapter of Adams's *Lameness in Horses.* (4)

The evaluation of movement should include noting a short stride, reluctance to bear weight when turning, intermittent lameness, or knuckling over. Listening is also important. Is the sound quality the same for each foot strike?

Manual palpation will assess whether the muscles are toned, flaccid, wasted, or irritable. Although nearly 80% of the body is muscle, this organ is often neglected in the initial veterinary exam. The equine therapist must make it a priority to examine the musculature for imbalances in tension, flexibility, weakness, or spasm. These imbalances often lead to injury, and they are the signposts of chronic injury. Learning to identify injury using acupuncture and trigger points helps greatly in getting to know your patient.

The value of observation can be illustrated with this example:

A groom was attempting to lead a yearling filly from her stall to the field, but she was so uncomfortable she could barely move. Her right rear ankle was swollen and she was palpably sore in her back and hips. Her stride length in the right rear was shortened significantly, and she moved her leg through only 40% of its normal range of motion. She had been fine before lunch, but now only an hour later, she was lame. Was she coming down with an illness? Was she going into colic? Was this an allergic reaction?

Examining the condition of the stall, we could see scrape marks on the wall where she had been cast and struggled to get up. The curious thing was that this filly always slept in the same place in her stall, a position that did not put her in danger of being cast.

After looking around outside we could see that the mowers had come by her stall during the lunch hour. The filly was known to react to the mower with great fear and had been seen to rear and wheel when the mower was near her stall. The clues lead us to reason that the filly had been frightened and had fallen backwards, getting cast in the process. She struggled against the wall, finally righting herself and standing up. We would never have understood the cause of her lameness if we had not looked for the clues. There was a happy ending to this story. After four treatments with electrical stimulation, the filly went from a grade 4 lameness to soundness.

The therapist must be able to see the total horse. Avoid tunnel vision, which allows you to see only a specific injury. The rest of the horse is attached to the injured area and is affected by it. Consider the breed of horse and type of activity in which he participates. Observe the eyes for clarity and the condition of the coat, teeth, and hooves. Check the pulse points in the lower legs. Observe the horse's conformation. Is there evidence of overuse of some muscle groups and under-use of others? Note the horse's disposition. Find out about his attitude toward his work.

Always take time to watch a horse move at a walk, trot, and at a faster gait, if possible.

How does he go on hard ground and on soft ground? Does he move differently under tack than when moving about his paddock? The therapist should be able to detect discomfort and subtle gait changes.

Much information about the horse's functional status can be gained by flexing

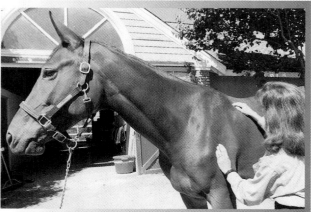

Manual palpation can help determine the condition of the muscles.

and extending the joints, comparing one side of the body to the other. Look for unequal musculature development and unequal range of motion of the joints; also notice signs of discomfort.

It is important for the therapist to get information about medications administered to the horse. Note dosage amounts and when they are given, and ask about radiographs or other diagnostic techniques that have been used.

Record Keeping

Keeping a daily treatment log is an impor-

Note the imbalance of the rider by following the line of the spinal cord from human to horse.

tant part of equine therapy. The log can be used to review the case with the owner, trainer, or veterinarian to inform them of the actions and observations of the therapist.

A basic record form includes the horse's name, the veterinarian, owner, and the trainer's names, billing address, barn phone number, and date of treatment. A history of the injury and present medications must be included. When getting the history of the injury, note the chief complaint, the condition you observe, the past condition that pertains, and any surgeries or drug reactions that relate. There should be space for a description of the daily treatment and changes noted by the therapist.

On a daily basis the therapist should note the eyes and the information they can give,

head carriage, attitude, and energy level. Manual palpation of the muscles will provide information on muscle spasms and fasiculations, the small local contractions of muscle bundles that are involuntarily contracting. Assess the degree of tension in the muscles. Assess the range of motion of each joint and compare it to the range of motion of the joints in the opposite limb. Note neurological signs such as ataxia or unwillingness to have a hoof picked up.

The daily record should include the tools and techniques used by the therapist that day. An assessment of the outcome of the treatment should be included.

Equistar Publications produces a record chart that includes anatomy drawings for injury location. Call their offices at 800-440-8064 to order it.

Rehabilitation using Controlled Exercise

There is minimal scientific documentation in veterinary literature on rest and exercise in the treatment of equine athletic injuries. Research data from human studies indicate that stall rest would have a deleterious effect on tensile strength and range of motion, as well as on muscle strength. Controlled exercise following the application of a therapeutic modality for pain relief would be preferable to stall rest or the uncontrolled activity of turn out.

A controlled exercise program is based on the principle of progressive resistance. The exercise regimen begins with the least stressful and most controllable form of activity. For the horse, this usually means hand walking. Hand walking in the barn aisle is not ideal because of the hard footing and the necessity of turning tightly at the end of the aisle. Repeated torsion on the joints is not conducive to repair. Automatic walkers are used to reduce the man hours necessary for this task. But walkers have some risk as horses might get entangled in the tether. Some walkers are constructed with a radius that is too small.

A new type of walker solves many of the problems of hand walking; it has a larger radius, and the horse is not tethered to the apparatus. Several horses can be walked at once, one per compartment. Free-hanging gates separate each horse from the other and keep them moving. It is natural for a horse to vary his walking speed. This type of walker allows this, adding to its safety and appropriateness for rehabilitation. Even with these innovations, an automatic walker falls short of optimal exercise if all horses are given the same exercise dose. Rehabilitative exercise must be tailored to individual needs in terms of duration and intensity.

Ideally, rehabilitative exercise gradually increases in intensity. It can begin with hand walking, followed by lunging, then both these exercises with tack added to increase the exercise stress. Later a rider is added for additional load. Slow jogging is followed by extended trotting, progressing to collected cantering, then extended cantering. "Ponying" the horse for the faster gaits is not recommended as the horse's head is inevitably pulled to one side in an effort to control speed. This interferes with the normal flight path of the legs and twists the muscles of the neck and back. Incorporating hill work in the later stages of progression increases muscular and cardiovascular strength.

Before increasing the level of exercise intensity, take time to assess the fitness of the horse. The point of therapeutic exercise is to regain strength and normal range of motion. Progression from each phase of exercise should be based on this criteria.

The time allotment for each exercise session is always a question. Typical prescriptions of 10 minutes or 30 minutes have no basis in research. The use of a heart-rate monitor gives a better indication of exercise stress or benefit. Thermography is another tool used to measure exercise stress; it documents the tissue temperature before and after exercise. Simply observing signs of fatigue such as head bobbing and change in lines of flight of the limbs are more appropriate guidelines than minutes on a clock.

A good horseman is a good observer. Therapeutic exercise should never be a negative stress. That outmoded phrase, "no pain, no gain," has always been incorrect. Pain inhibits gain.

Swimming pools and underwater treadmills can be effective rehabilitation tools in providing exercise without the concussion of work on the ground. The disadvantage of swimming is that it causes spine extension that can increase back pain in already stressed musculature.

Manually take joints through their range of motion to assess equality in range of motion.

The advantage of swimming is that weight bearing is decreased and the resistance of the water stimulates the cardio-respiratory and muscular systems. Swimming should only be considered useful in rehabilitation, rather than as a conditioning exercise. It does not tax the anaerobic metabolic system to the extent needed for competition. Limb range of motion and speed of motion are limited by water resistance. The muscle fibers do not

undergo appropriate stretching or contraction speeds for racing, also because of the reduced concussion forces on the leg, the bone is deprived of the stress-response remodeling necessary to withstand racing. The distinction must be made between rehabilitative exercise and conditioning for strength, speed, and endurance for competition.

High-speed treadmills offer a means of controlling the speed and intensity of exercise during rehabilitation and conditioning. A recent study showed that incorporating this type of treadmill into the conditioning program of thoroughbred racehorses improved their competition times over conventionally trained horses.[5] The authors observed a low injury rate in the treadmill-trained horses despite the fact that many of them were rehabilitating from previous injuries, such as bucked shins, osteochondral fragments in the carpus and fetlock, minor tendon problems, and osteoarthritic conditions of the distal forelimb, carpus, and tarsus. High-speed treadmills offer the safety of a non-slip surface. Another advantage is that the exercise bout is repeatable, with absolute control of velocity, distance, and time. The ability to increase the incline of the high speed treadmill allows for increased cardiovascular and respiratory work with less stress on the musculoskeletal system.

Trainers in the study used the treadmill as the only form of exercise early in the rehabilitation period, at speeds of a fast walk or slow jog for one to two miles. Exercise on a track was gradually added into the workload until the treadmill work made up only 30% to 50% of the total conditioning program. This approach would ease the transition from the treadmill to the racetrack as race-specific training progressed.

Interval training can be used in the advanced stages of rehabilitation as a transition from rehabilitation to athletic conditioning. The goal of interval training is to divide a demanding exercise bout into smaller, less demanding bouts to reduce the total stress yet achieve the same total amount of work. For example, a given distance such as one mile would be divided into three one-third-mile segments. Each of these segments would be covered in a specified time period with a specified rest period after each segment, allowing for partial recovery.

The goal is to maintain the same effort in each exercise bout. If this is accomplished, the total work output would be more over the three one-third mile distances than it would be if the horse were asked to run one mile. As the horse becomes fitter, the rest periods are shortened and the segment times are reduced.

Another form of interval training is interspersing long, slow distance with short bouts of speed. With either approach, the goal is to increase fitness. A principle of athletic train-ing is that training is specific. If your sport is sprinting, you must devote some of your training to sprinting the distance you race.

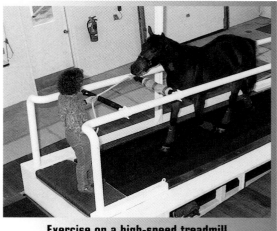

Exercise on a high-speed treadmill.

Interval training is used in the advanced stages of rehabilitation, when the horse has reached the end of recuperation and is ready to regain strength and endurance.

Problems and Equine Therapy Solutions

Muscle Pain

Muscle pain is a physical stress. It is a drain of both the physical and the mental energy. When there is pain, the body sets up protective mechanisms such as muscle contraction to guard the injured area. The metabolic processes necessary to maintain this chronic muscle tension take their toll on the body's physical energy.

Emotional stress is a very real component to muscle pain as well. Emotional stress is

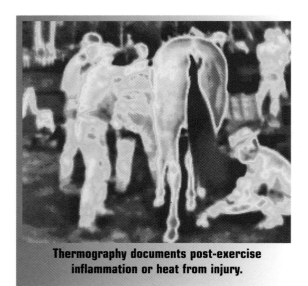

Thermography documents post-exercise inflammation or heat from injury.

the constant feedback from the pain site, which distracts the brain from full concentration on the athletic task at hand.

Solution

Electrical stimulation, magnetic fields, and massage provide relaxation to tense muscles and allow the horse to go into a state of deep relaxation. This state is vital to the restoration of full muscle function.

Muscle Spasm

Muscle pain sets up a reflex loop known as the pain-spasm-pain cycle. Spasm is the intense, involuntary contraction of muscle fibers. Muscle spasm is more severe than muscle tension, which can be relieved with rest. Spasm cannot be relieved until the self-perpetuating cycle of pain-spasm-pain is broken. When muscle is in spasm it feels hard and hyper-reactive on palpation, rather than

soft and vibrant. A muscle in spasm has reduced agility and strength. If spasm is allowed to persist, it results in marked loss of function, discomfort to the horse, and permanent joint contractures.

Solution

Equine therapy techniques as simple as stretching and ice massage can break into this cycle. The application of electrical stimulation, laser acupuncture, or trigger point acupressure disrupts this debilitating cycle, allowing muscle fibers to relax and begin to fire in a more functional manner.

Muscle Weakness

When the brain gets a message of pain from a muscle, an inhibitory loop is set up, preventing the body from using that limb to the extent that it normally would. We say this is Nature's way of protecting the injured body part. But reduced muscle force and reduced range of limb movement eventually results in muscle weakness or stiffness. When this situation is allowed to persist, the muscle fibers atrophy and lose their contractile power. Loss of muscle volume can be seen in as little as a few weeks.

Solution

Therapeutic ultrasound or high-frequency electrical stimulation can be used to combat restrictions of active range of motion (movement produced by volitional activation of muscle). In a study using humans as the subjects, one group carried out movement exercises designed to increase range of joint motion. These exercises were like the movements required in daily living. The other group carried out the same exercises, but received high-frequency electrical stimulation as well. The subjects in the stimulated group showed increases in extension that averaged 35 degrees, whereas the control subjects' joint extension improved by only eight degrees on average.

This study is pertinent to horses in that the injured horse is often turned out in a paddock to let nature take its course. When faced with recovery, the application of equine therapy is certainly better than turn out, which only asks the horse to use "movements required of daily living."

Trigger Points

Active acupuncture sites or trigger points develop in sore muscles. A trigger point is a small nodule of degenerated muscle tissue highly sensitive to pressure. Trigger points sometimes develop after chronic or acute injury and also result from chronic muscle spasm or muscle tension. An acupuncture point, which is also in the dermis, exists where cutaneous nerves emerge from deep fascia or along pathways of major peripheral nerves.

Solution

Stimulation from a therapeutic laser can deactivate these points and provide significant relief from muscle pain. Photon therapy is a non-invasive method of deactivating these points of noxious stimuli. The pain relief achieved from this modality is often long-lasting. This indicates an endogenous opiate mode of action. These pain-relieving hormones are produced by the body when the appropriate stimulus is applied.

A skilled equine therapist will address muscle pain as a major part of treatment. Sensitive manual palpation of the musculature will reveal sites and soreness that might not be evident when simply watching the horse move. Often, equine therapy can intervene in the progress of muscle degeneration and allow the horse to recover more quickly.

Observations for Consideration:

There are many old horseman's tales that, just like "old wives' tales" have a shred of truth based on a little observation and perhaps some misunderstanding. Here are a few for you to consider and to validate or discard:

• Secondary pain is often the easiest to find or to see in the way of going.

• A sore front foot will result in tension in the withers area and in the gluteal muscles.

• Subclinical hock pain will result in soreness at the tail head and gluteal muscles.

• Back muscle soreness results in a shortened anterior phase of the gait.

• Hip muscle soreness indicates stifle pain.

• Bursitis of the trochanteric bursa is often mistaken for stifle pain.

• Soreness in the sacrum indicates hock pain.

• Back pain can be a primary injury .

• Compare size of foot and frog to determine habitual weight-bearing stance.

• A change in attitude, behavior, or performance is always related to pain.

Conclusion

In this rapidly evolving field of sports medicine, new ideas are constantly challenging old ones. New techniques and tools are being developed, and research supports or refutes previously held ideas. We adopt a procedure because we see it work. At times we hold on to a procedure because we "believe" in it. Belief is for the realm of religion, not the scientific realm of medicine. Continuing to use a procedure because we believe in it obscures our view of whether it truly works. Likewise, if we fail to read the scientific literature on new techniques, we are preventing progress. Since the time of Hippocrates, it has been recognized that the proper study of the individual, whether it is man or horse, is on the man or horse himself, as a species. The most illuminating studies of any therapy for the horse would use the horse as a subject. The field of equine therapy is wide open for scientific study. This only enhances the excitement it holds for the curious mind.

Definitions

Abduction — To draw away from the midline.

Adduction — To draw toward the midline.

Analgesic — A substance that relieves or reduces pain.

Anesthetic — A substance that causes complete or partial loss of pain or sensation.

Extension — The act of straightening.

Flexion — The act of bending.

References

1. McNamara, K. and Mackintosh, S. 1993. Veterinary surgeon's perceptions of animal physiotherapy. *Physiotherapy.* 79:312-16.

2. Kahn, J. 1987. *Principles and Practice of Electrotherapy.* New York, NY.: Churchill Livingstone. 71.

3. Travell, J. and Simons, D. 1983. *Myofascial Pain and Dysfunction.* Baltimore, MD.: Williams & Wilkins. 21.

4. Adams, OR. 1987. *Lameness in Horses*, 3rd ed. Philadelphia: Lea and Febiger. 1-32.

5. Kobluck, CN. et al. Case control study of racing thoroughbreds conditioned on a high speed treadmill. *J Eq Vet Sci.* 16:1996.511-513.

Stretching for the Horse

Give the simple necessity of care

A HUMAN ATHLETE works to develop three major areas of physical fitness: building muscle strength, increasing endurance, and improving flexibility. Horse trainers recognize the need to develop muscle strength and the cardiovascular system, but how often do we consider the need for flexibility in the horse?

Speed depends on strength, but also on agility. Running straight ahead demands a certain amount of agility for rapid stride turnover. Agility is required in many other equine sports, as well, as the horse is asked to zig zag like a soccer player, leap like a high jumper, and bend like a ballet dancer.

Elasticity of the muscles, tendons, and ligaments allows for more controlled, quick movements and helps avoid muscle pulls. Stretching exercises will increase the stretch tolerance of muscles and connective tissue.

Flexibility is the ability of soft tissue to relax and yield to stretch forces. A better term might be extensibility. Flexibility can be limited by bone structure or soft tissues such as the muscles and their fascial sheaths, the joint capsule, or the tendons. Soft tissue stretching exercises, which extend the muscle and its connective tissues to their full

The flexible athlete is less injury prone and more likely to perform optimally than the inflexible one.

lengths, can significantly change joint mobility.

Tissue shortening around a joint results from prolonged immobilization, which can come from stall rest or wearing a cast. Trauma causes protective muscle splitting, which can result in muscle fiber shortening if it persists. Muscle strength is lost when soft tissue adaptively shortens over time.(1) The muscle is tight yet functionally weak and no longer capable of strong or ballistic contraction.

A more severe condition results when scar tissue is laid down between otherwise normal muscle fibers and ties down the motion and function of the muscle. Chronic inflammation in the muscle can cause fibrotic adhesions to form throughout the musculature, reducing its ability to contract and extend.

Stretching for Pain Relief

Stretching exercises can provide relief from pain in the muscles or the fascia. Fascial contracture occurs when muscles and their connective tissues tighten abnormally. Age, chilling, inactivity, and muscle strain cause contractures that put pressure on nerve pathways as they go across muscle. This abnormal pressure results in pain and limits the muscle's power.

When muscles are stretched with consistently repeated exercises, some of the elongation achieved remains after the exercise is completed.(2) The exercises must be gradual and progressively more demanding. Gentle and progressive stretching relieves pressure on local nerves, thus reducing discomfort.

Stretching has a beneficial effect on post-exercise soreness. This soreness is composed of muscle spasm, edema formation, increased stiffness, and resistance to stretch. Reducing the pain requires inhibiting muscle spasm, stimulating local circulation, and altering the function of the organs involved in the stretch reflex.

These organs include the Golgi tendon and the muscle spindle, which are located within the muscle or at the musculo-tendinous junction. The Golgi tendon wraps around muscle fibers and is sensitive to tension; it protects the muscle by causing it to relax. The muscle spindle is sensitive to stretch and reacts protectively by causing the muscle to contract when it is in danger of overstretching. A chronically irritated muscle spindle sets up a muscle trigger point, which is a source of pain. Slow stretching increases metabolism in the muscle spindle, elevating its oxygen consumption and allowing it to relax. This reduces the trigger point. Slow stretching also engages the Golgi tendon to inhibit muscle tension, allowing the muscle to lengthen.(3) These structures provide the individual with kinesthetic sense, or an awareness of the body, and protection from extreme muscle activity.

A human study examined whether cold or heat therapy combined with stretching would elicit the greater amount of muscle relaxation when post-exercise soreness was present.(4) The use of cold and slow stretching, holding for 10 seconds at the end point of the stretch, was more effective in reducing pain. Cold apparently decreases the activity of the Golgi tendon, allowing the muscle to be stretched. Cold also reduces nerve conduction velocity, inhibiting muscle spasm.

Manual stretching provides the chance to assess a horse's health in a unique way. It allows the therapist to detect imbalances in flexibility and extensibility that could indicate injury. If a horse resists gentle stretching, it could indicate that the muscle involved is not being used to full capacity. Such an imbalance is a part of the chronic injury syndrome or could lead to an acute injury.

Note the amount of tension at the end of a normal range of motion. It should feel soft, indicating extensibility in the soft tissue. It could feel firm, indicating that the joint capsule and ligaments are being stretched. You could detect a hard end to the stretch, indicating a bony block. Guarding muscle contraction could be activated to protect a joint with cartilage damage or pain from an acute injury. Prolonged muscle spasm will cause the horse to tense all over to protect the area.

Stretching in Rehabilitation

Exercises used to restore function after an injury serve the same purpose as conditioning exercises — to increase endurance and flexibility. Flexibility is lost quickly when

the body naturally limits motion to protect the injured part. As the injury repairs, scar tissue formation within the muscle inhibits full functional contraction and extension. Imbalance in flexibility produces strain on related joints and muscles, compromising their function.

Flexibility exercises should begin immediately after injury as long as they do not aggravate the injury. In the early stages, stretching should be gentle. Special attention should be paid to signs of discomfort in the horse. Consult with a veterinarian before beginning any rehabilitation routine to determine the extent and nature of the injury.

Stretching for Injury Prevention

Flexibility provides a certain amount of insurance against injury to the musculotendinous unit.(5) Stretching routines offer a fertile area for creative thought as injury prevention is still an undeveloped aspect of athletic training in equine sports.

Muscle fiber tears can occur when heavy loads are placed on shortened, tight muscles. Using stretching exercises for injury prevention became popular with professional and college football teams many years ago. Football is a game of short bursts of effort with very little extension of the joints. Muscle strains and tears were and remain common, although this type of injury has been significantly reduced with the advent of supplemental stretching programs, according to many athletic trainers.

Stretching for Efficiency of Movement

The principles of physics and biomechanics have shown that the degree of stretch in a muscle before contraction will affect the strength of that contraction. A muscle will contract with maximum efficiency when it is stretched to 100% of its functional length. This is the reason for the various take-off positions in track and field events. A typical conditioning routine for the horse involves exerting muscles at only about 60% to 75% of their maximum

Muscle elasticity or stretchability is important in efficient movement.

length, as the horse is kept collected to keep his speed under control. Repeated workouts without the opportunity to extend the muscles to their maximum length can create muscle contractures and tightness. Research into the effects of stretching for soccer found that regular soccer training resulted in a decreased range of motion.(6) Stretching exercises added to the end of the warm-up improved flexibility and reduced the number of strains, the study showed.

Muscle elasticity or stretchability is important in efficient locomotion. In running, the muscle first is stretched in the leg extension phase, then contracted to move the body over the leg. Elastic energy from the extension phase can be used in the contraction phase, reducing the metabolic demand for work. This energy is increased with the stretch intensity of the cycle's extension phase.(7)

A horse with great reach and rapid stride turnover certainly will cover ground more rapidly than his shorter-striding stalemate. This was a factor for the great Secretariat as he was going stride for stride with Riva Ridge, outdistancing him in three powerful strides in a famed performance in the Marlboro Cup Handicap. Secretariat's greater reach allowed more power production per stride.

Certainly, muscles that have become contracted due to injury could benefit from gentle stretching exercises, but what about the apparently healthy horse? We often see horses stretching themselves in their stalls. A good roll in the dust can give the torso muscles a bit of a stretch. But historically, horses are not the great stretchers of the animal kingdom. Domestic cats and dogs, who often stretch, are descendants of den dwellers for whom a good stretch was essential preparation for subsequent activity.

The ancestors of today's highly regimented equine roamed the plains and forests freely, rarely staying in one spot long enough for the muscles to get stiff. Equus kept one nostril to the wind to stay ahead of his predators through continuous movement or short bursts of trotting. Running at top speed from a standstill was not part of his usual activity. Had he done more of that, surely would have been more inclined to long, luxurious stretches. As it is, horses who are passively stretched by their handlers

soon learn to enjoy it and stretch spontaneously more often.

When to Stretch

Stretching to improve flexibility is best done after a warm-up. Trying to stretch cold muscle could result in small tears in the muscle fibers. The muscles of a specific area can be warmed with a hot pack, electrical stimulation, or ultrasound, but a warm-up of walking and slow trotting is most effective. Before stretching, use joint mobilization techniques to free movement. Joint mobilization is described in Chapter 5.

Have you ever noticed that your muscles are especially inflexible in the morning? The body temperature is usually lower then

A horse with great reach and rapid stride covers more ground.

than at any other time of the day. This decreases the ability of interstitial fluids to flow through muscles, tendons, and joints, making movement more difficult. Human runners have learned to reduce morning stiffness by stretching after their workout. There is no proof that this will help horses, but it is food for thought and careful experimentation.

A mild muscle strain can be confused with post-exercise muscle soreness. A strained muscle, which is characterized by localized pain and swelling, involves overstretching and tearing of muscle. Post-exercise soreness, a more generalized discomfort that occurs when the activity level increases, is thought to be caused by microtrauma to the fascia and muscle fibers. Gentle stretching helps distinguish between these two problems. Post-exercise soreness will decrease with stretching; a strained muscle will become more painful. Strains should be iced immediately and rested, but post-exercise soreness benefits from mild exercise such as walking and stretching.

The Warm-up

The warm-up is an activity or a series of exercises that raise the total body temperature, preparing the body for vigorous activity. Warm-up exercises include walking, slow jogging, and gentle stretching.

A good warm-up will improve subsequent physical performance by helping the cardiovascular and muscular systems adjust quickly to increased activity. Warm-up exercises increase blood temperature, which enhances the separation of oxygen from hemoglobin and myoglobin, making it more accessible to the cells for metabolism. Body temperature also increases, stimulating mitochondria to consume more oxygen. This serves to slow the initial depletion of oxygen in the muscles, making for a smooth transition to heavier workloads.

Whether exercise is taking place in the winter or summer, do not underestimate the value of walking. Include longer periods of walking before exercise in cold weather to enhance blood flow through the muscles, facilitating muscle function.

Walking for extended periods before athletic exercise will improve oxygen delivery and waste product removal. Walking uses mostly slow twitch muscle fibers. These fibers rely on oxygen from the blood for fuel so muscle capillaries dilate in response to their activity, benefiting the entire muscle. Brief, intense exercise will not raise cooled muscle temperature as that type of exercise is done by fast twitch fibers that use anaerobic metabolism.

Warming up usually takes about 10 minutes, but you must use your own horse as a guide. A larger, heavily muscled horse will take longer to become ready for increased muscle exercise. Observe the increase in respiratory and heart rates as your horse begins to exercise. When it has come to a steady state, elevate the walking to a more brisk pace. Once the horse adjusts to this, increase the pace again. Reduced peripheral blood flow, brought on by cold weather, could leave the joints, tendons, and ligaments stiffer than in milder weather. Taking adequate time to warm these structures will help prevent injury by increasing flexibility and extensibility.

Walking as a warm-up can be done in hand, on a longe line, or by using a treadmill or horse walker. This is followed by walking under saddle to ensure that your horse's muscles are fully ready for increased work.

The next step in a warm-up is to increase the speed by trotting, which increases the stretch of the connective tissues and recruits more muscle fibers into work. As the horse adjusts to slow trotting, proceed to a more brisk pace to increase the oxygen demands from the muscles. By gradually increasing the exercise stress, the horse will be able to tolerate the additional stress brought on by cold weather. This first phase of the warm up could take as long as 30 minutes in cold weather.

At this point, consider the specific sport activity the horse will perform. Mild sport-specific activities (low jumps, or collected cantering, for example) further prepare the horse for safe work in cold weather. Scientists looked at the effects of exercise at near maximal tolerance levels in temperatures as low as -25° C (-13° F) and found no evidence of tissue damage in the horse's res-

Walking before athletic exercise will improve oxygen delivery and waste product removal.

piratory tract or musculature.(8) This report would indicate that cold temperatures alone would not prohibit safe exercise if the horse is otherwise well cared for.

Cool-down

The post-exercise cool-down should mirror the warm-up. In winter, this again could take as long as 30 minutes. A gradual cool-down allows the body temperature to decline more slowly. To avoid excess lactate in the muscles, mild sport-specific activities, followed by trotting, then walking, and finally walking on a loose reign, will allow capillaries in the muscles to dilate and remove the waste products of exercise. As with the warm-up, the walking phase is critical in cold weather. Once the tack is removed and the horse has accommodated to in-hand walking, manual stretches will complete the cool-down. Manual stretches maintain or increase joint range of motion and should be included in every cool-down.

Tips for Safe Stretching

There are several things to keep in mind as you work to improve your horse's flexibility. Stretching should be done in a relaxed, easy manner. The limb is guided through a range of motion, held in that position briefly, then gently returned to the original position. Do not pull on the limbs. Overstretching produces microscopic tears in the tissues that can lead to scarring and eventual loss of elasticity, the opposite of your goal.

A successful stretching program requires a certain amount of sensitivity. The stretch should be done slowly until a slight amount of tightness is felt. Human athletes work up to holding the stretch for 30 seconds. No research has been done to indicate how long a stretch should be held with a horse, so it is up to you to be aware of what he is feeling. Human athletes repeat each stretching maneuver several times for best results. Be aware of your horse's comfort level before repeating the exercise. Ignorance and lack of attention to task will be the downfall of an effective stretching program.

• Never use a bouncing or jerky stretch. When a bouncing movement, called ballistic stretching, is used, the muscle responds by tightening to protect itself from overstretch. You will be working against the muscle with a bouncing stretch, increasing the likelihood of microtrauma.

• Never stretch an acutely torn muscle. Allow time for it to heal before starting a rehabilitative program. Your veterinarian can advise you on this.

• Avoid excessive traction and pressure on the joints.

• Avoid movements that twist the joints.

• Do not try to gain full range of motion in one or two sessions. It could take several weeks to see significant progress.

▮ Stretches for Specific Areas

Stretching exercises for the neck

Having a treat in your hand can encourage the horse to stretch enough to increase range of motion in the neck. Bring the head around slowly. Try to get him to hold the stretch a few seconds. Be aware of the way he bends his head around to his side. Is he bending evenly through all spinal segments? To avoid stretching at the base of the neck, a

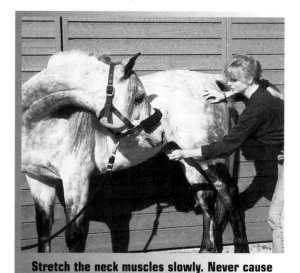

Stretch the neck muscles slowly. Never cause the horse to snap his head around.

horse will exaggerate the stretch at the poll. To avoid bending at the poll, he will twist the middle part of the neck. Neck stretches indicate the amount and distribution of tension in the rhomboideus, splenius, trapezius, omotransversarius, and serratus ventralis muscles.

Stretch for the withers

Place your hands on the withers and gently pull toward you, stretching the connective fascia on the opposite side. You might feel some resistance. If you do, stop the pull and hold for 30 seconds to re-set the stretch

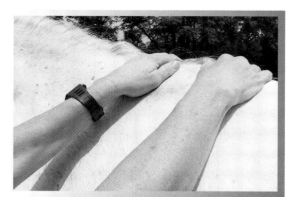

Place your hands on the withers and gently pull toward you to stretch the trapezius muscle.

reflex for more range of motion. Release after 30 seconds, rest for 10 seconds, and repeat three more times. Repeat this on the other side.

Stretching exercises for the shoulder, chest, foreleg, and ankle

When supporting the horse's foreleg, keep your knees bent and your back straight. Do not bend at the waist. Hold the leg firmly so that the horse feels secure and relaxes. Gently pull the forelimb through a complete range of motion in every direction it will normally move. Performing these stretches regularly provides an opportunity to compare joint range of motion in the left and right ankle.

Rather than tugging with your upper body, bend your knees and gently draw the leg forward and then downward. At the end of the stretch, place the hoof back on the ground, don't just drop it.

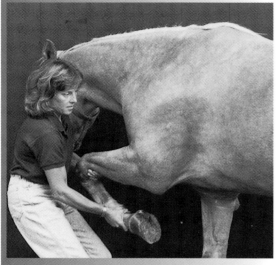

For the triceps, deltoid, trapezius, costal fascia, and latissimus dorsi muscles.

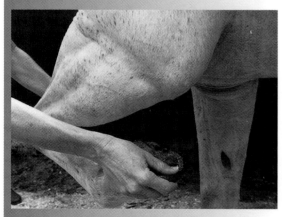

Flex and extend the fetlock joint and move the leg medially and laterally.

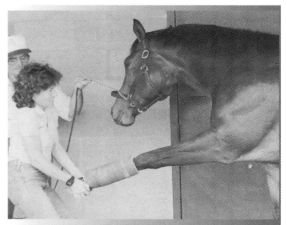

For the muscles of the shoulder: the trapezius, latissimus dorsi, thorascalis, deltoid, and serratus ventralis.

apply light pressure to the middle of the belly or just behind the girth. This should cause him to contract his stomach muscles and flex the spine. To cause spinal extension, apply light

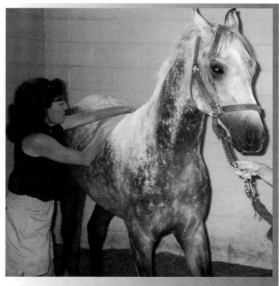

To cause spinal extension apply light pressure to the back just behind the withers or at about the 14th or 15th rib.

Stretches for the torso

Although there is little range of motion in the thoracid spine, the horse should be able to flex and extend it through at least 10 degrees. To cause the horse to flex the thoracic spine,

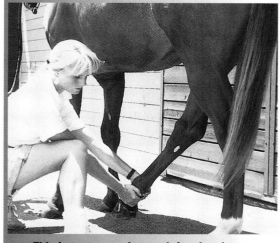

This is a very good stretch for the glutes, semimembranosis, semitendinosis, and the tensor fascia lata.

Gently pull the tail with steady pressure to stretch the hips: the superficial gluteus, semi-tendinosis, and semimembranosis.

pressure to the back just behind the withers or at about the 14th or 15th rib. The horse should move away from this pressure, extending the spine. If your pressure is too aggressive, the horse might tense his muscles, making the spine more rigid rather than allowing it to flex or to extend.

Get the horse to move the spine laterally by placing one hand on the middle of the spine and grasping the tail with the other. Alternately push and pull to move the spine to and fro.

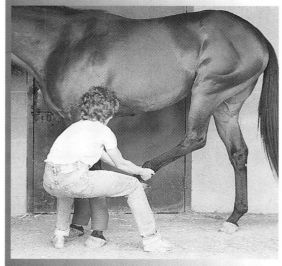

For the muscles of the hip and hamstrings; the superficial and gluteus medius, semitendinosis, semimembranosis, and the biceps femoris.

Stretches for the low back, hip, and hamstrings

To get the horse to rotate his pelvis, run your fingernails or an ink pen down the glutes. The horse will rotate the hips, stretching out the low back.

Pulling the tail also causes pelvic rotation and stretches the top line of the hip. Stand directly behind the horse and firmly grasp his tail in the middle. Gently but firmly, pull it straight out to the back. Hold for a few seconds, then slowly release the tension.

Definitions

Contracture — Shortening of muscle or other soft tissues which results in limitation of joint motion.

Flexibility — Mobility of the soft tissues and the joints. Ability of the muscles or other soft tissue to yield to stretch force.

Golgi tendon — Structure in a muscle that is sensitive to the tension of the muscle fibers whether from stretch or from contraction. This organ fires when there is excessive tendon in a muscle, causing it to relax.

Range of motion — The full motion possible for the joint structures and the surrounding muscles.

References

1. Kisner, C. and Colby, LA. 1990. *Therapeutic Exercise Foundations and Techniques,* 2nd ed. Philadelphia: FA Davis Company. 109.

2. Morehouse, LE. and Miller, AT. 1971. *Physiology of Exercise,* 6th ed. St. Louis, MO.: CV Mosby. 73.

3. Kisner. 114.

4. Prentice, WE. 1982. An electromyographic analysis of the effectiveness of heat or cold and stretching for inducing relaxation in injured muscle. *J Ortho Spts Phys Ther.* 3:133-40.

5. Klafs, CE. and Arnheim, DD. 1977. *Modern Principles of Athletic Training,* 4th ed. St. Louis, MO.: CV Mosby. 37.

6. Moller, MHL. et al. 1985. Stretching exercises and soccer: effect of stretching on range of motion in the lower extremity in connection with soccer training. *Intl J Sports Med.* 6:50-52.

7. Aura, O. and Komi, PV. 1986. Effects of prestretch intensity on mechanical effeciency of positive work and on elastic behavior of skeletal muscle in stretch-shortening cycle exercises. *Int J Sports Med.* 7:137-43.

8. Dahl, LG. et al. Effects of a cold environment on exercise tolerance in the horse. *Proceedings Int'l Conference on Equine Exercise Physiology.* 1987. San Diego, CA.

Heat Therapy

*We've got to get back to the basics of life...*Waylon Jennings

HEAT plays a vital role in the rehabilitation of chronic injuries because of its effects on circulation, metabolism, and nerves. A chronic injury results when symptoms persist or they develop over time. An acute injury, on the other hand, is caused by sudden trauma. Acute injuries are treated with ice and compression, which will be discussed in the next chapter.

Successful treatment of chronic injuries begins with an accurate diagnosis. The horse presents a special challenge to diagnosis and treatment because he can adapt and compensate. When faced with pain in one area, the horse shifts his weight. This results in more strain elsewhere and disuse atrophy in the painful area. Eventually the compensatory changes are exhausted and lameness results. When the horseman finally recognizes the discomfort that has developed, the injury has become chronic and involves several structures.

Tools such as thermography, ultrasound, and scintigraphy can identify the inflamed structures with an accuracy not previously possible. Chances of successful treatment are greater if an injury is addressed in the acute phase, which can be as short as two days. During this time ice, rest, support, and

proper veterinary treatment can control symptoms. Once the condition becomes

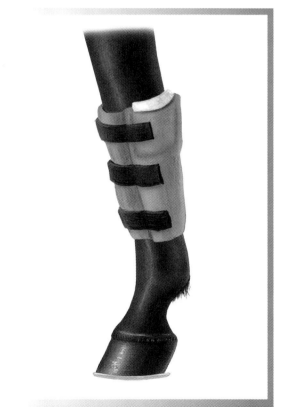

Chronic injuries can be treated with chemical hot packs, such as the Tempra Technology hot pack.

chronic, a combination of disorders can arise, none of which will subside until they all are addressed.

With chronic injuries, it is essential to address the cause of pain and dysfunction, not just the symptoms. Among the types of injuries and conditions which can benefit from heat therapy are:

- arthritis
- tendinitis
- bursitis
- adhesive capsulitis.

Arthritis, perhaps the most common chronic disease, begins as an inflammation in the joints, then degenerates due to wear and tear and metabolic influences. There is a progressive loss of cartilage and bony over-growth. The soft tissue around the joint is weakened through pain inhibition of muscles and inflammation in surrounding tendons and bursa. Tendinitis, bursitis, and arthritis can overlap and exist simultaneously, which can make diagnosis baffling and treatment frustrating.

Tendinitis is an inflammation of the structure that connects muscle to bone. The tendon is not generally as extensible as muscle and is susceptible to strain. The muscle-tendon junction also can be a site of strain. Tenosynovitis is a more appropriate term for the condition if the inflammation occurs in the tendon sheath, rather than the tendon itself. Should this condition persist, fibrosis can occur in the sheath and extend to the tendon, restricting motion.(1)

Bursitis is an inflammation of the structure that produces lubricating fluid to reduce friction between a muscle or tendon and a bone. When acutely inflamed, the bursa is distended. It is highly vascular, so heat can be felt on the skin surface. When chronic inflammation is allowed to persist, scar tissue forms in the bursa. The bursa itself is rich with nerve endings, so this tissue causes pain. Bursitis often is secondary to tendinitis or longstanding arthritis and results from overuse strain.

Injury to a sensory nerve results in pain, while injury to a motor nerve results in reduced function. The mildest type of nerve injury, neuropraxia, is often caused by over-stretching or compressing the nerve. It also can be caused by inflammation to the tissues around the nerve. A pinched nerve is subjected to vascular ischemia when the surrounding fascia is constricted. Nerves can show fiber atrophy if the condition persists. Local toxins from injury can cause nerve scarring, resulting in a conduction block or slow-down.(2) Heating can relieve the fascial restrictions on the nerve and its vasculature, increasing nerve conduction velocity.

Adhesive capsulitis, another troublesome condition of the joint structures, can result from chronically reduced joint function. When pain restricts motion, the fascia and connective tissue surrounding the joint shorten. Range of motion is reduced by the tight joint capsule, setting the stage for further muscle atrophy.

As you can see, the degenerative cycle of chronic injury is not easy to escape. The most efficient approach is confronting the process in the earliest stage possible. This means daily assessment of the horse's health status and early diagnosis when a problem is suspected.

Effects of Heat

Heat, being a form of energy, increases metabolic activity in the cells. This increased activity produces more demand for oxygen locally. As a result, capillary vasodilation increases the amount of blood bringing oxygen and nutrients to the area. Membrane diffusion and enzymatic activity also increase, enabling cell to use oxyget and metabolize waste. The waste products of injury include prostaglandin, bradykinin, and histamine, all implicated in nerve fiber sensitization and pain.

Pain is caused by muscle spasm, connective tissue ischemia, and shortened fascia that put pressure on nerves. Heat can address all of these causes and stimulate the repair process. Heating the tissues prepares them for mobilization exercises, facilitating a greater range of motion through reflex pain relief and connective tissue softening.

Heat can neutralize trigger points, nodules of tender muscle that can be a source of pain. This treatment increases local circulation so the irritated muscle spindle at the heart of the trigger point can relax. Heat also causes relaxation of the muscle fibers, which can be augmented by stretching to relieve the tight band of muscle that contains the trigger point.

Arthritic joints respond favorably to applications of external heat. Joint stiffness is reduced because of a decrease in the thickness of the synovial fluid and an increase in the amount of stretch in the surrounding connective tissue. A reflex pain-inhibiting effect also is created by increasing the temperature of the sensory nerves. The message of heat travels rapidly to the brain, where its recognition blocks out the pain message. The threshold of sensory nerve endings rises, resulting in long-term pain relief.(3)

When connective tissue contractures or scar tissue limit joint movement, heating before exercise will make the activity more comfortable. Heating dense, connective tissue affects bonds between collagen molecules, making the tissue more pliant. This allows more even distribution of force throughout the tissue, reducing focal points of stress, rupture, and inflammation.(4) The ability of joints to extend will increase when heating and stretching are carried out repeatedly over time.

Applying Heat

How much heat is enough? To achieve a significant change in metabolic rate and collagen distensibility, the target tissue's temperature must rise at least 5° F. Increases greater than 12° F can be painful. Unfortunately, by the time pain registers and the horse tries to move away, some damage already might have occurred. A horse's skin temperature is generally 90 to 92° F. Obviously, the heat source must be warmer than this to increase tissue temperature. It is well documented in human therapy, however, that heat applications of more than 133° F for prolonged periods will cause skin dam-

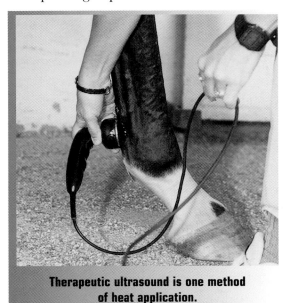

Therapeutic ultrasound is one method of heat application.

age. For humans, there is a nine-degree "window," or therapeutic range, between effective heating and surface tissue damage. Using this as a guide will prevent overheating the horse's superficial tissues.

Methods of heat application include heating pads, hot water bottles, hydrocollator packs, instant chemical heat packs, heating lamps, hot water whirlpools, hot towels,

counter-irritating liniments, and therapeutic ultrasound. Of these, only ultrasound can penetrate the skin to reach the deeper structures such as joints, bursa, tendons, and muscles. All the others heat only the skin and perhaps the underlying connective tissue, structures not involved in most sports injuries.

When using any heating modality, it is important to understand the depth of penetration. Temperature in the injured tissue must increase to have a significant effect on the problem. There is little change in deep skeletal muscle blood flow with superficial heating agents.(5) Superficial heat combined with exercise, however, can have a greater effect than either modality alone. (6)

To illustrate this point, I'll draw an example from a lecture given by Britain's renowned equine therapist, Mary Bromiley.(7) When a horse or human has muscular back pain, it is the multi fundi muscles that are likely to be irritated. These are a series of small bundles of muscle fiber that extend from the transverse processes of a vertebra to neighboring vertebral spines. They lie under the larger structure of the longissimus dorsi muscle, which is covered by fascia and skin. Heat from most of the therapeutic sources will be absorbed mostly in the skin and fascia; the multi fundi muscles might not get any direct benefit. In this case, exercise directed at the multi fundi can improve the back's comfort level and strength. A heating modality can facilitate the exercise.

Use of Superficial Heating Devices

Consider the pros and cons of the available products when equipping your barn with a heating device. Electric heating pads, although comforting for people, might not be a good choice for equine use. Because they must be plugged into a wall outlet, there is the danger of the horse stepping on the cord. In addition, metal horse shoes have been known to cut through electric cords, causing fatal shock. Another problem is that the handler does not know exactly how much heat is being delivered and absorbed. The skin could burn without frequent checks during the 20- to 30-minute recommended treatment time. Once the skin is burned, you have two injuries to contend with instead of one.

A hot water bottle can present problems as well. Their size and shape make them difficult to use on a horse. When wrapped on the limbs or tucked under a blanket, they have a tendency to slip down or fall out from under the blanket. Should the stopper accidentally come out, you have the danger of scalding.

Whirlpools provide gentle massage and superficial heat. Single-leg whirlpools are designed specifically for horses. The agitation of the water can loosen scar tissue on the skin surface and help remove debris from a wound. An iodine concentrate added to the water will reduce the possibility of transmitting infections and aid in cleansing abraded skin. Of course, the horse should be as clean as possible and the whirlpool boot disinfected before use if the horse has an open wound. A thermometer to check water temperature is essential for safe and effective treatment; the water should be between 103 and 110° F. If a tank is used it must be plastic or rubber, never metal, to avoid shock hazard. The motor should be grounded and protected with a ground fault interrupter at the wall plug. The danger of shock from ungrounded metal whirlpools is great.(8)

Hydrocollator packs provide an efficient means of superficial heating. These cotton packs contain a gel that absorbs heated water and becomes soft to conform to body contours. Although they are heavy enough to stay in place under a blanket when used to treat a horse's back, they are a bit heavy and bulky for the leg. The packs become quite hot, as the heating unit can bring water to 150° F. The packs must be wrapped in towels before they are applied to avoid burning the skin. They will hold their heat for about 20 minutes, which makes them much more efficient than hot towels.

Instant chemical heat and gel packs might be the most efficient form of delivering heat. These packs consist of a plastic pouch containing chemicals that produce heat when mixed. They stay hot about 90 minutes. This self-contained heat source becomes quite hot at first and should go in the accompanying cloth sleeve quickly. Sleeves are available to fit various areas of the horse. Soaking the sleeve before inserting the heat pack provides moist heat, which can be applied for 20 to 30 minutes twice a day.

Gel heating packs were used in a study with horses. The wrap was heated to 40° C (104° F) and applied to the metacarpal region for 30 minutes. Thermographic images were taken immediately after the wrap was removed, then every 15 minutes for two hours, and every 30 minutes for an additional two hours. Although the wrap cooled over the treatment period, the heat-treated legs were 5° C warmer than the untreated controls when the wrap was removed. The heat application also increased hoof temperature in the treated leg by 1.7° C. Although the metacarpal area cooled quickly after the wrap was removed, the treated leg remained more than 2° C warmer than the controls, and the vasodilating effects lasted nearly four hours. An interesting phenomenon of secondary reflex vasodilation was observed 30 to 45 minutes after the wrap was removed. The authors speculated the relaxation of the vas-

cular smooth muscle could have caused this response. Mild edema was noted in the treated legs, suggesting the benefit of a compression wrap after heat treatment. This study also showed that applying heat to the horse's leg increases circulation in the foot.(9)

Heating lamps have several disadvantages. They pose a fire hazard, and they do not provide enough therapeutic heat when suspended from a barn rafter over a horse. Equine solariums have been built so several lamps fixed to a metal arc can be lowered closer to the horse's back. Horses seem to enjoy standing under them, particularly when it is cold and they are sore.

Liniments and analgesic balms are counter-irritating agents. These lotions, creams, or liquids contain cutaneous nerve-irritating chemicals, usually Caspian from the pepper plant. The irritant causes skin capillaries to dilate, making the skin feel warm. This, of course, does nothing for the deeper structures. The massaging required to rub the analgesic balm into the skin could have benefits, and the sensory nerve stimulation could block out some pain message recognition. These agents do not really warm joint structures such as the capsule where restrictions occur, and their use is not a substitute for pre-exercise warm-up.

It has been shown that whereas dry heat can raise surface temperatures to a greater degree, moist heat can penetrate to a slightly deeper level of tissue.(10) A heat pack can be placed over a damp towel if moist heat is desired. For muscle soreness, try adding two cups of Epsom salts to a bucket of warm water. Soak towels in the water, ring them out so there is no dripping, and place them on the sore area. If used with a heat lamp, chemical heat pack, or other form of heat, the towels will maintain their warmth longer. The magnesium in Epsom salts, some of which will be absorbed through the skin, is an excellent muscle relaxant and sedative for the nervous system.

Ultrasound — the Deep Heating Device

Therapeutic ultrasound can increase tissue temperature at depths ranging from 3 to 5 centimeters (cm) without overheating the skin and superficial tissue.(11) The effects of therapeutic ultrasound are the same as superficial heating modalities with the addition of a "micromassaging" oscillation of molecules. Sound waves create rapid oscillation that disrupts collagenous fibers and increases cell metabolism. Ultrasound is described in more detail in Chapter 7.

Effects of Heat

- Increases cellular metabolism
- Increases muscle spindle activity
- Increases muscle contractility
- Increases inflammatory response
- Increases extensibility of collagen
- Increases nerve conduction velocity
- Reduces synovial fluid viscosity
- Stimulates vasodilation

References

1. Currie, DM. 1985. Self-directed learning and medical education: a comparison. *Arch Phys Med Rehab.* 66:454.
2. Robinson, AJ. and Snyder-Mackler, L. 1995. *Clinical Electrophysiology.* Baltimore, MD.: Williams & Wilkins. 389.
3. Michlovitz, SL. 1986. *Thermal Agents in Rehabilitation.* Philadelphia: FA Davis Company. 270.
4. Currier, DP. and Nelson, RM. 1992. *Dynamics of Human Biologic Tissues.* Philadelphia: FA Davis Company. 68.
5. Michlovitz, 102.
6. Greenberg, RS. 1972. The effects of hot packs and exercise on local blood flow. *Phys Ther.* 52:273.
7. Bromiley, M. 1998. Facts about backs. Proceedings Bluegrass Laminitis Symposium. Louisville, KY.
8. Porter, M. and Porter, J. 1981. Electrical safety in the training room. *Athletic Training.* 16:263-64.
9. Turner, T. et al. 1991. Effects of heat, cold, biomagnets and ultrasound on skin circulation in the horse.

Proceedings American Assocation of Equine Practitioners. San Francisco, CA. 249-57.

10. Abramson, DI. et al. 1967. Comparison of wet and dry heat in raising temperature of tissues. *Arch Phys Med Rehab.* 48:654.

11. Michlovitz, 99.

Cold Therapy

*Honor the healing power of nature...*Hippocrates

PEOPLE who work with horses have long recognized the value of cold in reducing swelling and pain. I have heard many a horseman attest to the benefits of turning out a horse with lower leg problems in deep snow. The combined effects of muscle activity and cold reduce edema and improve movement. Anyone who has turned out a horse for a romp in the snow has seen this.

Yet too few horse professionals recognize the usefulness of ice in preventing swelling or inflammation after exercise. Perhaps it is because many barns are not equipped with an ice maker or a freezer. Often the trainer turns to cold water hosing. Although this certainly cools the skin surface, the temperature is uncontrolled and might not be cold enough to affect the structures most often involved in sports injury. Effective cold therapy comes in the form of commercial ice packs, ice cubes or chips, bandages soaked in ice slush, and ice cup massage.

Cryotherapy is the therapeutic use of cold to treat acute injury. Commercial cold packs are a convenient way to apply this therapy. But perhaps because of the convenience, they often are misused, left on too long, or even forgotten. I often have taken off a cold pack to find it had become a "hot pack"

because the chemicals warmed to room temperature, then absorbed body heat.

As an equine therapy modality, ice has a broad range of application. Ice massage is used for:

• muscle pain, to break the self-perpetuating cycle of muscle spasm-ischemia-pain-more muscle spasm.

• a severe bruise or hematoma resulting from direct trauma such as a bite or kick.

• trauma from a concussion such as splints or bucked shins.

• a reaction to an intermuscular injection.

• acute tendinitis.

Effects of Therapeutic Cold

Cold therapy constricts capillaries at the site of application, reducing local tissue metabolism. Lower levels of chemical mediators of inflammation, such as histamine, leukotaxine, and necrosin, are liberated from damaged cells into the surrounding tissue. Pain message transmission is slowed through a lowered nerve conduction velocity. Although the inflammatory reaction is necessary to stimulate the release of neurotransmitters and to draw mast cells to the injured area to orchestrate repair, it should not be allowed to persist. (A mast cell is a granular connective tissue cell that releases histamine and an anticoagulant, heparin. (Histamine causes the red flush associated with injury.) The inflammation creates hypoxia in the tissues. Cryotherapy reduces the oxygen requirement of the cells around the injured tissue by lowering their metabolism, allowing them to survive the hypoxic condition.

Initially, cold causes vasoconstriction, decreasing local blood volume. Blood is shunted away from the cold area so the body can preserve its internal temperature.[1] Following prolonged exposure to cold, a

reactive vasodilation occurs as the body seeks to re-warm the cooled tissue to prevent damage. First identified in 1930, this reaction was called the hunting response, perhaps because it was often observed in the toes, ears, and nose of hunters.[2] This phenomenon, or reflex vasodilation, was not observed in a study of the cooling effect of a gel wrap applied to a horse's leg for 30 minutes.[3]

Cold applications have a direct effect on the conduction velocity of sensory nerves, which carry pain messages to the brain. In a classic study, a 20-minute application of ice packs slowed nerve conduction significantly enough to provide analgesia.[4] Slowing the conduction rate reduces the number of impulses per unit of time, and less "pain information" reaches the brain.

Cryotherapy is one of the most frequently used modalities for pain relief in orthopedic injury care. It decreases need for injected and oral analgesic medications following surgery.[5]

An interesting study looked at whether nalox-

Horsemen have long recognized the therapeutic benefits of cold.

one could be used to reverse the pain-relieving effects of cold. Naloxone is a narcotic antagonist that reverses the effects of endogenous opiates such as endorphin. Patients with rheumatoid arthritis of the knee who had previously gotten relief from cold pack applications found that they no longer felt pain-free after naloxone was administered, indicating that endorphins play a role in cold-mediated pain relief.(6)

Applying ice and a compression wrap to the site immediately after surgery helps prevent swelling. Tissue insult produces an immediate chemical reaction by the injured cells. Among the many other chemical activities, histamine produces local vasodilation and increases capillary permeability. Leukocytes migrate through the capillary walls and move toward the wound for phagocytosis (destruction of foreign matter). Large amounts of fluid, proteins, and fibrinogen seep into intercellular spaces, forming edema. When a joint is involved, blood and joint fluid accumulate within the joint capsule.

The combination of ice and compression causes capillary vasoconstriction and pressure on the connective tissue to restrict blood and fluid leakage from damaged tis-

sue. The first 48 hours after injury are critical to edema restriction. Polo bandages soaked in a bucket of ice slush are an effec-

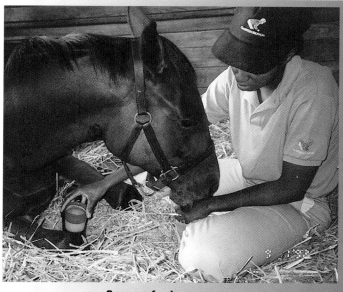

Cryocup for ice massage.

tive form of cold and compression for the horse's legs after exercise. When applied during the cool-down phase, they prevent post exercise inflammation and swelling. But when an injury exists, it will be that much more apparent — both in feeling and appearance — when the surrounding tissues are cooled.

One must remember that although the use of cold will reduce acute swelling and inflammation, tissue damage still might be present. A thorough veterinary diagnosis during the acute phase of any injury will provide crucial information about the nature and extent of the injury.

Applying Cold Therapy

The most efficient form of cold application is ice cup massage. For this you need to place Styrofoam cups filled with water in the freezer. When the water is frozen, peel away the cup's rim so you have a block of ice exposed. Hold the cup by the bottom and use slow, circular strokes to cool a 5-square-centimeter area in 10 minutes. This safe,

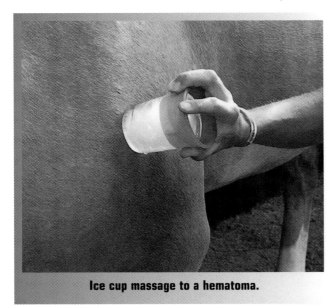

Ice cup massage to a hematoma.

effective, and inexpensive way to relieve pain also limits tissue damage from injury.

A commercial product called the Cryocup is a handy item that you keep in the freezer and use when needed. These cups are made of cold-retardant polyethylene so the user's fingers don't get frozen. To use the Cryocup, assemble, fill with water, and freeze. When you need it, briefly place it under warm running water, twist the appli-

cator ring, lift it out, and apply. These cups, which are used extensively in human sports medicine, are reusable.

Ice massage is done for 10 to 30 minutes, depending on the size of the area and the depth of tissue involved. Deep muscle takes longer to cool than tendons or ligaments. Ice directly over a bony area can be painful. Do not hold a block of ice still on the skin; keep it moving in a massaging motion. Ice massage provides a pro-active way to address the symptoms of injury or post-surgical swelling and pain. Minimizing blood and cellular fluid leakage from injured tissue will reduce the size of the trauma area. It also will reduce the amount of post-injury debris that must be removed before repair can begin. Ice limits the magnitude of the injury.

Wet cold is thought to be more effective than dry cold. A dry wrap under a cold pack will insulate the cold from the tissues. One study compared the ability of wet cold, dry cold, and commercial cold packs to reduce skin temperature in humans. Wet cold was ice chips in a towel; dry cold was ice chips in plastic (like those frozen peas often used in the barns); and commercial cold packs were gel packs that required refrigeration. The various forms of cold were applied for 15 minutes to the human calf muscle. Wet cold (ice in a towel) proved the most efficient means of reducing skin temperature, with skin remaining cold the longest and with the greatest reduction in nerve conduction velocity. (7) The commercial cold packs were the least efficient.

Some commercial cold packs are too stiff and do not conform to the horse's leg. If you use these packs, make sure they have softened enough to conform.

Although some people use a bag of frozen peas, this probably is not the most efficient choice. Air space around the peas reduces cooling effectiveness. This is also true for a bag of ice cubes. Break the cubes into smaller chips and place them in a wet wrap to cool the tissues more uniformly.

In human sports medicine, cryotherapy is used three or four times a day after injury or surgery. It is rarely prescribed for horses. In a recent veterinary newsletter, Dr. Larry Bramlage writes, "Treatment during the acute stage (0-48 hours) should be focused toward the control of the inflammatory response to the injury. Cold therapy will inhibit the inflammatory reaction, cause vasodilation, slow hemorrhage, reduce the amount of inflammatory mediators released into the surrounding tissues, and reduce the perception of pain. Applications of 30 to 60

minutes should be repeated three to four times a day." (8)

Cold therapy is indicated following many acute injuries and can be useful following surgery. According to a human study, the

This product offers an instant self-contained source of cold that will last about 30 minutes. Ice and refrigeration are not needed.

use of cryotherapy after arthroscopic knee surgery resulted in decreased medication use and improved weight bearing. (9)

The beneficial effects of cooling are achieved without freezing the tissue. Ice applications longer than 30 minutes should be avoided. Hours of continuous ice application will not increase the effectiveness of tissue cooling or extend the period of analgesia; in fact, cold that is too intense or used for too long causes pain. At the racetrack, horses are sometimes made to stand in a tub of ice water for hours. This is unnecessary and can be harmful. Excessive use of cold can cause such a decrease in metabolic activity that local asphyxia occurs; both the larger motor fibers and the sensory fibers can be damaged. Nerve palsy, or loss of ability to move or control movement, could result from over-cooling a major nerve branch.(10) Overexposure to cold can result in increased edema caused by tissue damage.

Uses for Cold Therapy

Whether in training or just playing, the horse has many opportunities to sustain an acute trauma. A few applications of ice and compression can significantly reduce the early symptoms of many injuries. Four common injuries that respond well to cold application are bucked shins, splints, hematomas, and tendinitis.

The early stage of dorsal metacarpal disease (bucked shins) is characterized by heat and tenderness on the anterior aspect of the cannon bone. Compressive forces stress the anterior aspect of the foreleg, stimulating new bone formation and remodeling of the cortex. The beginning stages of this adaptation involve inflammation and pain. At the first sign of ten-

derness, heat, or swelling over the dorsal aspect of the cannon bone, apply an ice cup massage at least twice a day until the area is completely cold. Follow this with a compression wrap to eliminate space for intertissue bleeding.

In addition to therapy, give the injury time to repair by reducing exercise. This allows the tissues to recover, yet continue to remodel. A hand-held infrared thermographic scanner can help determine the amount of exercise by measuring skin surface temperature. This reflects the amount of inflammation present and should replace repeated squeezing of the foreleg for a pain reaction.

Commercial ice and compression boots.

As with all injuries, many factors can play a role in the development of bucked shins. Investigate the cause by starting from the ground and working up, observing the running surface, hoof balance, and shoeing. Hock or stifle soreness often predispose a horse to shin pain. Muscle soreness in the gluteal area perhaps plays the most significant role in the development of bucked shins.(11)

The archaic practice of blistering or firing the shins, which forces stall rest, only furthers muscle weakness and does nothing for bone remodeling. Thermography has shown persistent inflammation in shins eight months after firing.

Human athletes in the early stages of training suffer from shin soreness as the tibia remodels in response to the stress of running. The accepted therapy includes ice massage once or twice a day, compression wraps, and strength training to condition the muscles to withstand the increasing work load. After a few days of ice therapy, electrical stimulation, photon therapy, or magnets are used to stimulate metabolism, further reduce pain, and promote repair.

Early applications of ice shorten the inflammatory response and reduce pain. Using this type of treatment, the horse can continue in a reduced exercise program, avoiding muscle atrophy, while the tissues of the foreleg heal. Thermography can monitor the progress of bucked shin repair and give the trainer insight into the appropriate amount of exercise. Radiographs also are necessary to rule out metacarpal fractures.

Splints, which can involve direct trauma to the periosteum of the second and fourth metacarpals, can be managed successfully with ice massage and compression. Another

This unit provides a temperature control and pads designed to conform to the treatment area.

mechanism involves tearing of the interosseous ligament due to concussive forces coming from the ground up and from the metacarpal bones pushing down and back when the leg is loaded.(12) The body responds to the excessive load by producing extra bone to stabilize the stress point. Reducing the work load and applying ice and compression will control the symptoms and allow remodeling.

A hematoma is a deep contusion or bruise that results in bleeding within the muscle. The accumulated fluid increases intermuscular pressure that eventually compresses the blood vessels and stops the bleeding, but also might result in ischemic damage and muscle degeneration. At the first sign of heat or swelling, apply ice cup massage to reduce the inflammation. Vasoconstriction will inhibit intertissue bleeding, reducing the amount of debris the body must absorb. Applying ice two or three times a day will minimize the wound size.

Cold must be applied immediately to tendon injuries to minimize the size of the hematoma. The goal during the acute stage, which lasts up to 48 hours, is to minimize inflammation. If inflammation is uncontrolled or allowed to persist, excessive edema and subsequent scar tissue can develop. Ice cup massage followed by a compression wrap will control the amount of debris allowed to accumulate around the tendon.

Several good products provide uniform cold and compression to the tendons without the need for tubs of water and ice. A thorough veterinary exam that includes diagnostic ultrasound is vital, however, in assessing the extent and nature of the injury.

One study examined how cold therapy gel wraps affected horses. The wraps were applied to one front leg of each of 10 horses, leaving the other front leg as the control. Cold was applied for 30 minutes, then the wraps were removed. Thermographic images were made of both forelegs immediately after the wrap was removed, then at 15 minute intervals for two hours, followed by 30 minute intervals for another two hours. The cold-treated legs averaged 6 degrees cooler than the untreated legs when the wraps were removed. The hoof on the cold-treated side was also about 2 degrees cooler. The dorsal metacarpus, which was the slowest area to warm, remained nearly 4 degrees colder than the untreated legs for four hours. This would support the use of cold gel wraps for pain relief and swelling reduction in acute dorsal metacarpal disease.

The study also noted that the palmar metacarpal artery and veins began warming almost immediately, indicating that effective cold therapy application to the flexor tendons should be applied repeatedly. This study did not see a reflex vasodilation occur after 30 minutes of cold therapy at 4° C. The authors suggested that because of the prolonged effect of cold on limb temperature, it's better to delay applying a compression wrap to avoid counteracting the cold through a bandage's insulating effect.(13)

Effects of Cold

- Lowered cell metabolic rate.
- Vasoconstriction.
- Lowered inflammatory response.
- Lowered nerve conduction velocity.
- Lowered muscle contractility.
- Raised pain threshold.
- Lowered collagen tissue extensibility.
- Lowered response of muscle spindle to stretch.
- Increased viscosity of synovial fluid.

Cautions

Commercial cold packs can be colder than ice, so be careful when using them. When cold is too intense, it is painful and can result in damage to nerves or skin. Do not use ice or cold packs on open wounds or over area where nerves have been damaged.

Definitions

Histamine — An enzyme that produces redness of the skin associated with injury.

Leukotaxine — a nitrogenous substance that increases capillary permeability.

Necrosin — An enzyme that destroys cells surrounding an area of trauma.

References

1. Olson, JE. and Stravino, VD. 1972. A Review of Cryotherapy. *Phys Ther.* 52:840-53.
2. Lewis, T. 1930. Observations upon the reaction of the vessels of the human skin to cold. *Heart.* 15:177-208.
3. Turner, T. et al. Effects of heat, cold, biomagnets and ultrasound on skin circulation in the horse. Proceeding American Assocation of Equine Practitioners. San Francisco, CA. 249-57.
4. Lee, JM. et al. 1978. Effects of ice on nerve conduction velocity. *Physiotherapy.* 64:2-6.
5. Cohn, BT. et al. 1989. The effects of cold therapy in the postoperative management of pain in patients undergoing anterior cruciate ligament reconstruction. *Am J Sports Med.* 17:344-48.
6. Utsinger, PD. et al. 1982. Efficacy of cryotherapy and thermotherapy in the management of rheumatoid arthritis pain: evidence for an endorphin effect. *Arth Rheum.* 25:s113.
7. Belitsky, R. et al. 1987. Evaluation of the effectiveness of wet ice, dry ice, and cryogen packs in reducing skin temperature. *Phys Ther.* 67:1081-84.
8. Bramlage, L. Rational approach to treating equine tendinitis makes dif-

ference. *DVM Newsmagazine Special Supplement.* 609.

9. Lessard, L. et al. 1977. The efficacy of cryotherapy following arthroscopic knee surgery. *J Orth Spts Phys Ther.* 26:14-22.

10. Drez, D. et al. 1981. Cryotherapy and nerve palsy. *Amer J Spts Med.* 9:256-57.

11. King, C. and Mansmann, R. 1997. *Equine Lameness.* Grand Prairie, TX: Equine Research. 736.

12. Rooney, JR. 1974. *The Lame Horse, Causes, Symptoms, and Treatment.* Millwood, NY: Breakthrough Pub. 65.

13. Turner, T. et al. 249-57.

Other Reading

Farry, PJ. et al. 1980. Ice treatment of injured ligaments: an experimental model. *New Zea Med J.* 91:12-14.

Kaplan, PE. and Tanner, ED. 1989. *Musculoskeletal Pain and Disability.* Norwalk, CT: Appleton & Lang. 82.

Levy, AS. et al. 1997. Penetration of cryotherapy in treatment after shoulder arthroscopy. *Arthroscopy.* 13:461-64.

Schauble, HJ. 1946. The local use of ice after orthopedic procedures. *Am J Surg.* 72: 711-14.

Tauber, C. et al. 1992. Measurement of reactive vasodilation during cold gel pack application to nontraumatized ankles. *Phys Ther.* 72:294-99.

Walker, RH. et al. 1991. Postoperative use of continuous passive motion, transcutaneous electrical nerve stimulation, and continuous cooling pad following total knee arthroplasty. *J Arthroplasty.* 6:151-56.

Hands-On Therapies for Horses

*The level of your communication determines the level of your relationship...*Mr. Ed

PERHAPS no other modality of equine therapy has grown as rapidly in recent years as the "hands-on" therapies. This therapy is patterned after human physical therapy, in which the use of the hands to relieve soft tissue discomfort and joint movement restrictions has expanded over the last 20 years. The many techniques of massage, acupressure, and joint mobilizations have long been used but only recently studied scientifically and refined. The use of hands can help reduce pain and swelling, as well as increase joint range of motion and muscle function.

Physical therapy began as a largely "hands-on" profession. With the development of therapeutic equipment, manual techniques fell out of favor in the early half of the century. This is changing as we approach the beginning of a new century.

Manual Therapy Tools

The equine therapist's most vital tools are the eyes, hands, and state of mind. With the eyes the therapist looks at both the horse's posture and the way he is put together. Beginning with the horse's head, we observe the position of his ears and the eye expression to determine his state of mind. We look

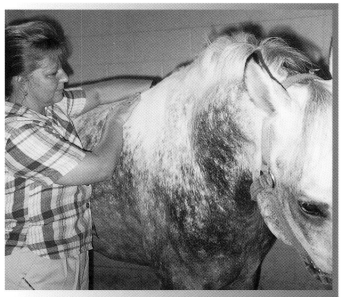

The use of hands can help reduce pain and swelling, and increase range of motion and muscle function.

for tension in the head carriage and around the muzzle. Muscle tension is often visible, and imbalances in muscle conditioning can be seen. Does the horse stand in a straight line from head to tail, or is he standing in a

"C" shape, habitually curving his body to the side? Resting postures can say a lot about body imbalances. Do the muscles of the top line look rounded and lively, or flattened and strained? Does the horse overuse the musculature along his bottom line, the triceps and the biceps femoris?

Looking down the legs, notice whether the horse stands with equal weight on all

Sensitive hands can detect imbalances in muscle tension or energy.

four feet. Is one hoof carrying more weight than the others, manifested by splayed walls or a larger frog? Are the heels contracted due to lack of weight bearing over sustained periods? After making this initial observation, watch the horse move. Look for uneven strides, for lack of or uneven pelvic

motion. Notice the motion of the head. The ears become helpful here, as the eyes can only observe movement, not forces. Listen for uneven hoof strike, or an uneven rhythm in the cadence of the hoof strikes, to gain insight into the muscle force used with each movement.

Visual gait analysis has certain inadequacies. The eye cannot observe high-speed movement. And because of the horse's great ability to compensate, visual gait analysis is very subjective. Also, you are observing an effect, the net result of a pathological process, and the horse's attempt to compensate for it. When a horse is visibly lame, the horse has exhausted all of the available mechanisms for compensation. Unless the injury occurs suddenly, someone failed to use the power of observation months or even years before, when the original insult occurred.

The hands can provide information the eyes cannot detect. A systematic exploration with sensitive hands can provide information about imbalances in muscle strength and tension. The hands can differentiate between atrophy from lack of use and atrophy from misuse. The hands can feel heat or an area of lower temperature. Sensitive hands also can detect excess or insufficient energy.

Manual therapy requires more than manipulation of joint and tissue: A key ingredient in an effective session is the therapist's state of mind. Manual therapy is noticeably less effective if the therapist feels no compassion. Controlled experiments have shown that human patients can tell the difference between a therapist in a healing frame of mind and one performing identical hand motions while doing distracting mental arithmetic. An equine therapist must cultivate true compassion for his or her patients and enter each therapy session in a healing frame of mind.

Benefits of Manual Therapy

Imbalances in muscle tension or energy are very early warning signs of injury. By using your hands on your horse regularly, you can see into the future and change it. Manual therapies can effectively prevent injury by keeping the soft tissues mobile. When connective tissue mobility is lost there is more strain on surrounding tissue, increasing the likelihood of fiber damage.

Manual therapy brings the horse and handler into close and intimate contact. A horse is able to detect kindness and love conveyed through touch and develops trust in the handler. When a horse is in critical ill health or discomfort, hands-on therapy can encourage survival. As Ric Redden, a veterinarian who has cared for many horses with chronic laminitis, says, "Those loving hands can talk them into living."

Techniques of Manual Therapy

It would be a very big job to list and describe all of the manual therapy techniques that have been developed over the last 20 years. In this book, several of the popular techniques will be discussed. All of them share the physical connection between therapist and horse, a means for evaluation, and a channel for energy flow.

Massage

Massage is the use of the hands and fingers, and even the elbow, to manipulate the soft tissues. Its goals include promotion of tissue drainage, muscle relaxation, and pain relief. Conditions that would benefit from massage include tight and contracted tendons, ligaments, muscles, chronic inflammatory conditions, scar tissue, and chronic edema. Massage loosens and stretches dense connective tissue, has a sedative effect on the central nervous system, and can enhance lymphatic and blood circulatory activity. For massage to work, the affected structure must be superficial enough to benefit from the force imparted by the therapist's hands.

Tools that provide a low frequency vibration, such as rollers, vibrators, or percussion devices, are available. They could save the operator some work, but also might prevent him from achieving the full benefit of massage. Hands-on contact can heighten the therapist's awareness of the horse's physical state.

When to Use Massage

Soft tissues are susceptible to injury from overuse or from a suddenly applied force. Such forces result in a "sprain" if ligaments are involved and in a "strain" if muscle and tendon fibers are involved.

The body's response to injury is inflammation followed by repair. The early stage of inflammation is marked by heat, redness, and swelling. The synovial membranes, those that line the joint capsule and produce its lubricating fluid, thicken. Adhesions develop between tissues that are not normally joined. Ice massage can help shorten this stage of the injury process. This cooling reduces the rate of chemical activity, restricting blood flow through vasoconstriction, and reducing the release of inflammatory substances such as bradykinin and histamine. Ice massage is so simple that its value is often overlooked. It simply requires freezing water in a Styrofoam cup, then using this block of ice for five to 10 minutes over the injury site. Use ice to reduce injury debris that contributes to scar tissue formation.

Manual massage usually is applied after the initial inflammatory phase is under control, at least 24 to 48 hours post injury. In this stage young fibro-blasts begin to migrate to the area and lay down new collagen fibers. These new fibers initially have a random orientation but later acquire definite arrangement. Tension plays an important role in this phase of the healing process because collagen fibers re-orient themselves in line with the tensile forces applied to the tissue. New collagen fibers not only fill the gap but also form transverse and oblique adhesions that could become binding to the connective tissue and prevent full movement of the body part. A sprain can heal with shortened connective tissue when pain prevents use. Massage can be used with stretching exercises to maintain normal range of joint motion.

A muscle strain also can result in shortened connective tissue. Injury leaves the muscle fibers in spasm. If this spasm persists because of repeated stress, muscle splinting could result. This occurs when dense connective tissue accumulates in a muscle that is in a chronic state of tension and strain. Massage increases a strained muscle's flexibility and softens the area of spasm. A study of the effects of a 12-minute massage on hamstring flexibility found a significant increase in flexibility immediately afterward.(1) Seven days later, the range of motion had returned to pre-treatment levels. This indicates the need to repeat massage until the horse can maintain the increased flexibility through his daily exercise routine.

Surgery or injury often results in an accumulation of edema around the wound. A stall-bound horse often will develop edema in the lower legs, which is known as "stocking up." Because the lymph vessels of the horse's lower leg do not have valves to counteract the effects of gravity, muscle movement is needed to assist blood and lymph circulation. Massage can assist the circulatory systems and aid in edema reduction.

Techniques of Massage

Before beginning a massage, the therapist must examine the area for broken skin or inflammation. The horse should stand squarely in a clean, dry stall, preferably his own. Lighting should be adequate and the surroundings quiet. A lubricant is not necessary; in fact, using oil or lubricant could cause the hands or fingers to slide, reducing the applied pressure. If a lubricant is desired, try baby powder because it can be easily brushed out of the coat.

All massages should begin with gentle stroking to accustom the horse to it and to allow the therapist to search for areas of spasm and tenderness. The strokes should be of even pressure and run longitudinally along the muscle following the direction in which the hair lies. The initial stroking should be superficial to create a sedating effect and avoid creating protective muscle contractions.

As the horse relaxes, the strokes can become deeper, stimulating blood vessels and lymph channels. Deeper stroking

Equine massage therapist Robert Altman says, "Massage is basically hard manual labor."

should be in the direction of venous flow, toward the heart.

It is usually recommended that the massage begin away from the problem area. As the horse relaxes, the therapist can work toward that area. Massage should not go on so long that it irritates the horse. With purposeful movements, 10 to 15 minutes per large area should suffice.

Recommended pressure is 15 pounds for compression-type stroke. To become familiar with the various pressures, practice with a bathroom scale. Twenty pounds of pressure is the maximum one should apply in practice. It is really not the amount of pressure but the intent, your own mindfulness, that is important. Before beginning a massage, take a moment to become grounded and summon the vital energy.

Types of Strokes

Several stroking techniques have specific application. These basic moves are common to all massage techniques.

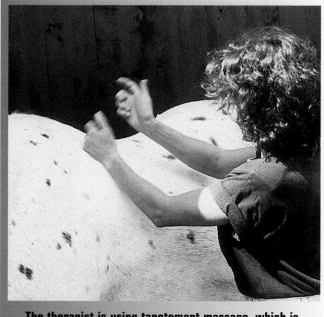

The therapist is using tapotement massage, which is intended to stimulate nerves and skin capillaries.

Effleurage are strokes that glide. This stroke is used to begin and end a massage. The pressure is firm and even as the fingers seek tender or tight areas. The palm of the hand often is used in a firm, gliding motion. In areas of extreme tenderness, it may be the only stroke used. Effleurage stroking accustoms the horse to the therapist's touch.

Petrissage are strokes that knead. Small areas of skin and subcutaneous tissue are grasped and lifted as the fingers are brought together with firm pressure. Theoretically, this stroke aids in removal of waste products and helps free adhesions.

Tapotement are striking movements. This technique can have a stimulating effect on superficial sensory nerves and skin capillaries or a sedating effect on the whole horse. Using the hypothenar surface of the hand (fleshy area below the little finger) the body part is struck with gentle, rhythmic blows. There are several variations of this move, one being a clapping movement using the palm of the flat hand. Clapping is done on muscle areas, not bony areas. To relax spasm, use the clenched fists in a beating manner. This must be done without tension to avoid alarming the horse. Controlled, purposeful blows can be comfortable and relaxing. A variation on this is to use the palm of the cupped hand. Cupping blows have a sedating effect.

Friction makes use of compression. Small, circular movements are made using the tips of the fingers, the heel of the hand, or the elbow. The fingers should move the tissues beneath the skin. The purpose is to separate the fibers that form adhesions in the deeper tissues. The horse's muscles must be warm and relaxed for friction to work.

Vibration strokes shake the tissue. The fingertips or palms stay in contact with the skin while a vibrating motion is created with the forearm and hands. This motion can follow the path of nerves or circulatory channels.

Knuckling uses the dorsal, or back side, of the hands. This gliding stroke is used when the fascia is thick or the problem area deep. Greater pressure can be applied by clenching the fist and rolling the back of the hand and knuckles over the affected area in an upward sweep.

Deep friction massage applies pressure across the muscle fibers rather than along their length. This technique is used to improve range of joint motion by breaking down scar tissue. Transverse adhesions are pulled apart as the longitudinal fibers are pushed back and forth or in small circles. This technique can be uncomfortable for the horse but effective when done by a skilled therapist. If the massage is not applied at the exact site of the lesion, no benefit occurs.

This technique, sometimes called transverse friction, is contraindicated in any situation in which inter-tissue bleeding could result. It is reserved for focal areas of adhesion where mobility has been lost. Warm the area with a hot pack or ultrasound before beginning the deep friction and apply an ice massage afterward. This will minimize inter-tissue bleeding and eliminate pain.

One study sought to determine whether deep transverse friction helped prevent transverse binding of collagen fibers in ligaments.(2) Histological analysis revealed that deep friction massage did not affect fiber orientation within the ligament. This finding goes against the theory under which this massage technique was developed, making its value a controversial topic. I think adhesions and dense connective tissue are better addressed with ultrasound and electrical stimulation. These tools soften the adhesions without the aggressive mechanical action of deep friction massage.

Before leaving the topic of manual massage, I would like to mention massage to the face, ears, and inside of the mouth. To massage the gums inside the mouth, first wet your hand, then gently slide it into the mouth over the upper gum. Massage gently, keeping your fingers together and out of the way of the teeth. Wet your hand again and slide it over the lower gum. It might be easiest to go over the nose and into the mouth rather than straight into the mouth. The horse's jaw should relax, and his head should drop. This is an ideal time to connect mentally with the horse and bring about deep relaxation.

Massage can be part of the warm-up before exercise or competition. Work your way from the head to the tail and down each leg to prepare the horse for pre-exercise manual stretching. Active stretching and sport-related movements done once the rider is up complete the warm-up.

When the workout is over and the horse's body temperature has returned to normal, massage can be used to prevent stiffness and aid in removing the waste products of exercise. Just as with the warm-up, stretching exercises should be a part of this routine. Massage and stretching provide an opportunity to detect post-exercise tightness or heat.

As Robert Altman, a renowned professional massage therapist, says, "Massage is basically hard manual labor." Massage therapists run the risk of developing arthritis in the wrists and fingers and must possess a fitness level suitable for the job. The American Massage Therapy Association has set standards for massage therapists and recommends attending an accredited school before using the title equine massage therapist. Again, in Altman's words, "Anyone can rub a horse and maybe even make him feel better, but massage therapy is a very scientifically accurate treatment and you do need quite a bit of training to become proficient at it."

Massage for Flexural Deformities in Foals

Massage is often prescribed for flexural limb deformities in newborn foals. This is not one condition, but several that are clearly described in King and Mansmann's *Equine Lameness*, from which this discussion is taken.(3)

The flexural deformity might be the result of a flexor laxity. This condition occurs in the rear legs where there is lack of tone in the flexor muscle and tendon, allowing hyperextension of the fetlock and hock joints. The deformity might be a flexural contracture, which occurs in the front legs. The flexor muscles are hypertonal and transmit this tension to the tendons, causing abnormal joint flexion, often called contracted tendons. With either problem there is an imbalance of tension in the opposing muscles: tightness on one side of the limb and weakness on the other. The flexor and extensor muscles should work together evenly to stabilize the carpal joint. The lengths of these muscles adapt to the position at which they are habitually held. For treatment to succeed, it must start as early as possible.

Gently massage the lax or weak muscle

group. You can use a grooming tool such as a "Unigroom," working for 30 seconds to two minutes at a time. The purpose is to stimulate the muscle fibers and establish neural pathways to the muscle bundles.

A stretching massage is used on the tight muscle groups to elongate the muscle fibers. Use a deep stroking massage with your fingertips to pull the fibers in a steady, longitudinal direction. As you work, begin to straighten the leg just until the tense group feels the first bit of stretch. Back off slightly on the stretch and hold for at least 30 seconds. Relax and repeat the stretching massage and manual stretch several times. You are trying to reset the resting tension in the tense group so the pull is not so strong that it overpowers the weaker group. Overstretching will cause more tightness and tension in the muscle, so always back off the stretch for the hold phase. Muscle shortening is a response to lack of stretch rather than lack of movement.

Tightness often can be found in the muscles and fascia of the neck, chest, and shoulders, or hips. To reduce fascial tension, focus your attention on the area and place your hands lightly over the chest and withers or the stifle and sacrum. Gently compress the tissue between your hands, using more mental energy than actual physical pressure. Hold the "pressure" lightly and feel the tissue warm and pulse. You might feel an "unwinding" sensation as the tension is released.

This could take as long as 30 minutes, depending on the extent of the restrictions. This tissue release technique also can be used on the carpal fascia to soften constricted joint capsule fascia at the back of the knee.

Sports Massage

Sports massage is designed to improve athletic performance by increasing muscle response and flexibility. These therapists primarily use deep strokes and cross-fiber friction to increase the efficiency of limb movement. The goals of sports massage are to alleviate muscle tension, remove lactic acid, increase pain threshold, increase flexibility, and stimulate circulation.

Few of the claims are based on laboratory studies, however. One study using humans as subjects sought to determine the physiologic responses during submaximal exercise following a 30-minute sports massage. The results indicate that massage had no effect on cardiovascular measures, such as cardiac output, oxygen consumption, heart rate, blood pressure, and lactic acid responses. It was not found to improve exercise performance or provide the subjects with increased oxygen flow to the muscles.(4)

One study with human sprinters reported that sports massage did not increase stride frequency. Participants in the study, however, said they felt relaxed and better able to cope with physical exertion after massage.(5) A contrasting study on the effects of massage on hamstring muscles reported that range of motion can be improved significantly.(6) This finding would validate the theory that massage can be used for preventing injuries such as strains and sprains. Confirming the effects of massage on blood flow, a thermographic study showed increases in skin temperature after massage to areas overlying muscle spasm.(7)

Sports massage is designed to improve athletic performance.

Sports massage might not be measurable by standard means. Instead, it could help put the human athlete in an appropriate frame of mind for competition. No one knows precisely the value of mental relaxation and preparedness for competition horses. Skilled riders know what their horses need before competing, but these needs cannot be subjected to laboratory analysis.

A discussion of sports massage cannot end without mention of Jack Meagher, who can be credited with bringing massage to the attention of horsemen. Meagher's book, *Beating Muscle Injuries*, has been the Bible for massage therapists for 15 years. His philosophy involves seeking the stress points in the muscles and working to remove them.(8)

TTEAM

Linda Tellington-Jones developed the techniques that have come to be called TTEAM after studying the Feldenkrais method of body awareness exercises. TTEAM, which stands for Tellington-Jones Equine Awareness Method, or more recently, Tellington-Jones Every Animal Method, is aimed at elevating the animal's awareness of its own body, but it also succeeds in fostering communication and bonding between human and animal.

The techniques are simple and easily

mastered in workshops given around the country. Ground exercises for coordination and focusing are combined with variations of the TTouch, gentle circles using the tips of the three middle fingers. TTouch is unlike massage, in that only the skin is moved in a small circular pattern.

Although there is very little pressure involved, sensory nerves in the skin are stimulated and a cascade of physiological events takes place, ultimately affecting brain wave pattern in both patient and therapist. All areas of the body are addressed with TTouch techniques, including the ears, belly, and inside of the mouth. The techniques are helpful in stressful situations. Horses accustomed to TTouch are more willing to have dental or farrier work or other potentially objectionable tasks performed if they are preceded or accompanied by this technique.

Trigger Point Therapy

Trigger point massage is sometimes called myotherapy or myofascial trigger point therapy. Before these terms became popular, this technique was called ischemic compression, which describes the mechanism of action. This technique involves sustained pressure from the thumbs, fingers, or elbow on myofascial trigger points. The firm, sustained pressure causes skin blanching due to capillary compression. Deep pressure causes ischemia in deeper tissues, fol-

lowed by reactive hyperemia when the point is released.

When an area of the body is stressed repeatedly, the local nerves become over excitable or hyperirritable — a process known as facilitation. Once an area is facilitated, any additional stress could produce an increase in neural activity. For example, if you have a hyperirritable spot just below your scapula and you get the flu, that spot might ache more than the rest of your body. Facilitated areas of the horse's body sweat more than the surrounding area because of sympathetic nerve and motor reflex excitement. A localized point in the facilitated area will be painful on palpation and might be responsible for pain in a distant area. This point could be in the muscle, the tendon, or the fascia. It might lie superficially or in deep tissue. Trigger points are a component of any chronic pain problem and of the pain-spasm-pain cycle. A high degree of correlation exists between trigger points and acupuncture points.

Janet Travell's work has brought us the most detailed information on trigger points. She describes the points as containing an irritated muscle spindle at their core. A metabolic crisis takes place, which increases the temperature in the trigger point, shortening a small portion of the muscle. This compression reduces oxygen supply and nutrients to the trigger point. During this disturbed episode, an influx of calcium occurs and the muscle spindle does not have enough energy to pump the calcium outside the cell where it belongs. A vicious cycle is maintained — the muscle spindle can't relax, therefore the muscle can't relax.(9) The muscles containing trigger points are held in a shortened position. For a therapist to affect a trigger point, the horse must be relaxed. If the compression hurts, the horse will tense the muscle to guard against the discomfort, making the treatment ineffective.

Trigger point therapy is begun by examining the musculature for taut bands and other evidence of trauma or imbalance. Associated with trigger points, taut bands are regions in muscle tissue that have increased resistance to palpation. The trigger point is a zone of maximal tenderness that will twitch when pressure is applied. Tender trigger points correspond to an injury in the underlying muscle and fascia.

The goal of trigger point therapy is to deactivate the point and thus eliminate a source of pain. Unlike acupuncture points, which can be mapped on charts of the body, trigger points are not in the same place in everyone. Also unlike acupuncture points, trigger points are sources of pain, rather than access points to energy channels.

To eliminate an active trigger point, apply steady, gradually increasing pressure to the point at a 90-degree angle to the skin surface. If the muscle tenses under the point, gently release the pressure, then resume applying pressure until you feel the point "turn to butter." When you feel this phenomenon, the point has released.

Trigger point therapy uses ice as another means of deactivating the points, followed by stretching to help the muscle return to its normal resting length. Icing and stretching might need to be done several times to deactivate the point.

Acupressure

Acupressure is an ancient technique in which the fingers press specific points on the skin to stimulate repair processes. Acupuncture and acupressure use the same points, but acupuncture is a veterinary procedure using needles while acupressure can be done by the therapist and is non-invasive. Shiatzu massage is often called acupressure because the spots for compression are acupuncture points. "Shi" is the Japanese word for finger and "atzu" is the word for pressure. Although this technique is widely known and practiced in Japan and China, it was virtually unknown in America until acupuncture began to receive attention. While acupuncture can be used as a medical treatment for injury or illness, acupressure is used to maintain well-being.(10) Firm, but gentle pressure with the fingers, hands, or elbow is used to release muscle tension and promote circulation. As pointed out by M. R. Gach in his excellent book, *Acupressure's Potent Points*, the acupressurist considers local tenderness an expression of the body's condition as a whole. Horses exhibit tension in the poll area to express pain and stiffness in the hip and rear leg. Tenderness in the longissimus dorsi muscle at the back's midpoint is a sign of muscle soreness and connective tissue tension throughout the body. According to Gach, acupressure focuses on relieving pain and discomfort before it develops into a "disease;" that is, before the constrictions and imbalances can do further damage.(11)

Acupressure massage is similar to trigger point massage in technique, but different in theory. The treatment approach for acupressure centers on the Chinese meridian theory, which posits that all organs are connected by a network through which energy flows. This vital energy, or chi, becomes blocked by injury or illness, and its functional flow is inhibited. According to acupuncture theory, specific areas on the skin surface relate to specific organs or remote parts of the body through a system of channels. Systematic pressuring of these points keeps the channels open and maintains the energy flow.

A more Western view of this concept describes the electrical nature of fascia. Nodes of fascial contraction interfere with electrical conduction and interrupt cell-to-cell communication.

Acupressure inhibits the transmission of pain signals to the brain through two mech-

Equine therapist Mary Bromiley performing acupressure on a rear limb point.

anisms. When superficial stimulation such as finger pressure is perceived by the brain's recognition centers, a "gate" — using Melzack and Wall's description(12) — is closed to other sensations. Acupressure massage requires accurate location of acupuncture points. Stimulating these points releases endorphins and other chemical catalysts for pain relief. This relief is long-lasting and can relax the whole body.

Acupressure technique can be firm and a bit aggressive as in Shiatzu, or steady and non-aggressive. The point is held for a few seconds up to a minute, then released. The thumbs, fingers, elbow, or knuckles are used to hold a steady pressure without movement. Humans would say this pressure "hurts so good." Horses can experience the same reaction, but caution must be used to avoid bruising the tissue. Although it might sound esoteric, this can be accomplished by focusing your intent through the skin to the deeper structures. When this is done successfully, the session evokes relaxation rather than testing pain tolerance.

Apply pressure in a steadily increasing manner until you feel the point release or relax. If you feel the area tightening, release the pressure a bit. A steady rhythm of pressure, release, and slightly increased pressure, coordinated with your breathing, should bring the feeling of a pulse at the point after a minute or two. As you become more skilled, you will begin to discern differences in the pulse. Repeated sessions, followed by stretching, should bring a consistent, firm pulse at the point.

Physiotherapist Mary Bromiley

uses the acupressure point demonstrated in the photo for an all-purpose rear limb point. She has been able to relieve pain in the hind quarters with this point alone.

Joint Mobilizations

Joint mobilization, sometimes called passive mobilization, involves moving the joint to the end of its normal range of motion, then flexing and extending the limb, but only to the point where resistance is met. Gliding movements are used to restore normal joint movement The movement is passive, meaning that the therapist moves the

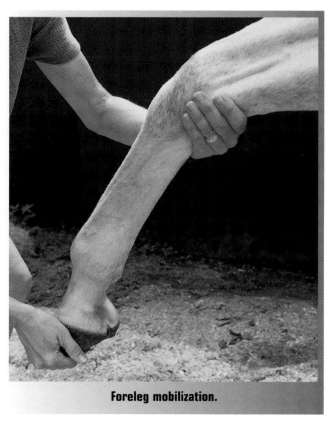

Foreleg mobilization.

limb un-assisted and un-resisted by the horse.

The mobilization movements are repeated as many as 10 or 20 times, depending on the horse's tolerance. Continuous Passive Motion machines that move the joint for hours at a time are now available in human physical therapy. Without this gentle, natural tension, collagen fibers tend to have a more random and less linear arrangement.

This manual therapy has its roots in a 1955 Swedish study that found that the articular cartilage is nourished from both the underlying epiphysis and the synovial fluid. The study also demonstrated that joint motion promoted cartilage nutrition.(13)

Joint mobilization uses low velocity (slow movements) and large amplitude (large range of motion, but within normal limits), in contrast with joint manipulation, which uses high velocity (quick, forceful thrusts) to extend the joint beyond its normal limits. When a horse is the patient, joint manipulation is in the domain of the veterinary chiropractor.

Joint mobilizations can stimulate biological processes within the joint, increasing range of motion and reducing tension in connective tissue. They help prevent and reduce pain if it is of brief duration. Chronic pain and joint restrictions that have existed a long time do not respond consistently to mobilization, but may respond when other therapies also are used. This technique should be used as a preventive therapy, to keep your horse flexible and fully functional.

Joint mobilization is carried out within what is called the zone of physiological movement. This zone includes the range of

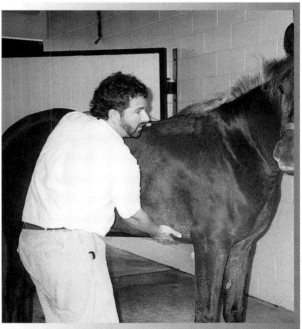

Mobilizing the vertebrae of the back.

normal active joint movement, or movement that the muscles can normally accomplish, plus a small range beyond this. To demonstrate the zone of physiological movement, extend one finger as far as the muscles will extend it. Now use the other hand to push that finger back farther, stopping when you feel tension. When a joint is moved to the end of its physiological zone, the resistance encountered is due to tensing of the joint capsule. Should a joint be taken beyond its limits, the joint capsule could tear, resulting in a sprain. Normal ranges of flexion, extension, abduction, and adduction as well as rotation are used in joint mobilization.

Joint mobilizations are slow, careful

Pulling the tail gently causes the horse to rotate the top of the pelvis cranially.

movements using the long lever of the horse's leg to mobilize lower joints. Fluid, circular motions are used. The leg is picked up, flexed and extended, and moved in a rotary manner both clockwise and counter clockwise. Each leg joint is flexed and extended, repeatedly and slowly, through the normal plane of motion to the point

where tension is felt. The process is repeated until free movement is achieved or until no further gain is apparent.

Mobilization of the horse's spinal joints involves pushing and pulling or rocking motions along the vertebral column. Begin at the horse's head and move down the vertebral column, pressuring alternately the left and right sides of the neck so the vertebra are moved left and right. Move to the withers and rock the dorsal spine back and forth using alternately your fingers and the heels of your hands in a slow, rhythmical manner. Use enough pressure to actually move the vertebrae. When you get to the hips, use the tail to mobilize the sacrum. Standing behind the horse, pull the tail gently to cause the horse to rotate the top of the pelvis cranially. Hold the tail pull briefly, then release.

One goal of joint mobilization is neurologic reprogramming to help the horse regain awareness of an area it guarded because of injury. The benefits include improved health and healing of the intra-articular structures, especially the cartilage, and reduction of soft tissue contracture associated with immobilization. Cartilage nutrition could be improved due to increased circulation and production of synovial fluid. Following surgery, fibrosis of periarticular structures can be reduced when repeated gentle movements are manually assisted. Passive mobilization should not be performed until the surgical incisions are healed sufficiently. Joint mobilizations are contraindicated where inflammatory arthritis is present. Never mobilize or stretch a swollen joint; the joint capsule is already stretched by the extra joint fluid.

Chiropractic Manipulations

Chiropractic joint manipulations are specific, high velocity, controlled thrusts directed at a joint. These movements can take the joint beyond its initial barrier of resistance to the limits of its physiological range of motion. The joint surfaces suddenly separate and a "crack" is often heard. The sound, often associated with a successful "adjustment," results from gas being released from the synovial fluid, much when a cap is popped off a carbonated drink. Indeed, there is great similarity as the synovial fluid contains hydrogen and carbon dioxide. This phenomena of a dramatic alteration of pressure within the joint space distinguishes chiropractic manipulation from therapeutic mobilizations. This is a veterinary procedure because it requires detailed knowledge of anatomy.

Chiropractic terminology has led to confusion about what the manipulations are attempting to accomplish. An adjustment is characterized by a specific force applied in a specific direction to a specific joint or vertebra.(14) Because the target lesions are termed subluxations, the idea that a bone is out of place has persisted and the notion that a bone can be put back in place remains controversial. Chiropractic manipulations must take into account the whole of the organism — the nerves, fascia, muscles, tendons, and ligaments, as well as the osseous structures. The spinal adjustment affects all the tissues around the joint. The goal of the adjustment is not to put a vertebra or the bone back into place, but to reduce fascial and muscular restrictions that put torque, or force, on the bone, affecting its normal movement.

Joint "fixation" can be traced to fascial shortening and muscle spasm. The "adjustment" is a release of soft tissue tension. The chiropractic manipulation stretches the fascia, nerves, and muscle by rapidly forcing the joint beyond the fixed region of joint motion. The process inhibits the relentless neural bombardment that has maintained the spasm, allowing relaxation around the joint. Chiropractic manipulations have been documented to reduce electrical activity in the muscle much like local anesthetic injection.(15) This technique is contraindicated in the presence of arthritis, bone disease, calcification around joints, ankylosing spondylitis, and any undiagnosed pain.

Myofascial Release

Fascia is a single structural entity that extends from the tip of the horse's ears to his feet and supports and envelops every organ. A gelatinous substance in the normal state, fascia can become rigid and fibrous. It is elastic but susceptible to shortening and forming fibrotic bands when subjected to chronic stress. It is piezoelectric, meaning that when pressured or stretched, it gives off electromagnetic signals. Fascia is richly endowed with nerve endings and produces burning pain. Trigger points exist in taut bands of muscle or tendon tissue and will twitch when pressed. The area of a trigger point is tight but not fibrosed, and will soften and relax with the appropriate treatment. Myofascial release aims to soften and relax fibrotic fascia anywhere in the body.

Myofascial release maintains that tension, shortening, or thickening anywhere in the fascia can affect total body functionality and might set up a chain of malalignments and restrictions. Fascia can place enormous tensile strength on painful structures. Because all musculoskeletal trauma involves the fascia and the fascia extends throughout the body, stressed areas are viewed in the context of their effect on the body as a whole. For example, tenosynovitis of the deep digital flexor tendon could inhibit full extension of the pastern joint. Without full extension, the stride could be shortened,

the shoulder musculature is not fully engaged, and the musculature of the opposite shoulder is overused as a stabilizer. The musculature of the affected side weakens and that of the opposite side becomes hypertonic.

Without full range of motion, fascia on the affected side shortens and thickens, further reducing functionality and placing pressure on nerves and muscles. Fascial restrictions begin to pull on the muscles and nerves, causing pain. Contracted fascia in the neck and shoulder can pull on the cervical vertebra. A change in the nature of the fascia might lead to tissue congestion and reduced metabolic waste removal, resulting in edema. The effects of the trauma reach throughout the body.

Myofascial release seeks to intervene in this chain of degenerative events with steady, increasing pressure and range of motion movements to soften restrictions. The goal is to allow the fascia to release its tension. Prolonged light pressure is used, although deep pressure can be used in some cases.

Craniosacral Therapy

Craniosacral therapy is sometimes called energy work because some of the techniques suggest that the therapist direct his or her own energy to the patient. This may sound esoteric, but as one practices this form of manual therapy under the guidance of skilled teachers, one soon feels capable of doing just that. John Upledger, the major

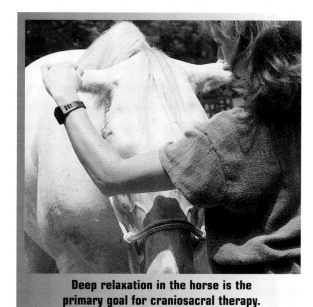

Deep relaxation in the horse is the primary goal for craniosacral therapy.

proponent of this technique, suggests that the electrophysiological potential of the therapist's hands might directly influence electrical activity in the patient. This technique is ancient, perhaps originally called laying on of hands.

The craniosacral concept is based on identifying the craniosacral rhythm, or the movement of the cerebrospinal fluid in the spinal canal. The body moves in a subtle motion that corresponds to the movement of the cerebrospinal fluid. The strength and synchronicity of the rhythm can be used to detect restrictions in the body. The removal of these restrictions is called a release.

In craniosacral therapy, the therapist places his or her hands gently on the patient and senses subtle body motions. The therapist follows the movement to its greatest range without any attempt to influence it. When the body movement begins to return from this point, the therapist presents resistance by being immobile. No pushing or overt movement is involved. Movement of the tissues will again move away from the therapist, and the therapist will move with it. At the end of this excursion, the therapist again becomes immobile. After several cycles of this, the tissue will soften and a release will occur. The theory behind this approach is that a small force over a long time can do more for the body than a strong force over a short time. Some experts believe that a small force produces much less resistance in the patient's body.

Deep relaxation in the horse is the primary goal for craniosacral therapy. There are many techniques in this classification of manual therapy. For the therapist wanting to improve tactile skills and awareness, a course in craniosacral therapy is a must.

Contraindications for Manual Therapy

As with any other modality, one must have experience with any manual therapy before applying it to a horse. There are few contraindications for manual therapy, but a few cautions should be kept in mind. Avoid manual therapy when bacterial or viral lesions are present. Massage should not be applied over a torn muscle or to an area of internal bleeding, such as an acute hematoma. Massage can cause further damage to an acute injury and should be avoided in the presence of phlebitis, thrombosis, or inflammatory arthritis. Massaging areas of calcification in the soft tissues will increase the inflammation in these areas and should be avoided.

It was once thought that the positive benefits of touch were reserved for humans alone. The sensitivity of horses to our loving touch is now widely recognized. A horse can feel the rider's subtle changes in body position and tension right through the saddle. They easily detect tension in the handler and are aware of the rider's emotional state. The therapist using manual techniques must be aware of the horse's response to tactile stimuli. Some people transmit confidence with their hands and attitude; others transmit distrust.

The therapist should have a complete knowledge of the horse's state of health before applying manual therapy. Manual therapies are appropriate for injury prevention and can be combined with other therapeutic modalities for rehabilitation.

Definitions

Active range of motion — Range through which the horse willingly moves a joint.

Ligament — Connective tissue attaching bone to bone.

Manual therapy — Procedures by which the hands directly contact the body to treat health problems.

Manipulation — A manual procedure involving a directed thrust to move a joint past the physiological range of motion, without exceeding the anatomical limit. This is reserved for veterinary practice.

Mobilization — Movement applied one time or repetitively within the physiologic range of joint motion, without imparting a thrust, with the goal of restoring joint mobility.

Muscle spindle — The major sensory organ of muscle. Monitors the velocity and duration of stretch.

Passive range of motion — Range through which the therapist is able to move a joint without resistance or assistance from the horse.

Physiologic movement — Movement that a horse normally can do, such as flexion, extension, rotation, and adduction.

Strain — Overstretching of a muscle or its tendon. May be mild or result in fiber tearing.

Sprain — Overstretching of the joint structures such as the joint capsule or ligament.

Tendon — Connective tissue attaching muscle to bone.

Traction — Slowly drawing or pulling.

Trigger point — A hyperirritable point lying within a taut band of muscle that is painful on compression and that refers pain to a distant site.

References

1. Crosman, L., et al. 1984. The effects of massage to the hamstring muscle group on range of motion. *J Ortho Sports Phys Ther.* 6:168-72.

2. Walker, JM. 1984. Deep transverse frictions in ligament healing. *J Ortho Sports Phys Ther.* 6:89-94.

3. King, C. and Mansmann, R. 1997. *Equine Lameness.* Grand Prairie, TX.: Equine Research. 578-88.

4. Boone, T. et al. 1991. A physiologic evaluation of the sports massage. *Athletic Training.* 26:51.

5. Harmer, P. 1991. The effect of pre-performance massage on stride frequency in sprinters. *Athletic Training.* 26:55.

6. Crossman, L. et al. 1984. The effects of massage to the hamstring muscle group on range of motion. *J Orthop Sports Phys Ther.* 6:168.

7. Mead, TW. et al. 1990. Low back pain of mechanical origin: randomized comparison of chiropractic and hospital out-patient treatment. *Br Med J.* 300:1431.

8. Meagher, J. 1985. *Beating Muscle Injuries.* Hamilton, MA.: Hamilton Horse Associates.

9. Lewit, K. and Simons, D. 1984. Myofascial pain-relief by post isometric relaxation. *Arch of Phys Med and Rehab.* 65:462-66.

10. Irwin, Y. *Shiatzu.* 1976. Philadelphia: JB Lippincott.

11. Gach, MR. 1990. *Acupressure's Potent Points.* New York, NY.: Bantam Books.

12. Melzack, R. and Wall, PD. 1965. Pain mechanisms: a new theory. *Science.* 150:971-79.

13. Ekholm, R. 1955. Nutrition of articular cartilage. *Acta Anatomica.* 24:329-38.

14. Willoughby, S. 1998. *Chiropractic Care in Complementary and Alternative Veterinary Medicine.* A. Schoen and S. Winn, eds. St. Louis, MO.: Mosby Co. 185-200.

15. Haldeman, S. 1977. *What is Meant by Manipulation? Approaches to the Validation of Manipulation Therapy.* Buerger and Tobis eds. New York, NY.: Appleton-Century-Crofts. 229-302.

Further Reading

Denoix, JM. and Pailoux, JP. 1996.
Physical Therapy and Massage for the Horse. North Pomfret, VT.: Trafalgar Square.

Hourdebaigt, JP. 1977. *Equine Massage.* New York, NY.: Howell Book House.

Travell, JG. and Simons, DG. 1984.
Myofascial Pain and Dysfunction. Baltimore, MD.: Williams and Wilkins.

Zidonis, N. et al. 1991. *Equine Acupressure.* Parker, CO.

Therapeutic Electrical Stimulation

I sing the body electric... Walt Whitman

ELECTRICAL STIMULATION is used to reduce pain and promote healing. Electrodes applied to the skin deliver low-voltage, intermittent stimulation to surface nerves in the skin. The transmission of pain signals is blocked, and endorphins, the body's natural pain killers, are released. This type of stimulation is non-invasive and non-addictive. It has no side effects and can be used to treat acute or chronic pain.

Electrical fields have been used to stimulate growth of both the hard and soft tissues. It has been known since the 1940s that bone emits electrical potentials when stressed. In the 1950s, electrical currents in the soft tissues were recognized. These discoveries led to the use of these currents to stimulate tissue repair.

Using electrical stimulation to improve muscle function also dates to the 1950s. The

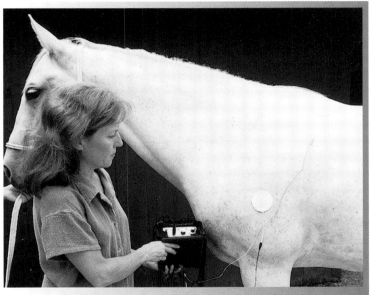

Electrical stimulation can help reduce pain and promote healing.

invention of the cardiac pacemaker and the use of electrical current to produce functional muscle contractions in paralyzed patients opened wide the doors of exploration into the uses of this modality. For the horse, electricity provides a comfortable modality with a broad range of applications. Horses tolerate the treatment well; in fact, they often sleep through it. An endorphin response is usually apparent within a few minutes. The treatment does not require high current levels; in fact, levels that are too high can be counter-productive.

A primary goal of equine therapy is to reduce the pain and discomfort brought about by injury or surgery. Most of us have a good idea what pain is because we have experienced it. But what is pain to the horse? Because they do not verbalize discomfort, as we so readily do, we often disre-

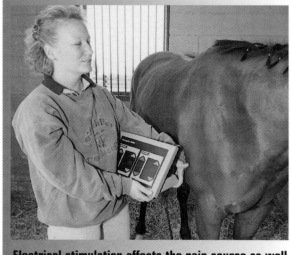

Electrical stimulation affects the pain source as well as the symptom.

gard the importance of pain and its effect on the horse. The horse's sense of pain is the same as ours — it is an unpleasant and emotionally distressing experience.

Acute pain is of sudden onset and short duration; there is a distinct cause of recent occurrence. This type of pain has a purpose: to warn the body of damage so the injured

part will not be used. Pain is nature's means of enforcing rest so repair can take place. Electrical stimulation minimizes the pain response after acute injury, but it does not completely block it out. This type of stimulation is an analgesic, not an anesthetic, so pain's warning signals come through when they are needed.

Chronic pain is another story. It is discomfort that endures beyond the acute injury incident, and it can become self-sustaining. Chronic pain can be energy-depleting, and it reduces the production of endorphin and other natural pain-relieving chemicals. Chronic pain causes muscle tension and leads to muscle atrophy. It does not stimulate any repair processes. Indeed, it can inhibit repair.

Therapeutic electrical stimulation is now widely recognized as playing a role in chronic pain management. An effective and practical treatment approach involves placing one electrode on the dermatome (area of the spine where nerves serving the injured area exit) and the other electrode on the injury site. Electrical stimulation of acupuncture points is another effective and non-invasive means of pain relief; it can be as effective as acupuncture if the therapist is familiar with point location and electrode placement is accurate. Low pulses per second (less than 10) are thought to simulate the ancient technique of needle twirling and pulsing. High pulse frequency (more than 100 pps) is sometimes used, as well, to deactivate a point in five minutes.

Pain Theory and Equine Therapy

The placebo effect is a confounding factor in all studies of human pain management. Horses are not thought to respond to the placebo effect, however, so it was quite satisfying when I first observed that athletic training techniques had the benefit of pain relief for these animals.

There is a neurological system for pain perception that consists of a series of pain-control "gates" from the dorsal spinal horns to the cortico-limbic recognition centers of the brain. This attempt to describe the system is taken from Charman's scholarly and detailed description published in 1989. (1)

The pain pathway ascends from all parts of the body to the recognition centers in the cerebral cortex through this series of "gates" that are not under conscious control until the level of the thalamus. From this point upwards, conscious activity can come into play. The nociceptor system, or pain sensing system, begins with free nerve endings that are embedded in all tissues where pain can be registered. These nerve endings detect insult to the body and carry the sensations on thin, mylenated (A delta) fibers, conveying fast pain messages or in unmylenated (C) fibers conveying slow pain messages.

Fast pain includes cold and heat, pressure, and acute pain. Slow pain includes chronic pain, dull pressure, or dull trauma. These fibers, called afferent fibers, enter the spinal cord through an area termed the dorsal horn and it is here that the first gate to pain inhibition exists.

The complex layers of the dorsal horn process incoming signals before sending them on to a higher level. Rubbing a sore area to reduce pain is an example of pain modulation on this level. Afferent nerves carry messages to the brain and have a low threshold for superficial stimulation, such as cold, touch, and electricity, meaning that these signals are transmitted preferentially over dull pressure or pain. Electrical stimulation causes cells in the dorsal horn to modulate afferent signals so that painful stimuli is inhibited and the sensation of mild electricity is sent on for recognition. The Gate Control Theory was proposed in 1965, by Drs. Melzack and Wall, who suggested that input from large diameter afferent fibers "closes a gate" or inhibits input from small diameter fibers at the level of the spinal cord. (2)

Farther up the pain pathway, the sub cortex of the brain provides another area where pain signals can be modulated. Here, neurotransmitters or neuromodulators such as enkephalins, endorphins, carbon monoxide, nitric oxide, and others close the gate to pain transmission. Charman relates that there are at least 18 endogenous opiates that might play a role in pain relief. These brain chemicals create a wide spectrum of feelings, thoughts, emotions, and moods. Acupuncture, photon therapy, magnetic therapy, and electrical stimulation cause a release of these chemical and gaseous compounds from blood proteins, affecting pain perception at the sub-cortical level.

Practically everything we do affects brain chemistry, including eating, exercising, sleeping, even thinking. High frequency electrical stimulation has a profound effect on the activity of neurotransmitters, increasing the production of beta-endorphins, serotonin, ACTH, epinephrine, norepinephrine, and somatostatin. (3)

A third means of pain inhibition is provided in the cortex of the brain, where the patient has the ability to distract attention away from pain. The cerebral cortex handles complex mental tasks, such as memory, speech, and thought. Nerve tracts that descend from this area can close the gate to pain under certain circumstances. For example, biofeedback techniques teach the patient to remove conscious focus from the pain site. When electrical stimulation is used, a patient becomes aware of a sensation from the electricity, and pain is not "felt" or recognized by the brain.

Other pain gates exist farther up the central nervous system, but they are less well understood in their relation to physical therapy input, and certainly unexplored where the horse is concerned. Charman mentions a therapist-to-patient, mind-to-mind interaction, which is certainly possible with a horse. Countless stories can be told of mind-to-mind interactions between horse and human, suggesting that pain control from higher centers could be activated.

The superficial stimuli from electrical stimulation, massage, ice, and other modalities activates the spinal cord gate, controlling ascending pain messages by overriding them or by moving conscious focus away from pain. This system is easily appreciated in the horse. His brain, ever on the alert for signals from the sensory system, such as smells or sounds, would sublimate pain to heed external signals that might signify danger.

Effects of Electrical Stimulation

A benefit of electrical stimulation over opiate drugs, designed to mimic natural opiates, is that it affects the source of pain as well as the symptom. This section will discuss the effects of electrical stimulation.

Analgesic Effect

Electrical stimulation has many applications, but pain relief or electrical analgesia probably gets the most research. Management of surgical wound pain is of great concern to human physical therapists. Studies have shown that an analgesic nitrous oxide-oxygen mix and electrical stimulation are equally effective. Electrical stimulation has the advantage of not having side effects, and patients preferred it.(4) In another study, post-operative pain was reduced and coughing after surgery was found to be less painful when electrical stimulation was used.(5)

There appears to be a strong preference among human patients for pulse rates of 50 to 80 per second at low intensities for post-operative pain. Electrodes are placed around the surgery site in the recovery room, using appropriate sterile techniques. Post-surgical electrical stimulation reduces the need for medication and improves patient comfort. Opioid drugs are well known for their analgesic properties, but they have side effects and are not always effective. Passing electrical current through the surgical site not only will reduce painful sensations but stimulate the repair process.

Post-Exercise Soreness versus Muscle Pain from Strain

Too many horsemen do not know when a horse is sore and do not understand the danger of allowing post-exercise soreness to persist. Muscle soreness often develops 24 to 48 hours after exercise and is thought to be due largely to microtrauma — microscopic

tearing — to the muscle fibers and connective tissue. Electron microscopy has shown that the muscle fibers themselves are actually torn. Although lactic acid has traditionally been blamed for post-exercise soreness, it is now thought that other metabolites, such as histamine, acetylcholine, serotonin, potassium, and bradykinin, play a role.(6) The pain can be reduced with warm-up and cool-down exercises, which include stretching. Until this pain disappears, the muscle is in a weakened condition, predisposing it to injury that can have more lasting consequences.

Muscle strain, a more severe problem, can vary from the tearing of a few fibers to complete rupture. Extensive muscle strain involves intertissue bleeding and inability to contract normally. Damaged muscle can regenerate without the formation of fibrous scar tissue if the blood and nerve supply are maintained.(7) The initial treatment is to stop the intertissue bleeding and inhibit hematoma formation through the use of ice, compression, and rest.

The first phase of recovery can take three or four days or more than a week, depending on the severity of the strain. Following this stage, electrical stimulation can be used to reduce pain and increase blood flow for the removal of injury debris. The rhythmical contraction and relaxation of a slow pulse mode (less than 10 pps) will help keep the muscle fibers more mobile. Gentle stretching exercises, preceded by electrical stimulation, will prevent shortening of the muscle fibers.

Treating Back Pain

I often treat horses that are sore from daily training. In many cases it seems the discomfort began in the lumbosacral junction, the most flexible area of the back. The lum-

Trigger points indicate site and extent of pain.

bosacral junction must flex and extend repeatedly as the horse runs, resulting in repeated stress injury to this area. The musculature involved is massive and might not receive adequate warm-up before exercise, leading to micro-tears in the tight structures. The obvious discomfort is in the back and hip musculature. The conformation starts to "flatten out" when the horse begins to favor muscles along his bottom line — the triceps and pectoralis, and the biceps femoris and quadriceps.

Because the larger, more powerful muscles of the gluteus and torso are sore, the horse no longer will round his back and drive from his hips. Pain in the back musculature is usually chronic and often secondary to another problem, or perhaps more than one problem. A complete veterinary diagnosis will help put all the pieces of the puzzle together. The primary problem must be treated for a successful outcome, but in this discussion I will focus on how I treat the musculature of the back.

Electrical stimulation to the trigger points in the musculature will effectively relax the spasm and pain, enabling the horse to round his body again and use its natural spring action for propulsion. I use a low pulse rate, one to five pulses per second, to evoke rhythmical muscle contractions. Endogenous (internal) opiate is released, and the horse relaxes and drifts into a semi sleep. Carry on the treatment for as long as the horse is asleep. When he awakens, usually in 30 to 45 minutes, the treatment is over. No further benefit will be gained from continuing.

Back muscle pain due to a poorly fitting saddle will show up as performance problems, rather than as overt sores on the back, according to Dr. Joyce Harman, a holistic veterinarian in Middleburg, Va. She lists the most common behaviors associated with poor saddle fit as objection to being saddled, resistance to work and to training aids, front leg lameness, stumbling and tripping, not traveling straight, tail swishing, ear pinning, and hypersensitivity to

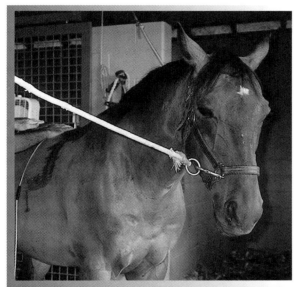

Electrical stimulation evokes deep relaxation.

being brushed. All these symptoms are reduced with electrical stimulation to the back musculature, but getting to the cause requires taking a close look at your saddle and how it fits your horse. Treating back pain can include an extensive investigation that includes checking everything from the horse's teeth and the way the bit fits to the condition of his feet.

Muscle soreness in the gluteal area often accompanies shin splints. In this case, icing the shins twice a day with an ice cup massage reduces the pain and inflammation. (This technique is discussed further in Chapter 4.) To allow the horse to rebalance his weight bearing, use electrical stimulation on gluteal trigger points. Mid to high frequencies can be used, 20 to 50 pps, for 12 to 30 minutes per site, depending on the severity of discomfort.

If you are using a direct current unit with carbide electrodes, you can use the electrodes as probes to locate sites of soreness and active acupuncture and trigger points. To probe for muscle soreness, first wet the area with warm water so the coat is saturated. Place the positive pole on the withers and move the negative pole around over the hips and back to identify sites of tenderness. Observe the horse's body language and be sensitive to the feel of the muscle contractions. The horse will move his ears or his eyes, or turn and look at you as you cross sensitive areas.

Exertional Rhabdomyolysis

Muscle soreness related to tie-up, exertional rhabdomyolysis (ER), has recently been the subject of considerable research. A University of Minnesota study describes a new classification system for ER.(8) Classic tying-up symptoms include sweating, stiffness, and reluctance to move due to muscle pain. Tying-up is not a single disease, but a collection of clinical signs that can have several causes. Horses can be classified as having sporadic ER or recurrent ER, depending on whether it happens once or repeatedly.

Electrical stimulation can greatly relieve sporadic ER. When a horse exercises more strenuously than normal or after a layoff, his muscles will be strained. The inflammatory process causes ischemia in the muscles, resulting in pain and cramping. A similar situation can occur after surgery when a horse has been lying on his side for several hours. Compression leads to painful muscle damage and cramping that can last for days after surgery. Using electrical stimulation to massage the muscles at a low intensity and a low pulse per second rate (less than 5pps) aids in muscle fiber relaxation and increases blood flow through the muscle, relieving the hypoxic state. The treatment should evoke relaxation and result in the horse's being able to move more normally. In my experience, tying-up doesn't recur the next day of exercise, as it often does when this treatment is not used.

The second form of ER can be caused by inherited defects in muscle metabolism. Muscle pain results from abnormal polysaccharide and muscle glycogen storage in muscle fibers. Another suspected cause is abnormal intercellular calcium regulation.

The membranes of nerve and muscle cells consist of a phospholipid bilayer containing a variety of protein molecules. These proteins could serve as receptor sites for neurotransmitters or as a channel or transport site for the passage of ions through the membrane.(9) Electrical stimulation possibly opens the channels for calcium transport into the cell, normalizing its movement through the cell membrane. An increase in intracellular calcium would increase the rate at which ATP is produced in the mitochondria, an effect observed by Cheng following electrostimulation.(10)

Horses which have had a series of ER episodes respond positively to electrical stimulation, and the bouts of ER cease. The stimulation must be kept at a low level so damaged muscle is not irritated. It could be that the external electrical current activates the mitochondria to metabolize the excess glycogen in the muscle fibers while affecting calcium movement back into intracellular storage sites.

Establishing specific dietary and exercise routines for affected horses appears to be the greatest protection against recurrent ER, according to Amy Gill, an equine nutritionist with Equine Marketing and Consulting, Inc., in Versailles, Ky. She suggests high-quality alfalfa/grass hay as the basis for the diet and a balanced feed mixture with vitamin and mineral supplements.

Digestible energy from vegetable fats, including corn or soybean oil, are recommended over high carbohydrate diets of grain and sweet feed for these horses. Once the horse recovers, exercise should be consistent and regular. Turn the horse out as much as possible and avoid stall rest.

Nervous or young horses going into intense training are more prone to recurrent ER. Once again, electrical stimulation can be helpful because of its calming influence. High frequency stimulation of 20,000 to 30,000 Hz affects neurotransmitter release and brings about deep relaxation in less than 20 minutes. Stimulators such as the Synaptic can provide this frequency level with very little motor stimulation, so muscle fibers are not irritated. Partnered with appropriate veterinary care, diet, and exercise, electrical stimulation can be an important part of managing both classes of ER.

Edema Reduction

Edema is reduced by increased lymphatic flow, increased venous drainage, and improved blood flow. The physical therapy literature concerning the effects of electrical stimulation on edema reduction differ in their conclusion, depending on the subject used in the tests. When human subjects were used, the results generally were in favor of using electrical stimulation. In contrast, studies using rats found no significant edema reduction. No study using horses could be found.

When swelling is allowed to persist beyond 24 hours post-injury, it becomes more viscous because of protein infiltration and debris from damaged cells. At this point it is referred to as edema. The particles making up edema are too large to be absorbed by the blood circulatory system, so the

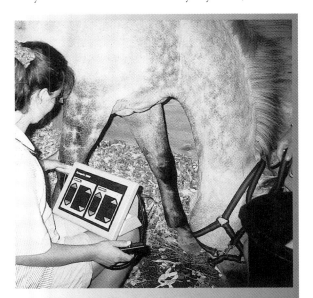

Electrical stimulation is useful in reducing edema.

lymph system handles extracellular fluid. Muscle activity plays a part in the pumping action necessary for lymphatic movement. Electrically stimulating the musculature to mimic rhythmic, voluntary muscle contraction helps the lymph capillaries absorb waste products. Because the lymph vessels in the horse's lower legs do not have valves to counteract the effects of gravity, the muscle pumps must keep extracellular fluid from collecting. In studies on venous stasis, a circulatory problem in humans, electrical stimulation prevented edema accumulation in limbs after surgery.(11)

I have observed that electrical stimulation reduces limb edema in horses as well. Treatment involves placing one set of electrodes on the muscle groups associated with the area of edema and another set on the edema, usually medial and lateral on the fetlock. The pulse rate is 20 pps or slower. If the current is increased over at least 20 min-

Human athletes can exercise isolated muscles, but horses cannot.

utes, the horse will be comfortable with levels sufficient to cause muscle contraction. The rhythmical muscle contraction and relaxation simulates normal muscle activity,

helping fluid uptake. The time needed for successful treatment can vary from 30 minutes to an hour, the longer treatments producing more favorable results. Treat only as long as the horse stands comfortably. The stimulation is soothing and evokes an endorphin response that most horses tolerate well. Using a brow band magnet might help calm the horse by stimulating the pineal gland. Following electrical stimulation, mobilization exercises are done to enhance circulation.

Improved Muscle Strength

A muscle increases in size and strength because protein in the muscle fiber increases as does capillary bed density. Increasing strength requires the muscle to confront a load that exceeds its metabolic capacity.(12) Injury prevents a muscle from contracting with maximum force and, indeed, can prevent muscle use. The horse, a master of compensation, simply shifts his weight to other limbs when standing, and uses other muscle groups for propulsion. Muscle in the area of discomfort begins to atrophy from lack of use, but this wasting usually is not recognized until the muscle has actually shrunk in size. Restoring muscle size and strength involves eliminating the discomfort as well as stimulating the muscle directly to improve its function.

Studies have compared electrical stimulation to voluntary exercise for the resulting increase in muscle strength. In the case of healthy muscle, strength usually increased in the stimulated group compared to the un-exercised group, but electrical stimulation at contraction strengths of 33% to 90% usually offered no advantage over natural exercise.(13) When electrical stimulation is used for strength gains in human physical therapy, stimulation above the comfort level often is used to simulate voluntary exercise. Just as with natural exercise, the muscle must confront an increased functional load. Electrical stimulation that is so intense that it causes discomfort and apprehension would not be tolerated for long by the horse. And horses do not require such levels to benefit. Remember that one of the laws of equine therapy is that it is always comfortable.

An abundance of evidence shows that when the muscle has been weakened by surgery or injury, electrical stimulation produces greater strength gains than voluntary exercise. This could be because of the pain-relieving component of electrical current or the selective recruitment of type II muscle fibers.(14) Electrical stimulation is effective for strengthening the muscles of a horse because muscle weakness is attributed to atrophy in type II muscle fibers. Electrically excited contractions are different from voluntary contractions. Voluntary contractions enlist smaller motoneurons, which enervate type I (slow-twitch) muscle fibers before larger motoneurons are activated. Electrical stimulation activates the nerve fiber at or near the motor end plate and takes the path of least resistance through larger diameter fibers, which enervate type II (fast-twitch) muscle fibers. All the motor units with nerve fibers originally activated by an electrical stimulus will be active throughout a contraction. They will be activated at the stimulation frequency and will contract until they fatigue.(15) Electrical stimulation superimposed on voluntary muscle contraction is superior to voluntary exercise alone in reducing muscle atrophy. Using electrical stimulation before exercise could help improve muscle function.

Electrical stimulation within the limits of comfort can be useful in maintaining muscle integrity following injury or surgery. To take an example from human sports medicine, profound inhibition occurs in the quadriceps muscle after surgery. Often the patient cannot lift his leg for several days. Patients receiving electrical stimulation have significantly improved muscle function and less atrophy than those doing exercise alone. Also, electrically stimulated muscle has higher levels of oxidative enzymes, which help muscles work.(16) This type of stimulation is considered important in the post-surgical rehabilitation of human athletes because it produces afferent sensory stimulation for pain relief and develops muscle tension. Certainly a combination of electrical stimulation and controlled exercise would be superior to stall rest for horses.

I once worked on a valuable breeding stallion who had shattered his hock kicking through the boards of a fence. The hock had been stabilized with pins, and the leg was cast from the ground to his stifle. This horse remained in the cast for an amazing 15 weeks. We used electrical stimulation to maintain blood flow and enzyme levels in the muscles of the injured leg by finding motor points and stimulating them directly. The rhythmical muscle contractions, which aid blood and lymph circulation, comforted this

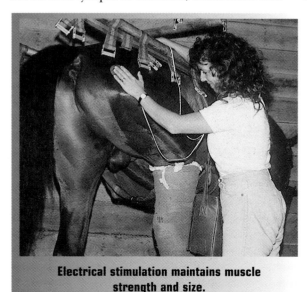
Electrical stimulation maintains muscle strength and size.

horse. The opposite leg also was stimulated to reduce muscle soreness from the constant weight bearing on the uninjured side. Because of the cast, this horse could not lie down, so the gentle massaging action kept the muscles supple and spasm to a minimum. When this horse was finally released from the cast, the gluteal muscles were symmetrical and he could walk with comfort. Extensive muscle atrophy would have made it difficult for him to resume his breeding career, so it was important to maintain the health of these muscles throughout recovery.

Surgery often leads to muscle inhibition. Hours of lying on the surgical table can result in myositis, inflammation of the muscle, where large areas of muscle become ischemic and unable to relax. The muscle feels hard, and the horse is uncomfortable.

Gentle, low-level stimulation increases circulation, bringing oxygen to the muscle fibers so they can relax and become functional.

By placing one electrode on a motor point in the hip and one in the shoulder, and using the acupuncture location BL18 (in the intercostal space between the 13th and 14th ribs), a significant relaxation response can be obtained. I usually treat post-surgical discomfort at a low level, just above sensory recognition, for as long as 45 minutes. I allow the horse to go into complete relaxation and sleep, ending the treatment when he wakes up. Hand walking can follow if the horse tolerates it comfortably.

Electrical stimulation applied at intensities that evoke muscle contraction increases blood flow velocity in the artery supplying the stimulated muscle. In addition, it increases the degree of microvascular perfusion in the stimulated skeletal muscle. These were the findings of a recent study of 30 minutes of electrical stimulation, which alternated 12 seconds of on time with 10 seconds of off time. Even with vascular denervation, the external stimulation would increase circulation enough to meet the metabolic demands of contracting muscle.(17)

Electrical stimulation can address another problem in equine rehabilitation — that of exercising specific muscle groups. Lifting weight to strengthen a specific muscle group is not an option with horses. The muscle work caused by stimulation will maintain blood flow through the muscle and prevent further atrophy. Pain relief afforded by electrical stimulation will allow the horse to use the limb in a more natural fashion, bearing weight earlier and moving the limb through a more complete range of motion.

Nerve Damage

When a motor nerve is stretched, torn, crushed, or bruised, the muscles it enervates cannot contract. Atrophy begins quickly and the muscle loses elasticity. The muscle soon will become unable to recover to its full strength potential if this condition persists. Weight-bearing stress to the opposite leg is of concern in paralyzing nerve injuries.

The case pictured on the next page involves a horse with radial nerve paralysis caused by hitting a fence. The photograph on the left shows the musculature of the right shoulder before treatment was begun. The photograph on the right shows the same area after a month of treatment.

Electrical stimulation was applied to the motor points in the atrophied muscles beginning five days after the injury. If stimulation is begun too soon, muscle inhibition could occur. The advantage of using electrical current in cases of nerve damage are:

• a large muscle mass will be stimulated to move rather than allowed to remain dormant.

• peripheral circulation will be augmented in the area of the damaged muscle and nerve.

Place the electrodes over the motor points to stimulate weakened muscles selectively. The motor point is where a major motor nerve enters the muscle bundle. Stimulating these areas will elicit the greatest amount of muscle contraction per amount of current intensity. Using a low pulse rate (10 to 20 pps), the current intensity is gradually increased until muscle contractions are visible. The point is to simulate natural muscle contractions. While I am externally stimulating the muscle, I also

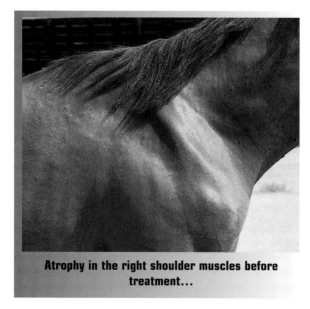

Atrophy in the right shoulder muscles before treatment...

attempt to cause internal stimulation by putting the leg in its normal position under

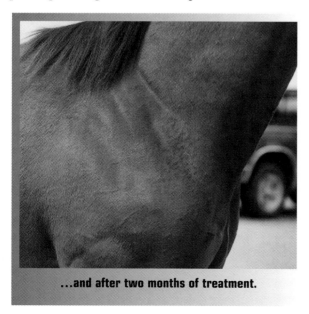

...and after two months of treatment.

the body. This can involve some work on the therapist's part. I use my knee against the horse's carpus to hold it in place while the electrical stimulation is given.

After electrical stimulation, do stretching and balance exercises. Stretch the injured foreleg forward and gently to the lateral and medial directions. Mobilization exercises are useful, as well, to re-educate the shoulder muscles. If the horse can bear weight on the injured leg, stretch the opposite leg forward so he must use the injured leg for balance. Gentle circles with the good leg activate muscles in the opposite leg as the horse seeks to maintain his balance. When the horse can walk comfortably, going up hills will strengthen the muscles and the cardiovascular system.

Do not be tempted to increase the intensity of electrically induced contractions to the point of discomfort. Overstimulation can result in increased damage to the muscle fibers and actually lengthen the re-enervation time. Also, painful overstimulation makes the horse resentful of the treatment and difficult to treat. An example from my experience illustrates this point. In treating a foal with shoulder nerve paralysis, I applied more current than the already weakened muscle fibers could handle. It was painful for the filly, so she sought to end the treatment session by lying down on the injured side as soon as I began to increase the current intensity. She was trying to tell me that it was uncomfortable. I soon got the message.

Keep the current in a comfortable range, and you will achieve a good response. Recovery time for shoulder nerve paralysis will be greatly reduced, assuming the nerve is not injured past the point of recovery. For the muscles to recover, the skeletal muscle fibers and the enervating motor neuron must be intact but non-functional due to trauma. Disuse results in atrophy, but allowing the atrophy to persist only lengthens the recovery period, affects joint health, and causes muscle pain and contractures.

The success of equine therapy for nerve injuries depends on the degree of nerve damage. If the nerve is bruised and mildly compressed, it should show signs of improvement in a few days. Hyperextension of the shoulder overstretches the nerve. If fibers are not completely torn, improvement should be seen in as little as a week. If two weeks go by with little improvement, there's a good possibility the damage is severe. At this point, diagnostic nerve conduction testing could provide information on the long-term prognosis for the injury.

Nerve Conduction Testing

Nerve conduction studies assess peripheral motor and sensory nerve function by recording the electrical potential evoked by external nerve stimulation. Motor nerve conduction velocity can be studied for most larger nerves of the foreleg. This physiological assessment is called electroneuromyography (ENMG), and its main purpose is to determine the location and extent of nerve injury.(18)

The nerve cell membrane is penetrated with a needle electrode called a microelectrode, and a second electrode is placed on the skin surface. Basically, electrical input is applied to the motor nerve, and an evoked potential is picked up from the muscle. The nerve may be stimulated at different sites where it is easily accessible from the skin surface. Transmembrane (across the membrane) electrical potential differences are recorded if there is nerve activity. The conduction velocity is calculated using the distance between the two stimulation sites and the time between stimulation and the onset of the motor action potential. Information about peripheral nerve function, skeletal muscle activity, and neuromuscular junctions will aid the therapist in electrode placement and in knowing the probable outcome of treatment.

Osteoarthritis

Osteoarthritis, or degenerative joint disease (DJD), is a chronic degenerative disorder of the articular cartilage of synovial joints. The American Association of Equine

Practitioners defines degenerative joint disease as any joint problem that has progressive degeneration of joint cartilage and the underlying (subchondral) bone. In horses, it occurs most frequently in the joints below the radius in the foreleg and femur in the hind leg. Some of the most common causes include repeated trauma, conformation faults, blood disease, traumatic joint injury, subchondral bone defects (osteochondritis dessicans), and repeated intra-articular corticosteroid injections.(19)

Once established, it presents an ongoing problem as bony overgrowth occurs at the edges of the joints (joint spurs) and the synovium and capsule thicken. The problem also extends to the musculature, with pain and unwillingness to move. Muscle trigger points and atrophy often result. Muscle pain

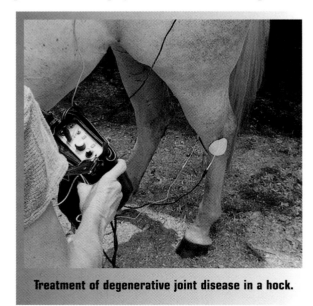

Treatment of degenerative joint disease in a hock.

is the major source of discomfort in the early stages as the joint itself has few sensory nerve endings. In the later stages, when the articular cartilage is destroyed, leaving only the subchondral bone, inactivity results in stiffness while too much activity results in pain.

Myofascial trigger points often can be found in muscles associated with the degenerative joint. The trigger points are identified by tenderness, a local twitch response, and a palpable band of tight muscle. Treating the points with electrical stimulation will greatly reduce the stiffness and discomfort associated with DJD.

Electrical stimulation has scientific support for use in treating joint symptoms of osteoarthritis as well as rheumatoid arthritis. Under experimental conditions, this treatment reduced the interarticular pressure significantly and reduced inflammatory reaction in the synovial tissue.(20) A related study showed stimulation improved the load-carrying capacity of affected joints and reduced pain.(21)

In one of the few published reports using horses as subjects, blood cortisol levels rose following electrical stimulation to appropriate acupuncture points.(22) Cortisol acts as an anti-inflammatory agent in arthritic conditions. It often is administered in the form of a cortisone, which can have serious side effects when injected. Its natural release by electrical stimulation of acupuncture points would be a safer form of therapy.

The treatment method I prefer includes placing electrodes on the medial and lateral sides of the joint and holding them in place with a stretch wrap. Two additional electrodes are placed on muscle trigger points. These points usually can be found easily with palpation. Gel might be necessary to maintain current flow at the joint. There might be more than two palpable trigger points, so I wet the hair coat in the area of the musculature so I can move those pads around. Because of associated muscle weakness, I also look for motor points in this area. Stimulating the motor points causes muscle contractions to maintain strength in the supporting muscles. I usually do not follow stimulation with stretching in cases of DJD because of the joint instability. If the musculature is tight and stiff, I use electrical stimulation to provide a deep massage, finding motor points and eliciting deep, slow, rhythmical muscle contractions.

Wound Healing

Electrical currents applied to a wound stimulate re-epithelialization and attract white cell activity.(23) Healing time is reduced, and there appears to be less scarring. The theoretical rationale for this includes improved circulation and lymphatic drainage. In addition, increasing the neg-

ative charge in the tissue creates an inhospitable environment for bacteria.

Electrical stimulation often is used as a bactericide as well as to hasten the regenerative process in wounds. Applying the negative electrode of a direct current unit to a wound or ulcer has been shown to be bactericidal or to retard the growth of common Gram-negative and Gram-positive microorganisms.(24,25) A reduction in microorganisms, namely *Escherichis coli*, *Staphylococcus aureus*, and *Pseudomonas aeruginosa*, have been documented in controlled studies.(26) The general treatment protocol uses the negative electrode over the wound until it is no longer infected, usually two to three days. At this point, a return to the positive electrode will continue the dermal cell and leukocyte migration toward the wound. Becker's "current of injury" theory holds that wounds are initially positive with respect to the surrounding tissue, that this positive polarity triggers the onset of the repair process, and that maintaining the positive polarity would promote healing.(27) This positive electrical potential attracts dermal cells, which possess a negative charge. Chronic, non-healing wounds no longer possess this electrical potential difference. The difference in electrical potential may be restored and trigger dermal cell movement by treating an unresponsive wound with the positive electrode.

Low-current intensity is used for 30- to 45-minute treatment periods. The electrodes should be cleaned and wrapped in sterile gauze that has been soaked in sterile saline. The active electrode should be directly over the wound. The ground electrode should be in a neutral place, such as the withers area. This electrode placement will ensure that the current is flowing through the wound and not around it.

When treating deep wounds, the electrodes can be replaced with a hydrogel conductive gel pad. The pad provides moisture, an aid to epithelialization. After treatment, these materials can be left in place, held by a dressing. When a wound cannot be held together by sutures, the hydrogel provides a moist, protective covering.

It might be even more important to treat sutured wounds with electrical current. Tight sutures that incorporate large amounts of tissue can strangulate the capillaries and compromise the blood supply.(28) This alone can be a reason for sutures to fail. The increased need for oxygen by collagen-forming cells can be satisfied through the use of electrically induced vasodilation.

Pressure sores result from pressure on bony prominence, but friction and moisture also play a role. Lying in urine-soaked bedding or padding can contribute as much to sores as constant pressure. Higher tempera-

tures because of the insulating effects of bedding or dressings increase tissue metabolism and oxygen consumption. It is said that for every one degree Celsius increase in

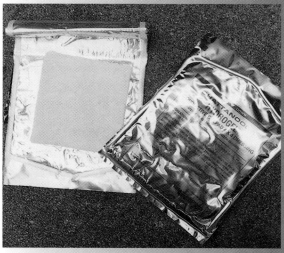

Hydrogel conductive gel pad can be used as an electrode.

skin temperature, there is a 10% rise in metabolic demand. The heightened need for nutrients and oxygen cannot be fulfilled because of blood vessel compression and resulting ischemia.

Thermography is used successfully to predict pressure sore formation. These deep sores start at the dermal and muscle layers and are only apparent at the skin surface when it finally gives way, opening a deep wound that can extend to the bone. Electrical stimulation is passed through the pressure ulcer by placing an electrode on either side of the wound. These wounds begin to close with the first treatment of electrical stimulation. Natural debridement takes place as waste fluids and dead cells are pushed out of the wound by muscle contraction and fluid shifting. Left untreated, pressure sores do not heal.

When a condition such as laminitis forces a horse to lie down, pressure sores, or ischemic ulcers, develop over the ileum, ulna, ribs, or other bony prominence. Chronic tissue ischemia causes dermal and epidermal erosion. These sores can be brought under control quickly with the use of the technique described. Infection from such wounds can be fatally toxic to a horse, so care must be taken to avoid further contamination of the wound during treatment. Post-surgical wounds also benefit from electrical stimulation, which reduces pain and decreases recovery time.

Electrical stimulation allows natural debridement of a wound. When electrodes are placed on the surrounding musculature and rhythmical muscle contraction occurs, wound exudate is pumped out. Less debris remains to be resorbed. An interesting case involved a yearling turned out with a paddock mate who was wearing a corrective shoe with a wide wing on the lateral side. The paddock mate came down on the yearling's back, causing a deep laceration with his shoe. Because of the wound's location, it drained poorly and exudate began to build up. Electrically stimulated muscle contrac-

tions pumped quantities of debris out of the wound, greatly reducing the potential for scar tissue formation. Because of the wound's location, wearing a saddle would have been uncomfortable for the horse if scar tissue had developed.

Tendon Repair

There are many approaches to caring for the injured tendon, especially in the flexor mechanism of the horse's lower leg. Because these injuries are common and range in severity, no single treatment satisfies all conditions. Equine therapy techniques could help ensure a more functional tendon after recovery and perhaps reduce the incidence of re-injury by enhancing its strength. The contribution equine therapy could make in the rehabilitation program for this injury, however, has largely been ignored.

Tendons display electrical properties and apparently have a current of injury just like the skin. Weak electrical currents have been used to re-orient the fibrin network in vitro, and it is well known that stretch forces placed on tendons aid in longitudinal fiber realignment. A study using low intensity, low frequency (10 pps) current stimulated surgically created tendon wound repair.(29) After two weeks, the tendons receiving stimulation withstood greater loads than the non-stimulated tendons. Another study looked at the tension required to re-break tendons, finding that tendons treated with anodal (positive) current were significantly stronger than those without any stimulation, measured 14 days after surgery. The authors suggested that other forms of electrical stimulation could produce the same results.(30)

Considering the number of digital flexor tendon injuries suffered by horses in training and the numerous techniques used to deal with these injuries, it is remarkable that electrical stimulation has not emerged sooner as a favored treatment. The most desirable tendon repair would limit adhesion formation and maintain the tendon's elasticity and ability to glide smoothly.

Trauma caused by hyperextension of the digital flexor tendons or fatigue failure can result in edema and discomfort. The symptoms of acute or chronic injury can be reduced through timely use of electrical stimulation. Place an electrode above and below the wound to allow current to pass through the tendon longitudinally. Stimulation will mimic the natural currents the tendon would produce from normal stretching when the horse walks. Ice cup massages or the use of gel cold packs and compression wraps will augment the effects of electrical stimulation in the early stage of injury. Continued passage of electrical current through the tendon could aid in the strengthening process as rehabilitation progresses. Mild, controlled exercise is essential

for the healing tendon. Electrical stimulation before exercise will make it more comfortable and prepare the structures for stretch forces. Remember to refrain from doing "too much too soon."

Laminitis

Electrical stimulation can benefit laminitic horses greatly because it reduces pain and increases blood flow to the foot. As laminitis occurs, endotoxins cause arteriospasm and a disruption in the blood flow through the hoof. The result is extreme pain and eventual death to the oxygen-deprived tissue. In 1978, Hood, et al. reported decreased perfusion of the capillaries of the foot in laminitic cases due to a significant arterio-venous shunting during the syndrome's onset.(31) Electrical stimulation has been shown to increase microcirculation, indicating a by-pass of the A-V shunt (arteriovenous shunt between the artery and vein). This effect and the ability to reduce pain make it a valuable therapeutic tool to use in treating laminitis. Stimulation shortens the acute inflammatory process and reduces lameness, hoof temperature, and associated muscle spasm in the upper body. It is far more comfortable and efficient than the traditional hot and cold water soaks. Combined with the appropriate medications, stable management, and hoof care, electrical stimulation is a valuable part of the care of laminitic horses.

In a report of eight cases, laminitis was treated with only electrical stimulation; no adjunctive medication or other forms of therapy were used.(32) Stimulation was started within two hours of the onset of symptoms and applied to the heel of the affected limbs twice daily for two hours. The treatment resulted in decreased clinical signs of laminitis and a rapid return to normal gait. Increases in blood flow will reduce the pulse pressure, and pain relief will reduce the stress to the horse (as well as to the worried horse owner).

An effective approach includes placing the electrodes on the medial and lateral aspects of the lower leg, over the digital vein and artery, at the fetlock. An alternative pad placement is using TH1 (the acupuncture location triple heater 1) on the anterior aspect of the foot at the coronary band and PC9 (the acupuncture location pericardium 9) on the posterior pastern. Using this pad placement, farriers have observed increased hoof growth. One farrier said he had observed a quarter-inch of new hoof growth over a six- to eight-week period using electrical stimulation.

Close veterinary supervision is vital in cases of laminitis. It is important to understand what triggered the syndrome in an effort to avoid recurring bouts.

The following photograph is a thermographic illustration of one treatment with electrical stimulation to the hoof of a horse with chronic laminitis. Thermographs of hooves affected with laminitis are character-

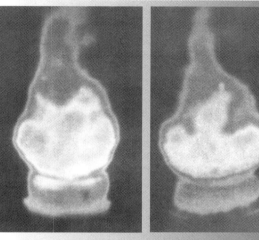

Thermographic picture showing increased blood flow to the hoof (left) after one electrical stimulation treatment, and before (right).

istically ghostly images of the foot and pastern. With increased blood perfusion the image is stronger, as seen in the thermograph on the left.

In an unpublished study using horses as subjects, I investigated the effects of blood flow through the common digital artery, a large artery that supplies most of the equine foot with blood.(33) A low pulse rate of 16 pps was used at an intensity just below perception, and blood flow was measured over 25 minutes. During this time, blood flow increased two-fold in the treated limbs compared with the non-treated limbs. Based on this observation, it seems likely that electrical stimulation to the major vessels in the lower leg could improve perfusion of the foot. The results of this experiment agree with Vasco's study. In this study, electrical stimulation was started within two hours of the onset of symptoms and applied twice daily for two-hour sessions. Low voltage TENS devices were used. Using a higher voltage device could have reduced treatment time, as less time is needed to accumulate sufficient charge in the tissues to cause vasodilation.

Iontophoresis: A New Mode of Drug Delivery

A product certain to change the way medications are delivered to animals was introduced at the 1997 meeting of the American Association of Equine Practitioners. Iontophoresis, also called ion transfer, uses direct current to drive water-soluble medications into subcutaneous tissue. Iontophoresis is an attractive drug delivery mode for the equine therapist because it is non-invasive and requires minimal ionic concentrations.

Historical Background of Iontophoresis

Although new to the equine industry marketplace, iontophoresis is not a new modality. Drugs have been introduced successfully into the tissues below the skin surface by means of electrical current since Fabre-Palaprat recovered iodide in urine following its electrical transfer in 1833. The safety and comfort of this method of drug transfer is illustrated by the use of zinc ion transfer for corneal ulcers in 1929, and in calcium ion transfer through the eye for the treatment of eye diseases in 1932. Bee venom was used in therapeutic iontophoresis in 1938. In 1940, epinephrine was administered to asthmatic patients by electricity. When the drug was deposited in the skin this way, it was absorbed gradually, and the supply was available for a period of time. Histamine ion transfer was advocated in 1944 for the treatment of subacromial bursitis. The versatility of this procedure is indicated in the broad spectrum of ions used in the early days. Because current levels are low, indications and contraindications of iontophoresis pertain to the ion selected and its physiological action in the tissues, rather than to the use of electricity. The electrical current merely repels the drug ion through the skin pores and the hair follicles.

Iontophoresis was approved by the FDA in the 1970s. The use of this modality is increasing in athletic training and orthopedic medicine for the treatment of injury, arthritis, and over-use syndromes. Each year more than 4 million people successfully receive drugs delivered by iontophoresis.(34)

Theoretical Basis of Iontophoresis

The Greek *ion* or *iontos* refers to an atom having a negative or a positive charge as a result of the loss or gain of one or more electrons. *Phoresis* refers to being carried. A direct electrical current provides the electromotive force to move the ionized particle of the drug past the barrier of the skin and into the deeper tissues. The route of entry is through the pores, sweat glands, and hair follicles. Additionally, the skin's overall resistance will decrease somewhat under the influence of electricity, allowing further passive passage of the drug into the dermal layers. The skin acts as a reservoir of the drug, extending its release into the deeper layers after the iontophoresis device is removed.

An iontophoresis device consists of:

• A low voltage direct current generator, the power source. Modern units are the size of the palm of the hand and powered by a 9-volt alkaline battery.

• Lead wires consisting of a positive lead and a negative lead. One unit has dual channel capability, enabling treatment of two sites at once.

• Electrodes, consisting of a buffered drug containment electrode for delivery of the drug, and the grounding electrode, also called the dispersive or return electrode.

The central process of iontophoresis is the movement of ions. The basis of ion transfer lies in the principle that like poles repel and unlike poles attract. Ions, being particles with a positive or a negative charge, are repelled into the skin by an identical charge the electrode places over it. When a direct electrical current activates the elec-

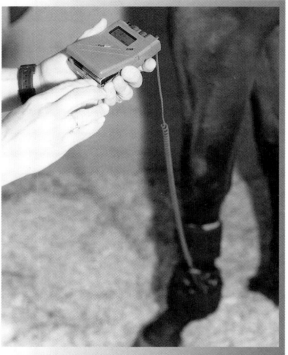

Treatment with iontophoresis delivers the drug right to the site.

trodes, anions in the solution — ions with a negative charge — move toward the positive electrode. Positively charged ions, called cations, move toward the negative electrode. The electrical current will drive ions through the skin that would not be absorbed passively. The quantity of ions made to cross the skin barrier is directly proportional to the current density and the amount of time the current flows through the solution. Current density is determined by the strength of electrical field and electrode size. Most units use a current strength of 0.4 milliamps (mA), or 1mA per square inch of electrode surface. This current strength is just below sensory perception. Smaller electrodes concentrate the current, making it more readily felt by the patient.

Another factor that determines ion flow is the weight of the ion molecules. Examining the delivery efficiency of three differently weighted drugs, Phipps et al.(35) found that sodium, the lowest weighted ion of a group that also included magnesium, potassium, and calcium, had the highest delivery efficiency. Elements of low atomic weight, less than 8,000 daltons, migrate much faster than those of high atomic weight. Such drugs include:

- local anesthetics such as lidocaine.
- antibiotics such as gentamicin and ceftiofur.
- corticosteroids such as dexamethasone.
- non-steroidal anti-inflammatory drugs, such as phenylbutazone and funixin meglumine.

A solution with a high concentration of ions will not increase the number of ions transferred. Indeed, a solution with a high concentration of ions could have a low delivery efficiency. Several investigators have demonstrated that medication at concentrations of between 1% and 5% are optimal for ion transfer.(36,37) An analogy could be made to a doorway through which a finite number of people can pass at any given time. Because of competition for space at the doorway, one way to allow more people to pass would be to keep it open longer. Increasing the number of people at the door would only create congestion. Optimal dosages for most drugs are achieved in treatment times of 10 to 20 minutes.

Continuous direct current is the current of choice for iontophoresis, since this mode ensures the maximum ion transfer per unit of applied current. It provides a constant, unidirectional electrostatic field between the electrodes to allow continuous transmission of drug. Other forms of current, such as high-voltage galvanic, sine wave, interferential, and microcurrent, are not effective in iontophoresis.

Application of Iontophoresis

In the past, human patients faced a risk of mild burning or a prickling sensation under iontophoresis electrodes. For this reason, lidocaine hydrochloride was added to the delivery electrode, along with the desired drug. Recent advances in electrode technology and current modulation have eliminated the need for lidocaine as no electrical sensation is felt. These advances also have made it possible to deliver more drug in less time. Skin pH at the electrode can affect ion transfer, so buffered electrodes provide the most efficient delivery. As with any other approach to drug delivery, iontophoresis must follow a complete veterinary evaluation and diagnosis to determine the nature of the injury, its location, and extent.

In iontophoretic drug delivery, it is critically important that the drug is applied through the electrode with the appropriate polarity. That means a drug with a negative charge is applied with the negative electrode. If the polarity is reversed, the drug won't be delivered.

Before applying the electrodes, inspect the area of skin to be treated. Look for abrasions, lacerations, scar tissue, or inflammation. Damaged skin is more sensitive to electrical current and could make the application uncomfortable or cause irritation at the delivery site. Clean the area thoroughly to remove oils, dirt, sweat, or other medications. Treatments should take place in a clean, well-lighted area where the horse can relax. Iontophoresis is well tolerated by the horse.

Prepare the delivery electrode by attaching the appropriate lead wire and filling the drug reservoir pad with at least 6cc of solution. Place it over the treatment site and apply a wrap to secure it in place. To prepare the ground, or return electrode, attach the wire of the opposite polarity and apply a dab of transmission gel on the karyra gum pad or wet it with water to increase its conductivity. This electrode is placed on the same side of the body, about four inches away from the delivery electrode, and wrapped in place. The electrodes have an adhesive backing to hold them in place, but additional wraps are recommended to ensure good contact and maintain electrode placement. Maintaining contact between the skin surface and the electrode is essential to obtain optimal current flow and to avoid uneven current density. Generally, shaving the hair coat is unnecessary, although a very thick coat may inhibit good contact between the electrode and the skin.

One device on the market today has a built-in ramping mode to increase the current slowly to delivery level. At the end of treatment, the current is automatically ramped down to 0. This ramping procedure allows a more gradual increase or decrease in current, resulting in a comfortable treatment without the sensation of being shocked. The delivery electrode can be left in place for additional time to allow for any passive absorption of the medication. Treatments are usually given every other day for one to eight weeks. Generally, results are seen within the first few treatments.

Iontophoresis can be used along with, and in many cases may enhance, other forms of equine therapy. Stretching exercises are used to increase range of motion and are useful in reducing muscle spasm or in elongating scars or adhesions. Electrical stimulation, photon therapy, or magnetic fields can be used to maintain pain relief and edema reduction. Therapeutic ultrasound increases membrane permeability, increasing absorption of the ions.

The drug is placed in the reservoir electrode.

To show the compatibility of iontophoresis and other equine therapy modalities, iodine was used for its softening effects in addition to ultrasound and stretching. The results of this case study of post-surgical tendon scarring were complete pain relief in humans and normal range of movement in five treatments.(38)

Specific Uses of Iontophoresis

Corticosteroids are the primary drugs used with iontophoresis in human physical therapy.(39) Formulated as a water-soluble salt, the corticosteroid molecule has a negative charge. Dexamethasone is often administered by iontophoresis to treat joint or musculoskeletal disorders. In a comparative study of three approaches to over-use injury of the shoulder, iontophoresis provided the quickest end to muscular pain. Orally administered muscle relaxant and analgesic medications were given to one subject group; another group received treatment with hot packs and ultrasound. The iontophoresis treated group received 1cc of 0.4% dexamethasone sodium phosphate and 2cc of 0.4% lidocaine hydrochloride. Although all three treatment procedures resulted in increased pain-free range of motion, the subjects receiving oral medication had the least increase, and those receiving iontophoresis had the most. The investigators think this was because the iontophoresis administered the medication directly to the target tissues.(40)

In another study, 50 patients with various musculoskeletal conditions, including epicondylitis and tendonitis, were treated with dexamethasone sodium phosphate and xylocaine using iontophoresis. All showed positive results within 24 hours after the first treatment. Cumulative effects of up to three treatments in a week resulted in permanent relief in some cases.(41)

A case report of gouty tophi and osseous degeneration, which would be equivalent to degenerative joint disease in the horse, showed positive response to lithium iontophoresis. The patient reported immediate improvement following the first treatment. Subsequent treatments resulted in complete relief of edema and pain.(42)

Calcific deposits are amenable to treatment with the acetate ion found in acidic acid. A reduction in the deposit's size and density was confirmed by radiograph. Two investigators reported the results of applying acetic acid solution to bursal calcification, tendon sites, and myositis ossificans. Radiographs three months after treatments showed complete absorption of the heavy calcific deposits seen before treatment.(43, 44)

An unpublished study examined the consistency of iontophoretic drug delivery to the hock joint of the horse.(45) Using three horses, six hock joints were treated with betamethasone at three concentrations and three treatment durations. The data indicated a 2.4% solution of betamethasone administered in a 40 to 80mA/min. dose was optimal. These parameters were found to deliver betamethasone concentrations considerably above estimated therapeutic concentrations as

proposed by Lillich.(46)

Copper sulfate has been used to treat fungal infections such as tinea pedia (athlete's foot) in humans with marked improvement in 24 hours.(47) Perhaps this could prompt investigations of iontophoresis treatments for white line disease or fungal skin diseases in horses.

Benefits of Iontophoresis

Iontophoresis offers the benefits of being painless and non-invasive. In addition, there is no danger of infection or damage due to needle insertion or impact from a bolus of fluid. The local concentration of the drug is high, while the systemic concentration is minimal. Only minute amounts of the drug reach the systemic circulation, greatly reducing side effects. Drug dosage is regulated by controlling the quantity of electrical current used to transfer the drug. For areas such as the distal tarsal joint or around the hoof, where injection is difficult, iontophoresis offers an alternative mode of drug delivery. As the medication passes through the tissues, it bathes the peri-articular tissues, as well as the articular surface.

Exposure to mild electrical current provides added therapeutic effects. Contraindications with this modality pertain to sensitivity to the drug rather than to the modality itself. The manufacturer suggests that therapists avoid placing electrodes so that the current pathway crosses the heart or the brain. The eye area also should be avoided. In addition, abraded skin or new scars should be avoided because these areas are sensitive to electrical current.

The equipment available today is efficient and miniaturized. The possibility of shock or burns no longer poses a problem because of advanced electrode design and modulated current. Iontophoresis has the potential to provide substantial benefits. As with many new modes of therapy, however, more studies that document the use and effects of iontophoresis are needed.

Fundamental Concepts of Therapeutic Electricity

The therapeutic use of electrical currents dates to the ancient Greek and Roman eras. The first recorded electrical stimulation treatments documented the use of the electric ray fish in the treatment for gout. Fortunately, this modality has evolved considerably since then. The electrical output from today's units is smooth, comfortable, and suitable for use on horses, without any of the shocking or burning sensations of devices of the past.

The therapeutic electrical stimulator emits a type of energy with wavelengths and frequencies that can be classified as electromagnetic radiation. The electromagnetic spectrum contains wavelength and frequen-

cy outputs of other therapeutic tools such as magnets and therapeutic lasers and is discussed in Chapter 8. Wavelength is defined as the distance between the peak of one wave and the peak of the next wave. Frequency is defined as the number of wave oscillations occurring in one second and is expressed in hertz (Hz) units or in pulses per second. The wavelength and frequency of the output determine the biological effect of electrical stimulation. They can be adjusted by the therapist in some units and are set by the manufacturer in other units. Electrical stimulating currents that affect nerve and muscle tissue have the longest wavelengths and the lowest frequencies of any of the modalities.

Current is the rate of flow of electricity and is measured in amperes. Typical currents emitted by electrical stimulators are measured in milliamperes, or one-thousandth of an amp. Continuous currents in the milliamp (ma) range can harm the body. You can receive a painful shock with 8 to 100 mA of continuous current; 100 to 200 mA can disrupt the heart and cause fibrillation. Above 200 mA, tissues are destroyed by the rapid rise in tissue temperature and severe non-relaxing muscle contractions. How, then, can one expect to survive the standard treatment dose of 150 mA delivered by a therapeutic stimulator? It is because the current flow is modulated within the machine and delivered in very brief pulses, varying from several microseconds to several hundred milliseconds, depending on the unit. The total current flow is within the range of safety.

Before 1990, no system had been developed to standardize descriptions of electrical currents used in electrotherapy. Traditional designations for therapeutic currents were galvanic, sinusoidal, alternating, faradic, and high frequency. Manufacturers of the units influenced the language of electrotherapy with their designations of H-wave, high-voltage, and Russian current. In an effort to reduce the confusion, the American Physical Therapy Association developed the following designations for therapeutic electrical currents.

Direct current is the uninterrupted unidirectional flow of charged particles. A direct current unit will have a cathode, or negative pole, where chemical reactions produce an excess of electrons, and an anode or positive pole, with a deficiency of electrons.

Alternating current is the uninterrupted bi-directional (sometimes called biphasic) flow of charged particles. The polarity of this type of current is reversed periodically so that the current flows first toward one pole, then toward the other. Alternating current is expressed in hertz.

Pulsed current is defined as the uni- or bidirectional flow of charged particles that periodically ceases. This is the most commonly used form of current therapeutic units. A pulse is a finite period of charged particle movement.(48)

All units fall into one of these categories. The wave shape probably has little to do with the physiological effects of the device. The body has its own electrical currents, and these influence the form that external cur-

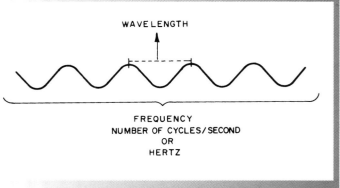

Wavelength is the distance between the peak of one wave and the peak of the next wave.

rent takes once it passes through the skin.

Voltage, also referred to as electro motive force, makes charged particles move, causing the current to flow.

To illustrate the relationship between voltage and current, think of voltage as the pressure in a water hose and current as the amount of water coming out of the hose. If great pressure is required to obtain only a trickle of water, there must be a kink in the hose somewhere or some connection is not snug. So it is with the flow of electricity. If the voltage must be increased excessively before a muscle contraction is seen in the area of the active electrode, there must be a bad connection somewhere. If excessive

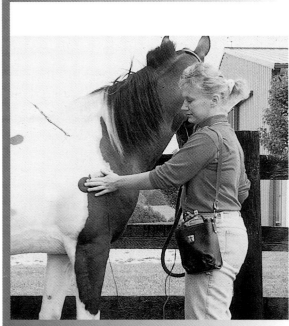

Therapeutic currents are comfortable and safe.

voltage is needed to elicit contractions, one might consider that there is poor electrode-skin contact. Perhaps the hair coat is too dry, oil or dirt are inhibiting the current flow, or there is a break in the circuit between the machine and the horse. Check for a problem rather than increasing the intensity.

Intensity

The intensity dial controls the voltage output and therefore influences the comfort and effectiveness of the treatment session. Generally, the higher the intensity, the greater the number of nerve or muscle fibers that are activated, but high intensity currents can be painful. Keep the intensity low and within the range of comfort by your choice of electrode size and placement and by maintaining a good electrode-skin contact. Uncomfortably high intensity levels are never appropriate for the horse. An effective electrotherapy treatment evokes a profound endorphin effect, and the horse should remain relaxed, even to the point of deep sleep, throughout the treatment session.

A good habit is to return the intensity control to the 0 setting at the end of each treatment. Before attaching the electrodes, check the setting to be sure the treatment will begin at the 0 setting.

The numbers on the intensity control have nothing to do with the actual voltage; they are simply relative guides of low to high intensity. The intensity control should be periodically checked by the manufacturer to ensure proper functioning. Most physical therapy clinics have their units checked annually.

Electrical stimulation at any current level will not penetrate through bone and can be uncomfortable in areas where bone is superficial. Lower current intensities will provide a comfortable and effective level of stimulation on areas such as the lower leg or on bony prominences.

Electrodes

Electrodes are the conductive interface that delivers current to the tissues. Those best suited for use on horses are made of carbon impregnated silicon rubber because they are durable and easy to keep clean. Although these electrodes last a long time, they do not last forever. In time the rubber will begin to deteriorate, and the electrode will not provide uniform current flow.

If the hair coat is kept wet there is no need to use conductive gel between the electrode and the skin. The wet hair serves as the coupling medium. Use gel when treating the lower limbs to ensure that air does not impede current flow.

Self-adhesive electrodes can be used on horses if the hair coat is short. The area should always be clean and damp. When the adhesive begins to break down, the electrode must be discarded because the contact will be difficult to maintain.

Air is a good insulator of electrical energy. The quality of contact between horse and electrode will affect the depth of penetration of the current. Although it is not necessary for current transmission, shaving the coat will increase the quality of contact since hair traps a great deal of air. When the coat is shaved, gel must be used for uniform coupling.

Wetting the hair thoroughly with water or an electrolyte gel aids transmission of current into the tissues. The electrodes should be wet, and if they are made of sponge they should be soaked. It may be necessary to repeatedly wet the electrodes and the horse's coat on a hot day to avoid losing current flow as the coat dries.

The current density, or amount of current per unit area, is inversely proportional to electrode size. The smaller the electrode, the more intense the current will be as it is concentrated in a smaller area rather than being spread out over the skin surface. Depth of current penetration can be affected by electrode size and electrode spacing. Most stimulators come equipped with large and small electrodes. The smaller surface area concentrates the current, providing the potential for greater depth of penetration. Some direct current units provide a large electrode called the dispersive pad. This electrode spreads the current over a large area; thus, it does not penetrate down to sensory and motor nerves and very little sensation or muscle movement is felt under it. Using a dispersive pad and a direct current unit enables the therapist to designate the active electrode as positive or negative for wound treatment.

Electrical current remains relatively

superficial if the electrodes are close together. Spacing the electrodes farther apart causes the current to flow through tissues providing the least resistance, the nerves and muscles. This tendency for current to flow in the areas of least resistance can be used to great advantage when the treatment goal is to stimulate deep muscle. Electrode placement can affect the current density in the deep muscle in another way, as well. Placing the electrodes parallel to the muscle fibers will produce a greater response than placing them perpendicular to the fibers.

Commercially Available Stimulators

Electrical stimulators go by several names and are categorized according to their intended effects. There are many units available, more than could be completely described here. The following units, some of which are more suitable than others for equine therapy, are those I have used on horses. Those described are not the only ones that could be used successfully, I am sure.

TENS units

During the 1970s interest in electrotherapy grew with the development of small, battery-operated stimulators that could fit into a shirt pocket. Repetitive stress disorders such as carpal tunnel syndrome and chronic back discomfort are treated with devices called TENS to reduce the patient's depen-

dence on analgesic medication. TENS stands for trans cutaneous electrical nerve stimulation. Skin surface electrodes stimulate sensory and motor nerves that lie directly beneath them. These devices are marketed specifically for pain control and produce a low level of smooth current. They are meant to be worn for several hours so the stimulation replaces some or all of the pain medication normally taken after surgery or with chronic injury. In a study of 200 patients with intractable pain due to peripheral nerve damage, anginal pain from ischemic heart disease, and musculoskeletal pain, TENS showed immediate favorable response that was maintained for more than six months.(49)

Originally TENS units were designed to be operated by the patient, rather than a trained therapist, and had few pulse characteristic options. More recently TENS units have come out with pulse width and frequency options as well as burst and ramping options. They are typically two-channel stimulators with independent amplitude controls for each channel and four treatment electrodes. The units usually offer stimulation in the 50 to 100 Hz range with a pulse width of up to 200 microseconds and an amplitude of capability of up to 100 mA.

These devices can be used on horses for pain relief, and the small size allows them to be attached to a surcingle and left on for an

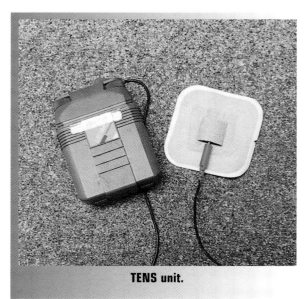

TENS unit.

extended period. Gel should always be used under the electrodes, which are held in place by a wrap. The therapist should regularly check to see that the electrodes are in place. Place TENS electrodes on acupuncture points for the best effect. Low frequency TENS, less than 10 Hz, has been shown to result in an increase in the endogenous opiod, beta-endorphin.(50)

NMES

NMES units also developed in the 1970s, when it was learned at the Olympic Games that the Soviets used electrical stimulation to produce rapid strength gains in their athletes. Subsequent studies in Europe and America did not substantiate these results and indicated the levels of current necessary for strength gains comparable to those pro-

duced in resistance exercise programs were beyond the limits of comfortable stimulation. This might be all right for the Russians, but it certainly would not do with horses!

NMES, or neuromuscular electrical stimulation, devices use a variety of waveforms, including rectangular, biphasic, pulsed or burst current. This modality is also often called FNS for functional neuromuscular stimulation. Some units designed for use on humans may not be comfortable enough or versatile enough for general equine therapy. A horse will rebuild lost muscle strength through regular exercise once pain has been relieved and the normal range of limb movement has been restored. Using electrical current strictly for increasing muscle mass in healthy horses may be impractical. These devices are used to exercise muscles of the paralyzed lower limbs of spinal cord injured patients. This type of stimulation improves muscle strength, endurance, girth, and appearance during rehabilitation.

Recently an FNS unit has been designed for use on horses. Based on technology used for rehabilitation of spinal cord injured patients, the Theraquine electrical stimulator uses a biphasic wave as well as direct current. Two of its three electrode pairs deliver a sinusoid shape wave of 250 microseconds on time and 500 microseconds off time.

Stimulus durations of 200 microseconds or more are likely to produce the greatest muscle contractions, but longer durations of stimulus on time can result in increased sensation. For this reason, the output is ramped so it gradually increases to a peak and then drops off. The ramping feature makes this output comfortable, and horses tolerate it well.

The biphasic waves in the Theraquine cross in a manner similar to interferential current while the middle electrodes deliver direct current. All three outputs are ramped in an effort to avoid "startling the horse," according to the instructions. The horse can be startled by a surge of current if the unit is turned on or off with the leg wrap plugged into the unit. Another way to startle the horse with this unit is to increase the intensity when the green light on the panel is not lit. As with any unit that has a ramping feature, there is an upward sweep of output intensity followed by a drop-off. To avoid surprising the horse, advance the intensity only when the output is at the peak of the upward sweep, indicated on this unit by a green light.

This device enables the therapist to evoke deep muscle contraction without discomfort. I have used it to stimulate atrophied shoulder muscles following nerve damage. The six-electrode pad was held in place so that the electrodes were over the target muscles. Increasing the current level gradually makes for a treatment that is easily tolerated by the horse. Holding the pad in place allows the therapist to feel the muscle contractions.

The electrode pad can be used over the horse's back muscles when soreness interferes with a stallion's willingness to breed. Using this technique, I have observed an immediate relaxation response in chronically sore back musculature. Placed properly, the pad can stimulate acupuncture points related to reproductive functions.

Interferential stimulators

Interferential stimulators were developed in the 1980s. These devices emit sinusoidal, symmetrical, alternating current at very high frequencies (2,000-5,000 Hz). The therapist sets the channels at slightly different values, and the electrodes are placed so the two currents cross at the pain site. Theoretically, the crossing allows deeper penetration and greater amplitude of the current where the currents intersect.

Interferential currents do not produce visible contractions unless the amplitudes are set high, so verbal feedback from the patient is important in setting the parameters correctly. These units can be complicated and expensive, but that doesn't mean they are better than other types. Interferential current is simply a different approach to achieve the same effects as other electrical stimulators that are less expensive and more user-friendly.

Microcurrent

Microcurrent stimulators produce very low amplitude currents that do not excite nerve or muscle tissue. Not even cutaneous sensory nerve fibers are stimulated, so the patient does not feel the tingling sensation of other devices. These units are used for pain relief and evoke an endorphin response. The same effect can be achieved by other units with the intensity kept low. Perhaps more important than the low amperage current (less than 1 mA of total current) are the high frequencies this modality offers. Current frequencies of 15,000 Hz may be responsible for the pain-relieving effects.

Perhaps the most popular microcurrent device for use on horses is the Acuscope, a device that measures skin impedance (resistance to electrical current) as well as delivering electrical output. These devices are designed to be used on acupuncture points, and accuracy is important for effective treatment. These units are expensive and require training. Because each acupuncture point must be stimulated for several minutes, treatments can take an hour or more. Skilled therapists often get good results, but other units can achieve the same outcome with less commitment of time and money.

\Direct Current High Voltage

Direct current high voltage stimulators are the foundation units of electrotherapy. They are versatile and can be battery-driven. These units provide a comfortable, pulsed, uniphasic current in the range of 25 mA at the maximum end. They usually offer variable pulse rates ranging from low frequency pulses of 2 pps for edema reduction and muscle relaxation to frequencies of 200 pps for pain relief and neuromodulation. A positive and negative switch allows the therapist to determine the polarity of the pads for wound healing or for iontophoresis. When a direct current unit is used, the unidirectional flow of ions travels from one electrode to the other. These units are usually easy to operate and are reasonably priced. A favorite unit, made by the Soken Company, comes in a carrying pouch, making it easy to use with a horse.

Neuromodulators

A high frequency, neuromodulating device called the Synaptic has recently been introduced. It offers continuous alternating current rather than the pulsed current found in most units. This device, developed for human physical therapy, emits very high frequency electrical current, 2,500 to 30,000

Hz compared to the 50 to 250 Hz used in other devices. This makes the stimulation virtually non-perceptible while it evokes a pleasant and sedating modulation of neurotransmitter chemistry. This phenomenon plays an important role in pain control. When this device is applied to a horse, the animal immediately relaxes as beta-endorphins and serotonin levels increase. Other blood chemistry changes include an increase in ATP and enkephalins to enhance tissue healing.

I had five of these units at the Olympic Games in Atlanta and could have used five more. This device has a profound effect on pain and muscle spasm. Many of the competing horses had severe spasm in the supporting musculature along the spine, keeping these muscles in a state of hypertension. This type of non-relenting muscle spasm causes fibrous ribbons to form through the muscle, eventually reducing its contractile power. Using a low frequency muscle stimulator on muscles in this condition could be uncomfortable and cause further spasm. Very high frequency currents evoke significant relaxation, allowing for more functional muscle contractions. If spasms are allowed to persist, muscles will atrophy as full functional contractions are inhibited by scar tissue. This had actually taken place in some of the competing horses. That they can still compete at the

Synaptic treatment at the Olympics.

Olympic level is testimony to the greatness of their innate athleticism and heart.

Neuromodulation, or therapeutic effects on neurotransmitters, is a rapidly growing area in physical therapy. Neurotransmitters are chemicals produced by brain cells that are responsible for transmitting messages within the brain and also messages from the body to the brain. Specific neurotransmitters are the basis of our moods, our ability to feel pain and to heal, and our ability to sleep and remember. This particular device is being used in Alzheimer research where improved memory, behavior, and elevated pain threshold have resulted. Studies have shown this device affects levels of such neurotransmitters as beta-endorphins, serotonin, ACTH, epinephrine, norepinephrine, and somatostatin.

Horses respond to treatment with this device by going into a state of deep relaxation that can be vital to their health in high-stress environments such as racetracks or shows. This relaxed state is more consistent and profound than with any other treatment I have used.

We generally use this device set on level 2 to evoke the peaceful resting state. To relieve muscle spasm and pain, higher levels such as 4 and 5 can be used. Although the intensity can be increased up to level 9, the upper levels are not used with horses. Treatment time is generally 20 to 45 minutes. An effective approach is to allow the horses to drift into sleep and end the treatment when they wake up refreshed and calm.

The Synaptic uses adhesive electrodes, making it easy to apply its four treatment pads as well as providing for good contact with the skin surface. This device can be used for muscle soreness and stiffness, for mental and physical relaxation, and for joint pain.

Electro Medicine in the Future

The future for electrical stimulation holds much promise. Electricity will be used to prevent the bone resorption that normally parallels disuse. Already specific electrical field parameters, between 50 and 150 Hz, are being used for an hour a day to maintain bone mass in the absence of function. Fields of 15 Hz are being used for osteogenesis. The electrical fields have been found to be more effective than the pulsed magnetic fields in initiating new bone formation and at only 0.1% of the electrical energy of the pulsed electromagnetic field.(51)

Electrical stimulation to paralyzed muscles allows spinal cord patients to walk. It is also being used to prevent lymphatic congestion in cases of chronically spasmed muscles. How these advances will be used to affect horse health remains to be seen. Since the body is an electrical entity, then electrical current can have an effect on how the body, and even cells, function.

Conclusion

The therapeutic electrical stimulator is perhaps the most versatile of the therapist's modalities, being capable of providing pain relief, stimulating edema absorption, promoting wound healing, and producing muscle contraction for the retardation of atrophy and spasm reduction. Profound relaxation can be achieved with electrical stimulation, affecting a horse's mood and behavior.

Although this is a safe modality with few

contraindications, it is often used as a last resort. Electrical stimulation can hasten recovery time and ensure a more comfortable rehabilitation from injury or surgery when applied early in the injury process. Horses enjoy being treated with this modality, and there are many conditions that will respond favorably to it.

There are many portable units suitable for use on animals. Before choosing one, consult a veterinarian and have your therapeutic goal clearly in mind.

Definitions

Adhesions — Abnormal adherence of collagen fibers to surrounding structures following trauma, immobilization, or surgery. Restricts normal elasticity of structures involved.

Arthritis — Inflammation of structures of a joint.

Atrophy — Muscle wasting due to disuse. Loss of muscle bulk and strength when it is not used.

Fast twitch fiber — A skeletal muscle fiber with fast reaction time and high anaerobic capacity.

Guarding muscle contractions — Muscle contractions that functionally splint the injured tissue against movement. Guarding ceases when pain is removed.

Hypertrophy — Increase in strength of a muscle related to the physiologic cross-sec-tional area of the muscle fiber. The diameter of the muscle fiber is called muscle bulk.

Ions — Atoms or molecules that have gained or lost electrons making them electrically charged.

Ischemic ulcers — Areas of chronic dermal and epidermal erosion in which local hypoxia plays a major role.

Membrane potential — The difference in concentration of ions inside the cell and the surrounding extracellular fluid. All body cells exhibit membrane potential.

Muscle spasm — Prolonged contraction of a muscle in response to local circulatory and metabolic changes.

Osteoarthritis (DJD) — A chronic degenerative disorder primarily affecting the articular cartilage with eventual bony overgrowth at the margins of the joint.

Relaxation — Conscious effort to relieve tension in muscles.

Synovitis — Inflammation of a synovial membrane, an excess of synovial fluid within a joint or tendon sheath.

Tendinitis — Scarring or calcium deposits in a tendon.

Tendon — Attaches muscle to bone.

References

1. Charman, RA. 1989. Pain Theory and Physiotherapy. *Physiotherapy*. 75:247-254.

2. Melzack, R. and Wall, P. 1965. Pain

Mechanisms: A New Theory. *Science.* 150:971-78.

3. Silverstone, LM. The use of a new, non-invasive neuromodulation device in the treatment of acute and chronic pain. Proc 3rd Int Cong Int Neuromod Soc. Orlando, FL:1996.

4. Jones, AYM. and Hutchinson, RC. 1991. A comparison of the analgesic effects of transcutaneous electrical nerve stimulation and entonox. *Physiotherapy.* 77:526-30.

5. Dougal, TS. 1991. Effectiveness of transcutaneous electrical nerve stimulation following cholecystectomy. *Physiotherapy.* 77:715-22.

6. Newham, DJ. 1991. Skeletal Muscle, Pain and Exercise. *Physiotherapy.* 77:66-69.

7. Ibid.

8. Valberg, SJ. 1997. Exertional Rhabdomyolysis. Annual meeting of the British Equine Veterinary Association.

9. Robinson, AJ. and Snyder-Mackler, L. 1995. *Clinical Electrophysiology,* 2nd ed. Baltimore, MD.: Williams & Wilkins. 84.

10. Cheng, N. et al. 1985. The effects of electric currents on ATP generation, protein synthesis and membrane transport in rat skin. *Clin. Ortho. and*

11. Doran, FS. et al. 1970. A clinical trial designed to test the relative value of two simple methods of reducing the risk of venous stasis in the lower limbs during surgical operations. *Br J Surg.* 57:20-30.

12. Kisner, C and Colby, LA. 1990. *Therapeutic Exercise Foundations and Techniques,* 2nd ed. Philadelphia: FA Davis Company. 11-12.

13. Snyder-Mackler, L. and Robinson, AJ. 1989. *Clinical Electrophysiology.* Baltimore, MD.:Williams & Wilkins. 111.

14. Delitto, A. and Snyder-Mackler, L. 1990. Two theories of muscle strength augmentation using percu-taneous electrical stimulation. *Phys Ther.* 70:158-164.

15. Rose, SJ. and Rothstein, JM. 1982. Muscle mutability: Pt 1. General concepts and adaptations to altered patterns of use. *Phys Ther.* 62:1773-87.

16. Eriksson, E. and Haggmark, T. 1979. Comparison of isometric muscle training and electrical stimulation supplementing isometric muscle training in the recovery after major knee ligament surgery. *Am J Sports Med.* 7:169-71.

17. Clemente, R. and Barron, K. 1996.

Rel. Res. 171:443-46.

Transcutaneous neuromuscular perfusion in anatomically denervated rat skeletal muscle. *Arch Phys Med Rehabil.* 77:155-60.

18. Snyder-Mackler, L. and Robinson, AJ. 361-431.

19. The American Association of Equine Practitioners. *Media Guide to Equine Sport.* Lexington, KY.

20. Levey, A. et al. 1987. Transcutaneous electrical nerve stimulation in experimental acute arthritis. *Arch Phys Med Rehab.* 68:75-78.

21. Abelson, K. et al. 1983. Transcutaneous electrical nerve stimulation in rheumatoid arthritis. *New Zealand Med J.* 96:156-58.

22. Cheng, R. et al. 1980. Electroacupuncture elevates blood cortisol levels in native horses; Sham treatment has no effect. *J. Neuroscience.* 10:95-97.

23. Borgens, R. et al. 1989. *Electric Fields in Vertebrae Repair.* AR. Liss.

24. Barranco, S. and Berger, T. 1974. In vitroeffect of weak direct current on Staphyloccus aureus. *Clin Ortho.* 100:250.

25. Rowley, B. 1972. Electrical current effects on *E. coli* growth rates. *Proc Soc Exp Biol Med.* 139:929-34.

26. Rowley, B. et al. 1974. The influence of electrical current on an infecting microorganism in wounds. *Annals NY Aca Sci.* 238:543-51.

27. Becker, RO. 1967. Electrical control of growth processes. *Med Times.* 95:657-69.

28. Bojrab, MJ. 1994. A Handbook on Veterinary Wound Management. *KenVet.* 6.

29. Katzberg, A. 1974. The induction of cellular orientation by low-level electrical currents. *Annals NY Aca Sci.* 238:445-50.

30. Owoeye, I. et al. 1987. Low-intensity pulsed galvanic current and the healing of tenotomized rat achilles tendons: preliminary report using load to breaking measurements. *Arch Phys Med Rehabil.* 68:416-18.

31. Hood, DM., et al. 1978. Equine Laminitis I: radioisotopic analysis of the hemodynamics of the foot during the acute disease. *J Equ Med Surg.* 2:439.

32. Vasco, K. et al. 1986. Laminitis Treatment with Electrotherapy. *Equine Practice.* 8:1986.28-31.

33. Porter, M. 1983. Electrical stimulation of blood flow through the equine limb. unpublished. University of Kentucky.

34. Data compiled by Empi, Inc., St. Paul,

Minn. 1996.

35. Phipps, JB. et al. 1989. Iontophoretic delivery of model inorganic and drug ions. *J Pharm Sci.* 78:365-69.

36. O'Malley, E and Oester, Y. 1955. Influence of some physical chemical factors on iontophoresis using radio isotopes. *Arch Phys Med Rehabil.* 36:310.

37. Murray, W. et al. 1963. The iontophoresis of C2, esterified glucocorticoids: Preliminary report. *Phys Ther.* 43:579.

38. Tannenbaum, M. 1980. Iodine iontophoresis in reducing scar tissue. Phys Ther. 60: 792.

39. Costello, CT. and Jeske, AH. 1995. Iontophoresis: Application in transdermal medication delivery. *Phys Ther.* 75:104-12.

40. Delacerda, FA. 1982. Comparative study of three methods of treatment for shoulder girdle myofascial syndrome. *J Orthopaed Sports Phys Ther.*4:51-54.

41. Harris, PR. 1980. Iontophoresis: Clinical research in musculoskeletal inflammatory conditions. *J Orthopaed Sports Phys Ther.* 4:109-12.

42. Kahn, JA. Case report: Lithium iontophoresis for gouty arthritis. *J Orthopaed Sports Phys Ther.* 4:113-14.

43. Kahn, J. 1977. Acetic acid and ultrasound for calcium deposits. 1990. *JAPTA.* 6:658.

44. Paski, C. and Carol, J. 1955. Acetic acid ionization: A study to deter mine the absorptive effects upon calcified iondinitis of the shoulder. *Phys Ther. Rev.* 35:84.

45. Dorian, R. 1996. Clinical investigation of iontophoresis of betamethasone in the horse hock joint. unpublished study. Edna Valley Veterinary Clinic/The Equine Center. San Luis Obispo, CA.

46. Lillich, JD. et al 1996. Plasma, urine, and synovial fluid disposition of methylprednisolone acetate and isofluupredone acetate after intraarticular administration in horses. *AJVR.* 57:187-92.

47. Haggard, HW. et al. 1939. Fungus infections of hand and feet treated by copper iontophoresis. *JAMA.* 112:1229.

48. Robinson, AJ. and Snyder-Mackler, L. 1995. *Clinical Electrophysiology, Electrotherapy and Electrophysiologic Testing,* 2nd ed. Baltimore, MD.: Williams & Wilkins.

49. Meyler, WJ. et al. 1994. Clinical evaluation of pain treatment with electrostimulation: A study of TENS in patients with different pain syndromes. *Clin J Pain.* 10:22-27.

50. Clement-Jones, V. et al. 1980. Increased beta-endorphin but not metenkephalin levels in human cerebrospinal fluid after acupuncture for recurrent pain. *Lancet.* 2:946-48.

51. Rubin, CT. et al. 1993. Optimization of electric field parameters for the control of bone remodeling: Exploitation of an indigenous mechanism for the prevention of osteopenia. *J Bone Min. Res.* supp 2. 8:S573-S581.

Recommended Readings

Cummings, J. 1987. *Iontophoresis. in Clinical Electrotherapy.* Roger Nelson & Dean Currier, eds. Appleton & Lang. 231-41.

Li, LC., Scudds, RA. 1995. Iontophoresis: An overview of the mechanisms and clinical application. *Arth Care Res.* 8:51-61.

Li, LC., et al. 1996. The efficacy of dexamethasone iontophoresis for the treatment of rheumatoid arthritic knees: A pilot study. *Arth Care and Res.* 9:126-32.

Wearly, L. et al. 1989. Iontophoresis: Facilitated transdermal delivery of verapamil.I. in vitro evaluation and mechanistic studies. *J Controlled Res.* 8:237-50.

Therapeutic Ultrasound

*One must develop an identity with both the instrument
and the target tissue, a sameness of therapist,
instrument, and target...*M. Porter

ULTRASOUND, a form of acoustic energy, is commonly used to treat musculoskeletal injuries. The popularity of this treatment can be traced to its large number of clinical indications, relative ease of application, and minimal number of precautions and contraindications. The effectiveness of ultrasound in the treatment of joint-limiting conditions, soft tissue injuries, inflammatory processes, and wounds has undergone considerable research scrutiny in the last decade.

Ultrasound acts as a deep heating agent and can produce temperature changes in tissues as deep as 1 to 5 centimeters (cm), such as muscle and tendon, without excessive heating of superficial tissues such as skin. A thorough understanding of the effects and proper use of ultrasound is necessary to ensure safe and effective treatment. A veterinary

evaluation is necessary to determine the involved tissue and the stage of tissue healing before treatment begins. This chapter will

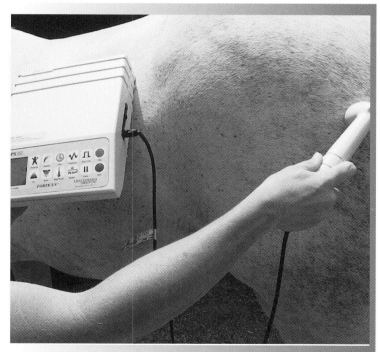

Ultrasound acts as a deep heating agent and is used to treat musculoskeletal injuries.

help educate equine therapists in the basic physics and physiological effects of therapeutic ultrasound, as well as the specific treatment techniques and clinical applications.

The use of ultrasound in medicine began in the 1920s with the discovery that strong, high-frequency sound waves caused damage to living cells. This led to its use for the destruction of cancer cells in the late 1920s. During the 1930s, lower intensity ultrasound first was used in the treatment of soft tissue injuries. In 1980, it was estimated that more than 15 million ultrasound treatments were given each year in hospital settings alone. It remains the treatment of choice for many musculoskeletal dysfunctions.(1)

The use of sound energy has expanded greatly in recent years to include burglar alarms and underwater identification. Medical applications include diagnosis (imaging of internal organs), tissue treatment (functional restoration and healing of soft tissues), tissue destruction (tumor irradiation), and obstetrics (fetal imaging).

Sound waves are mechanical pressure waves described in terms of frequency. Audible sound has a frequency between 16 and 20,000 cycles per second, or Hertz (Hz). Therapeutic ultrasound frequencies are much higher, usually from 1 million to 3 million Hz, or 1 to 3 Megahertz (MHz). While lower frequency sound waves (audible sounds) appear to spread out in all directions, ultrasound beams emanate in straight, parallel lines, similar to the light beam from a flashlight. This collimated sound wave is important in delivering treatment to the injured tissue selectively.

Originally, ultrasound units offered only one frequency (1 MHz) and allowed only for the continuous application of sound waves. This, coupled with the fact that most devices were used by technicians with no theoretical background, led to numerous cases of overheated equipment and damaged soft tissue. Today's units measure energy output and have automatic shut-off devices. New units also offer a range of frequencies from 1 to 3 MHz and both pulsed (interrupted) and continuous modes of ultrasound delivery. At the racetrack, however, the combination of outdated units in need of calibration and untrained users commonly result in deep tissue burns. Therapists must have a thorough understanding of the mechanisms by which ultrasound operates to achieve consistently good results.

Mechanics of Ultrasound Production

To understand the effects of therapeutic ultrasound, it is important to understand the sound wave itself. Ultrasound waves are pressure waves of mechanical energy moving in a straight line from the source. Because of their frequency, ultrasound beams are well collimated, which is important in the penetration of superficial tissues.

The velocity of the sound waves is related to the physical properties of the medium through which they travel and changes as tissue density changes. Sound waves travel best through solid mediums and cannot be transmitted through a vacuum. Ultrasound does not travel well through air; in fact, transmission of ultrasound waves through air could damage the ultrasound device's sound head (or transducer), which converts electrical energy to kinetic energy before it enters the body. Therefore, the sound head must never be held away or tilted away from the horse while the unit is on.

Sound waves multiply in the medium until the energy is absorbed. When applied to tissue, compression and rarefaction occur in each cycle of the sound wave (up to 3 million times per second). Compression is the point at which particle density is greatest, and rarefaction refers to making the sound wave less dense. The compressive forces mount as the wave moves deeper into the tissue. Absorption of sound waves increases as the frequency increases. Therefore, at very high frequencies, the superficial tissue absorbs all the energy and deeper structures remain unaffected.

Characteristics of Ultrasound

Reflection and refraction are two key terms in understanding therapeutic ultrasound. They occur when ultrasound is transmitted across tissues of varying densities, such as through muscle to bone. The angle of reflection equals the angle of incidence. This means that sound waves delivered at a 30-degree angle to the left will be reflected away from the tissue at a 30-degree angle to the right. If the angle of incidence is zero (perpendicular), the sound waves will be reflected directly back toward the source. If the ultrasound source is stationary, energy can be transmitted and reflected to and from the source. This process becomes hazardous to the tissue, which is subjected to both incoming and rebounding energy. This could result in tissue burns, often referred to as "hot spots." It is important to keep moving the sound head in a slow, steady motion to prevent "hot spots" and treat the area uniformly.

Refraction, the deflection of energy waves, depends on changes in velocity and wavelength as ultrasound passes from one medium to another. In the body, reflection and refraction occur largely at tissue interfaces, including fat to muscle, muscle to fascia, tendon to bone, and ligament to bone. The amount of reflection when ultrasound crosses from fat to muscle is minimal. The junction of tendon or ligament to bone, however, brings about a substantial increase in reflection of energy.

Bone is thought to reflect up to 70% of sound energy that reaches it. Thirty percent of the sound energy might enter the outer covering, or periosteum, of the bone, while the rest is reflected. This reflected energy interacts with the incoming energy, increasing the heat at the periosteum. Overheating is felt as a dull ache in the bone and can damage the periosteum as well as capillaries. Therefore, caution should be used when applying therapeutic ultrasound to joints or other areas of the body where bone is superficial.

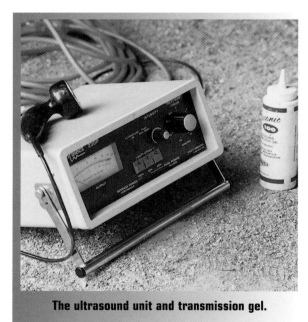

The ultrasound unit and transmission gel.

The Ultrasound Unit

The ultrasound unit produces ultrasound waves by applying electrical current to a specialized material housed in the sound head of the unit. Components within the unit transform 110-volt, 60-cycle electricity from the wall outlet to 500 volts or more and 3 million cycles per second. This voltage is applied to a crystal in the sound head that has piezoelectric qualities. The crystal, made of either natural quartz crystal (in older units) or a synthetic ceramic material (in newer devices), contracts and expands to alternating electrical current. Therefore, vibrations occur when rapidly alternating current is applied to the crystal. The crystal is glued to a metal plate that forms the outer surface of the transducer and acts as an interface between the transducer and the patient's tissue. This vibration typically occurs at a rate greater than or equal to 1 million oscillations per second. The electronic frequency of the ultrasound unit is matched to the natural vibration frequency of the crystal. Therefore, transducers cannot be interchanged from one ultrasound device to another.

The crystals in ultrasound units are delicate and must be protected from hard blows or overheating. In older ultrasound devices, transducers were changed for varying treatment frequencies and continuous wave-forms. More recent technology permits numerous frequencies to be generated with the same sound head. When using interrupted wave-forms, the duty cycle indicates the percentage of time the ultrasound energy is on.

Transducers are available in sizes from 1 cm2 to 10 cm2 to accommodate both large and small treatment areas. Transducer faceplate size often is referred to as the Effective Radiating Area or ERA. Newer units will indicate a value described as the BNR or Beam Non-uniformity Ratio. This number indicates how uniform the ultrasound beam is when leaving the transducer. Units with lower BNR values deliver more uniform ultrasound energy to the treatment area and produce more favorable treatment results. Beam Non-uniformity Ratios of two to three are ideal.

It is recommended that all ultrasound units be tested on a bi-annual basis and recalibrated as necessary to meet performance standards. This includes interchangeable transducers which purport to auto calibrate.(2)

Physiological Effects

Many of the therapeutic uses of ultrasound involve the delivery of heat to underlying soft tissues. This treatment, however, also delivers non-thermal effects, which involve physiological changes in tissues that cannot be attributed to heating. The combination of deep heating and non-thermal effects makes this a unique and versatile modality.

Thermal Effects

The principal use of therapeutic ultrasound is based on the knowledge that ultrasound can increase tissue temperatures at depths up to 5 centimeters. The physiological responses attributed to deep heating include increased collagen tissue extensibility, alterations in blood flow, changes in nerve conduction velocity, increased pain thresholds, and changes in contractile property of muscle. Ultrasound intensities that are too great have been known to retard long bone growth and destroy various tissues. The amount of heat produced in tissues depends on the intensity and frequency of the ultrasound, duration of treatment, type of tissue treated, and size of the treatment area. Tissues with high concentrations of collagen, such as bone and joint capsules, absorb greater amounts of ultrasound energy. Conversely, little attenuation occurs in the skin and subcutaneous fat.

The amount of energy absorbed into tissue and the subsequent tissue temperature elevation depend on frequency. Higher frequency, 3 MHz, delivers heat to tissues at depths of only 1 to 2 centimeters. Lower frequency treatments, 1 MHz, allow for deeper penetration of ultrasound energy and heat. Frequencies of 1 MHz are used most commonly to treat musculoskeletal disorders. However, 3 MHz frequencies prove valuable in treating more superficial tissues or areas of bony prominence. Specifics regarding tissue temperature increases and blood flow changes caused by ultrasound will be discussed later in this chapter.

Non-Thermal Effects

Non-thermal effects of ultrasound are those that cannot be explained by a thermal mechanism. Over the past several decades, significant research on the use of therapeutic ultrasound in tissue repair has emerged. These studies indicate that pulsed ultrasound at low intensities that do not produce measurable thermal effects in tissue might assist in accelerating healing, reducing edema and pain, and speeding the inflammatory phase of tissue repair.(3) These non-thermal or mechanical effects include cavitation, acoustical streaming, and micromassage.

Cavitation is the vibrational effect, brought about by an ultrasound beam, on gas bubbles found in blood and tissue fluids. The pulsation of these bubbles, when intense enough, causes changes in cellular activity. When the bubbles in the field pulse but do not increase in overall amplitude, stable cavities occur. This can result in diffusional changes along cell membranes, thus altering cell function. The opposite effect of stable cavitation is unstable cavitation. This condition occurs when the bubbles vibrate violently, causing collapse and tissue damage. Unstable cavitation rarely occurs clinically; however, it can occur when treatment is too intense or long.

Acoustical streaming, which can alter cell permeability and function, refers to the movement of fluids along the cell membrane wall as a result of stable cavitation. Finally, micromassage refers to the oscillation of tissues and cells within the ultrasound field. It can reduce edema and stimulate mechanoreceptors (receptor cells for touch and sound) in acute injury.

It is essential to use proper care in administering ultrasound; the philosophy "more is better" cannot be employed. While both the thermal and non-thermal effects of ultrasound can aid in recovery, improper use actually can slow the process. The treatment should be administered only by skilled operators and only after consultation with a veterinarian.

■ Therapeutic Uses of Ultrasound

Joint Mobility

Ultrasound can be used in treating joint mobility limitations, which often are a result of prolonged immobilization or scar tissue formation. The goal of ultrasound is to increase tissue temperatures before stretching. Experience has shown that heating deep tissue immediately before or during stretching results in a greater effect on tissue length and less risk of tissue injury than stretching alone. The joint capsule, which is made up largely of collagen, is responsible for limiting joint motion. When treated, the joint capsule absorbs large amounts of ultrasound energy, which increases the collagen's elastic property, making it easier to stretch. The use of continuous ultrasound at 1 MHz is ideal for reaching the deep tissues surrounding joints and increasing soft tissue elasticity to accommodate improved stretching.

Tendon Extensibility

Tendons, the fibrous attachment of muscle to bone, can become shortened in cases of joint immobilization or injury. Like the joint capsule, tendons are high in collagen fiber and benefit from the use of ultrasound accompanied by or immediately preceding prolonged stretching. A study by Draper determined that the "stretching window" following ultrasound treatment is about three minutes if the tissue temperature is raised 5° C.(4, 5) This stretching window applies to all soft tissue.

Research on humans shows that stretches must be maintained for a minimum of 30 to 60 seconds for permanent elongation of tissue to occur. Stretching for less than 30 seconds results in elastic soft tissue deformation, which means tissue is temporarily elongated then returns to its original length.(6)

Ultrasound and stretching can be applied to flexural deformity, a condition

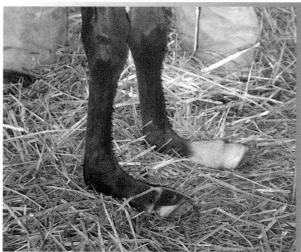

Ultrasound was applied to this foal, which suffered from hyperextension of the fetlocks...

seen in newborn foals. This condition is manifested as contraction of the flexor tendons or hyperextension of the fetlock, resulting from congenital factors, from malpositioning of the fetus in the uterus, or

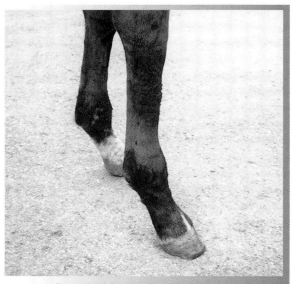

...and resulted in a noticeable improvement.

from nutritional deficiency of calcium, phosphorous, vitamin A, or vitamin D. The contraction might involve the superficial flexor tendon, the deep flexor tendon, and the suspensory ligament.(7) The flexor tendons also can contract due to injury in mature horses. Hyperextension in newborn foals results from excessive tension in the extensor digitorum muscle. Applying ultrasound to the tendon makes the collagen more susceptible to stretch forces. Applying ultrasound to the muscle reduces neural input from the gamma fiber, allowing relaxation. (Gamma fibers are special nerve fibers from the spinal cord that cause muscle fibers to contract.)

No research is available on temperature tolerance of tendons in foals; however, the tissues of young horses are more susceptible to damage by overstretching or overheating. Furthermore, ultrasound applied over the growth plates of long bones has been indicated in preventing normal growth. Close veterinary supervision is essential in such cases.

In mature horses, injury resulting in altered stride length or decreased joint range of motion could require veterinary consultation to determine the exact musculotendenous groups involved. Ultrasound treatments provide the therapist with a way to increase the tendon temperature and flexibility without overheating the skin. A combination of ultrasound, manual stretching, and gentle exercise (such as walking or swimming) will help the tissue regain elasticity.

Scar Tissue

After injury, tissues begin the repair process. The results are often imperfect, leaving scar tissue, called generic connective tissue, rather than specialized connective tissue. This tissue is mechanically inferior and adheres to bone or skin or to tendons and tendon sheaths. It prevents the normal motion of body tissues that should occur with movement.

Clinical evidence supports the use of ultrasound in softening scar tissue. The treatment can be applied before massage and range of motion activities to aid in destroying scar tissue and improving joint mobility. Studies by Griffin and Karselis reported a relaxation in peptide bonds after the application of ultrasound to scar tissue.(8) Scar tissue softening might be attributed to temperature increases in collagen tissue and the mechanical forces of cavitation associated with pulsed ultrasound.(9) The exact intensities, rates, and durations of ultrasound in the treatment of scar tissue are still being studied. Current research seems to support the use of continuous ultrasound, for its heating effects, or pulsed ultrasound, for its mechanical effects, in treating scar tissue.

The importance of addressing scar tissue

in horses is threefold. This tissue can lead to nerve entrapment and joint range of motion limitations, hindering athletic performance. Furthermore, it might be considered a blemish that will decrease a horse's sale potential. Starting treatment early is critical when using ultrasound therapy to reduce scar tissue. Young tissue is modified more easily and broken down by ultrasound, cross friction scar massage, and range of motion activities. Older scars present more difficult clinical scenarios with questionable outcomes.

Calcium Deposits

Calcium deposits — excessive bone growth secondary to trauma — are a common problem in horses. These splints or exostosis of the interosseous ligament often occur between the second and third or third and fourth metacarpal bones. This new bone growth might be associated with a single traumatic episode or repeated microtrauma from weight bearing on imperfectly positioned bones during growth. Ultrasound has been reported to ease calcium reabsorption and minimize the effects of deposits. The literature, however, fails to support this claim with substantial clinical research.

Using ultrasound to treat calcium deposits is most likely successful because it decreases inflammation around the

deposits, which decreases edema in the involved extremity.

Pain Relief

A primary use of ultrasound therapy is to help reduce pain by increasing the pain threshold. The therapist must recognize that the absence of pain does not necessarily mean complete healing. However, ultrasound has been advocated in reducing pain

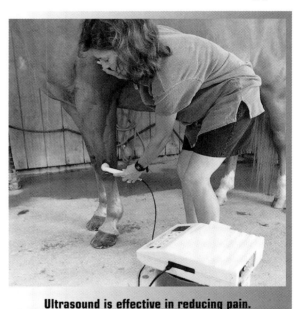

Ultrasound is effective in reducing pain.

associated with bursitis, tendinitis, osteoarthritis, and other musculoskeletal conditions. In these cases, ultrasound decreases inflammation of the involved tissue and affecting the nervous tissue conducting the pain message to the brain. Szumski described the effects of ultrasound on nervous tissue as selectively heating peripheral nerves, blocking painful impulse conduction, increasing membrane permeability, and increasing tissue metabolism.(10)

The effects of ultrasound on nervous tissue can be attributed solely to heating effects. Some authors have also noted the use of ultrasound to alter nerve conduction velocities in relaying painful messages to the brain. Still others suggest the deep heating effects of ultrasound act as a counter-irritant to block the transmission of pain. Although the exact mechanisms by which ultrasound alters pain perception are not fully understood, the literature clearly supports its use to reduce pain.

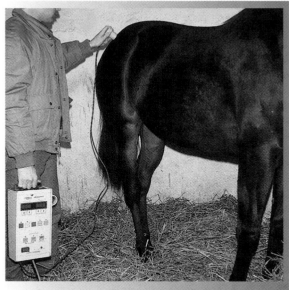

Ultrasound can help reduce muscle spasm.

Muscle Spasm Relaxation

Ultrasound relaxes muscle spasm through its direct effects on the gamma fiber activity. Gamma fibers originate in the spinal cord and terminate in specialized muscle fibers in the periphery called intrafusal fibers. Vigorous contraction of muscle heightens the electrical impulses from the spinal cord to the muscle. An increase in these impulses results in muscle contraction that stretches an organ called the muscle spindle. When this organ is stretched, reflex contraction of muscle fibers occurs. This constant tension in muscle creates ischemia, or lack of blood flow, which results in pain and spasm. This vicious cycle often is referred to as the pain-spasm-pain cycle.(11) Using ultrasound to heat these gamma fibers slows the transmission of electrical activity, which reduces stimulation of the muscle spindle and allows the muscle to relax. Pain reduction discussed earlier in this chapter also might be responsible for ultrasound's effect in breaking the cycle.

Edema Reduction

Edema often is implicated in slowing recovery following soft tissue injury. Rapid edema reduction can speed recovery. Typically, the old adage of RICE — rest, ice, compression, and elevation — is used to manage edema. Ultrasound can help treat this condition by increasing blood flow to capillaries in the injured area and increasing cell membrane and vascular wall permeability, all of which will allow for increased absorption of exudates. One study reported better reduction of edema, point tenderness, and pain with ultrasound than other forms of therapeutic heat.(12)

Ultrasound also might be indicated in the treatment of hematoma, a localized swelling filled with blood. Left untreated, a hematoma can take as long as eight weeks to go away. Applying ice massage when the injury is first noticed and following with ultrasound after the internal bleeding has stabilized can reduce a hematoma in two weeks or less. The need to lance or drain the hematoma is eliminated, as are all the complications that go along with these invasive procedures.

Ultrasound can enhance vasodilation, which in turn reduces edema. In a vasodilation study, 10 horses were treated with ultrasound to one clipped front leg while the other front leg served as a control. The metacarpal flexor tendon was the area treated for 10 minutes at three different intensities: 0.5 W/cm2, 1.0 W/cm2, and 1.5 W/cm2. After treatment the gel was removed and the leg was thermographed.

Thermography showed that therapeutic ultrasound increased skin temperature, supporting the concept that it causes vasodilation. Increasing the ultrasound intensity increased the heating effect. The leg treated

with 0.5 W/cm2 intensity had the least profound change. The 1.0 W/cm2 intensity treated leg had the most dramatic change, lasting more than two hours. The leg treated at an intensity of 1.5 W/cm2 had an initial temperature increase, but the tissues cooled to below the untreated skin temperature within two hours. The authors speculated that the drop in temperature could be due to heat loss through convection, conduction, and radiation. They suggested applying a wrap after ultrasound treatment to maintain increased tissue temperature.(13)

Tendinitis and Bursitis

Ultrasound is also commonly used to treat inflammatory conditions. While many studies advocate using ultrasound for both acute and chronic conditions, the literature indicates it is most helpful in the acute stages of tendinitis and bursitis.(14) The Falconer study suggests pain relief in acutely inflamed tissue is brought about by the increased pain threshold, increased blood flow, and increased cell permeability produced by ultrasound energy. In chronic inflammatory conditions, ultrasound can complement treatment if used to increase tissue temperature prior to stretching.

Use caution when treating acute conditions. Low intensity pulsed ultrasound will minimize tissue temperature increases while facilitating the healing process. Non-thermal effects, such as micromassage and alterations in cell permeability, might help enhance reabsorption of fluid between the cells.(15) Using ultrasound to treat tendinitis and bursitis apparently increases blood flow to aid in healing, increases tissue temperature to relieve pain, and increases tissue permeability to decrease soft tissue edema.

One study compared the effects of thera-

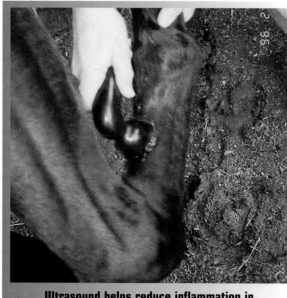

Ultrasound helps reduce inflammation in injured tendons.

peutic ultrasound with electrical stimulation in treating humans for painful shoulder syndrome, a condition involving the connective tissue, joint surfaces, and bursa around the shoulder. The two treatment groups also received heat and performed stretching and joint mobilization exercises. Success was measured by evaluating range of movement and pain. The study found that both types of treatment provided statistically significant relief from the syndrome, which is characterized by pain, functional impairment, and weakness. This condition is often treated with analgesics and non-steroidal anti-inflammatory drugs, as well as with local steroid injection.(16) Therapeutic ultrasound offers a non-drug alternative through vasodilation, increased metabolism, muscle relaxation, and increase in collagen extensibility (ability to stretch). Electrical stimulation provides analgesic electrical currents.

The ultrasound application used in this study is one I particularly favor for use on horses. The first few sessions consist of 10 minutes of ultrasound at 0.5 W/cm2. The ultrasound is increased each session by 0.1 W/cm2 until you get to 1.0 W/cm2. Subsequent sessions are at this level. The gradual increase prevents overdosing if the injury is still in the inflammatory stage. Electrical stimulation was applied with the electrodes placed on the anterior and posterior areas of the shoulder for 20 minutes with a mean frequency of 50 Hz. This low frequency would be tolerated well by a horse, and the pads could easily be held on the shoulder joint. Heat and mobilization exercises complete the package of modalities.

Tendinitis was found to be the most prevalent cause of painful shoulder syndrome in humans. Horses, particularly jumpers, exhibit a similar syndrome. Using a combination of ultrasound, electrical stimulation, heat, stretching, and mobilization exercises could reduce the need for drug therapy in this condition. Drug therapy characteristically needs to be increased as tolerance grows, whereas physical therapy is often reduced in frequency or intensity as the therapy progresses.

In my research, I found an interesting 1978 study that examined the histological picture of the repair process in surgically split tendons following treatment with ultrasound. The authors thought the treatment improved the quality of healing.

The horses in this study were subjected to radical surgical splitting of the tendons of one foreleg while the other foreleg was used as the control. Ultrasound was applied for 10 minutes six times a week for two weeks. The continuous mode was used at intensities of 1.5 W/cm2.

In the untreated legs, the flexor tendons showed areas of hemorrhage and inflammation. Degeneration of tendon tissue was found in the area of the incision, with fibrin still in the incision line. There were few fibroblasts with poor granulation and collagen, and vascularity was poor. The ultrasound-treated tendons didn't have the inflammatory reaction and degenerative areas observed in the control tendons. A network of newly branching blood vessels was crossing the incision line and passing into tendon tissue. Young fibroblasts were migrating into the incision gap from surrounding tissue. (17)

Wound Healing

The effects of ultrasound on tissue healing have been studied in both humans and animals. Numerous animal studies have shown that ultrasound enhances the tensile strength of collagen tissue following tendon injury and prevents the risk of future injury.(18-20) Other studies have examined the effect of ultrasound on wound contraction and wound healing.(21) Ultrasound applied in low intensities (0.1 to 0.5 W/cm2), usually in pulsed modes, consistently demonstrated benefits to healing tissue in open wounds, tendon repair, and closed trauma. Higher intensities, greater than 0.8 W/cm2, have been shown to retard wound healing.(22)

Pulsed ultrasound applied at a 20% duty cycle in very low intensities appears to be most beneficial in the healing of acute wounds. Treatment times should be brief, usually 30 to 60 seconds per ERA, and should be repeated daily.(23)

Stable cavitation and acoustical streaming play a significant role in healing wounds. Conversely, the risk of unstable cavitation delays the healing process and occurs with high intensities of pulsed ultrasound, even at duty cycles as low as 10%.

It is not advisable to use ultrasound during the first week of healing. However, beginning it during the second week of repair, when collagen formation and fibroblastic infiltration have begun, can help. Fibroblasts respond to therapeutic ultrasound with an enhanced rate of protein synthesis.

When treating an open wound, avoid contaminating the wound bed. Clean the area thoroughly before and after ultrasound treatments using gentle materials such as saline, which works well for flushing the site. Never use bleach, peroxide, alcohol, or betadine. Treating wounds with ultrasound requires further investigation and should only be done by the experienced equine therapist under a veterinarian's supervision.

Hoof Wall Abscesses

An infection that starts in the white zone of the hoof and progresses up to the coronary band is often called a "gravel." The resulting abscess beneath the hoof wall hurts and causes lameness until the pressure is relieved, either by its breaking out, usually at the coronary band, or by being opened and drained by the veterinarian. In either case, treatment involves draining the pus from the infected wall.

Ultrasound can provide a non-invasive means of drawing the infection out that takes less time than soaking and packing the foot. Because ultrasound can be applied with the sound head under water, it can be combined with the hot water soaking routine, reducing the soaking time to 10 minutes. Sound passes through water and tissue in much the same way.

Subaqueous ultrasound produces less tissue heating than direct application. An outdated method of application called for holding the sound head away from the hoof, which reduced the heating effects. The accepted new technique is to hold the sound head against the skin, which increases the heating benefits.

The hoof should be cleaned thoroughly, and the water and container must be clean. The tub must be deep enough to submerge the lower pastern completely. If the horse repeatedly takes his foot out or moves, the water will be agitated, interfering with sound wave transmission. When the water is agitated, you must turn off the unit immediately and wait until the water is calm again before continuing.

Application Techniques and Clinical Decision-Making

The misuse of ultrasound in equine therapy, which can result in such things as deep tissue damage, will increase as the popularity of the modality grows. The rest of this chapter will focus on proper clinical application and decision-making in the use of therapeutic ultrasound in equine therapy.

Many parameters must be considered to apply ultrasound treatment properly. A thorough evaluation of the type of injury and the stage of healing is important before beginning any treatment. This might require a veterinary consultation. Once the injury assessment is complete, decisions must be made regarding ultrasound frequency, waveform, intensity, duty cycle, treatment duration, and treatment area.

Furthermore, ultrasound can be applied using numerous methods. These methods include the direct contact technique, underwater technique, or fluid-filled bag procedure. Proper positioning of the horse and the sound head is crucial in delivering the most effective treatment.

Ultrasound Application

Before beginning ultrasound treatment, the therapist must clean and prepare the area, preferably a stall with good lighting. This involves assembling the transmission gel, a sponge, and water to wet the hair coat. A clean towel also is needed to remove excess gel and dry the area after treatment. It is important that the horse is relaxed; it might help to give him some hay to keep him occupied. Restraint such as twitching is never necessary during ultrasound application.

Because ultrasound units are designed for use in hospitals and clinics, there is a risk of dust and straw being drawn into the vents of the unit's cooling fans. A large, clean, plastic bucket or an overturned tub will serve nicely as a table for the unit, keeping it away from the dangers of the stall floor. Place it so the controls are in easy reach and the read-outs are in clear view.

When applying ultrasound, be sure to maintain constant contact of the sound head during treatment. This will increase the amount of energy transmission to the target tissue and decrease the likelihood of damaging the transducer.

The intensity should always be re-set to zero before turning the ultrasound unit on. Setting the timer to the desired treatment time and pressing the start button will activate the unit. Be careful to increase the ultrasound intensity slowly during the treatment, until the desired therapeutic intensity level is reached. Decrease the intensity to zero when discontinuing treatment.

Some sort of coupling agent, most commonly ultrasound gel, is required when applying ultrasound. Ultrasound waves do not travel well through air and are markedly diluted at air-tissue interfaces. Typically, coupling agents are compared with water, considered the best transmitter of ultrasound energy. The couplant must provide sufficient skin lubrication to allow the transducer to move easily over the treatment area. It also should absorb little to no ultrasound energy to provide for greater delivery of energy to the target tissue and less energy attenuation at the transducer-tissue interface.

The agent must provide a great enough viscosity to prevent runoff. Ideally, it should be water-soluble to make cleanup easy and prevent buildup in the hair coat. Finally, it is essential that the material resist bubble formation, which will interfere with energy transmission. (24)

The need to re-apply gel is common because of coat hair in the treatment field. A decrease in wattage or the presence of air bubbles in the gel will indicate the need for more. An accumulation of air bubbles will result in poor transmission of sound waves into the target tissues. Bubbles that collect should be wiped away during treatment. Applying alcohol to the skin and to the transducer will reduce the accumulation.

Remember that the horse should feel no discomfort; pain during the ultrasound treatment indicates damage to deep tissues. If uneasy behavior occurs, check the output of the unit before continuing. The intensity should be maintained well below the pain threshold.

Dosage

Treating the horse with the correct dosage of ultrasound is extremely important. The adage that "more is better" cannot be applied to this therapy. Overdosing the treatment area with ultrasound might retard the healing process or even injure healthy tissue. Conversely, the therapist must apply ultrasound at an appropriate depth, intensity, and duration to bring about the desired results.

The analogy of a fireplace can be used when discussing ultrasound dosage. A smoldering fire does not produce enough heat to heat the room effectively, while too intense a fire can endanger the room. There is an ideal "temperature window" within which the room is effectively heated. The same "window" applies to the use of ultrasound. The dosage must bring about the desired physiological change without endangering the target tissue or other structures in the treatment area. In attempting to locate this "therapeutic window," the therapist must consider the type of tissue to be treated, depth of the target tissue, and stage of target tissue healing. The therapist also must consider the desired physiological effects, size of the treatment area, and treatment duration.

Frequency

The frequency at which ultrasound is applied will determine the depth of penetration of the ultrasound energy. Many older units offer only the 1 MHz frequency. Ultrasound applied at 1 MHz can deliver energy to tissues at depths of 5 centimeters or greater. Newer ultrasound units offer the clinician a variety of treatment frequencies. Most commonly these include 0.8 MHz, 1.0 MHz, and 3.0 MHz. The 3 MHz frequency is valuable for treating areas where the target tissue is more superficial, or bony areas where deeper penetration could cause periosteal tissue damage.

Frequencies below 1.0 MHz allow ultrasound energy to reach depths greater than 5 centimeters. The therapist must be aware of the risks of overheating target tissue close to bone. The rule of thumb when considering therapeutic ultrasound frequency is the lower the frequency, the greater the depth of energy penetration. With the increased depth of penetration goes the increased risk of unstable cavitation and, therefore, the increased risk of tissue damage.

Wave-form

The decision about which wave-form to use depends largely on the goals of the therapeutic intervention. The therapist must choose between a continuous or interrupted (also referred to as pulsed) wave-form. The effects of continuous ultrasound include increased delivery of heat to the target tissues. Pulsed ultrasound produces more mechanical than thermal effects. Typically, the use of continuous wave-forms increases the ability of soft tissue to extend before manual stretching activities. Pulsed wave-forms at low intensities are indicated in the treatment of acute injuries to aid healing without greatly increasing the involved tissue's temperature.

Duty Cycle

Duty cycle refers to the percentage of the total treatment time the pulsed ultrasound energy is being delivered. Pulsed ultrasound refers to an interrupted wave-form that has well-controlled on and off times. The amount of time the pulsed ultrasound is on determines the amount of energy delivered to the patient.

Duty cycle can be calculated easily by the ratio of "on time" to total treatment time. For example, a duty cycle of 20% applied for a treatment duration of 10 minutes indicates that ultrasound energy is being delivered for a total of two of the 10 minutes of treatment. In this example, pulsed ultrasound delivered at an intensity of 1.0 W/cm2 and a duty cycle of 20% will deliver only one-fifth the amount of ultrasound energy to the target tissues as continuous ultrasound delivered at the same intensity.

Ultrasound delivered at a duty cycle of 20% and very low intensity is recommended to enhance tissue repair. It is important to describe pulsed ultrasound treatments in terms of both intensity and duty cycle to accurately reflect the amount of energy delivered to target tissues.

Intensity

Ultrasound intensity refers to the strength of the ultrasound beam. Intensity is the rate at which energy is delivered per unit area and is expressed in terms of watts per centimeter squared (W/cm2). Typical treatment intensities range from 0.5 W/cm2 to 2.0 W/cm2. The greater the intensity, the greater the resulting temperature elevation. The types of tissue in the treatment field and the degree of energy reflection and refraction that occur also can determine the amount of tissue temperature elevation.

The measurement of intensity is calculated by measuring total power output in watts and dividing by the area of the applicator face in cm2.

intensity (W/cm2) = total power output (W)/ applicator size (cm2)

Because the ultrasound beam is not uniform, some areas of the beam might be more intense than others. The intensity reported by the ultrasound unit's digital readout is an average intensity, also known as the spatial average intensity. It could help to know the greatest intensity within the beam, the spatial peak intensity. Elevated spatial peak intensities are responsible for "hot spots" that might cause tissue damage. Hot spots are best avoided by continuously moving the sound head during the ultrasound treatment.

Intensity must be great enough to bring about the desired physiological and therapeutic effects without causing damage to tissues within the treatment area. When treating areas where bone is superficial or little muscle or fat tissue is present, use lower intensities.

Treatment Duration and Treatment Area

Treatment time is determined by measuring the treatment area. The equation of five minutes of treatment time for every two times effective radiating area (ERA) is most commonly used.

treatment time (min) = ERA X 2

Effective radiating area is determined by the size of the sound head, with larger sound heads providing greater ERA. Other formulas commonly used to determine treatment time depend on the stage of tissue healing. In cases of subacute tissue healing, the size of the treatment area (in centimeters) is divided by 1.5 times the ERA (in centimeters). In the chronic stages of tissue healing, the size of the area (in centimeters) is divided by the ERA (in centimeters). Sound head diameters vary from 1 to 10 centimeters. Treating areas greater than two times the ERA is not recommended. In these cases, greater heating benefits might be achieved using other thermal modalities.

Treatment Frequency

There are no specific guidelines on the ideal frequency or number of ultrasound treatments needed to bring about therapeutic effects in the horse. Ultrasound is applied most commonly once or twice daily, although every-other-day treatments often suffice. Many clinicians suggest limiting the total number of treatments to between 12 and 15. If this amount doesn't bring the desired results, it is time to ask whether the therapy is the appropriate therapy.

Ultrasound also should be discontinued if no positive results are seen in the first three or four treatments. If pain or exacerbation of symptoms occurs, modify the treatment immediately. Mild increase in symptoms commonly occurs after the first or second treatment. This discomfort lasts only a few hours, and the original symptoms should begin to subside the following day. Soreness does not mean discontinuing ultrasound therapy, but should be regarded as "treatment soreness" resulting from increased activity in the target tissue. Ice might give some relief.

Contact Technique

The most common way of delivering therapeutic ultrasound is the contact technique, which is effective and convenient. This method requires the sound head to touch the skin. A coupling agent is used for proper lubrication of the treatment area and decreased energy attenuation at the transducer-skin interface.

To apply ultrasound successfully using this technique, three requirements must be met. First, the contour of the body part must allow for good contact of the sound head

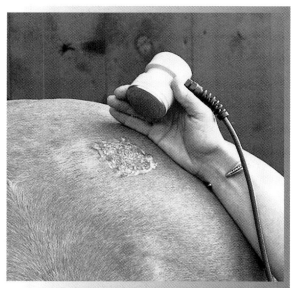

A coupling agent is used for proper lubrication.

throughout the treatment. This helps protect the ultrasound unit and ensures adequate delivery of energy to the target tissues. Secondly, the pressure of the sound head moving over the tissue must not irritate the treatment area. The sound head should be moved in overlapping circles throughout the treatment; each sweep should overlap the previous stroke by half. Move the sound head slowly and consistently; a speed of four inches per second is recommended.(25) Finally, skin in the treatment area must be intact, or blisters, skin eruptions, or infection can proliferate.

Underwater Technique

A second way of applying therapeutic ultrasound is the underwater technique, also known as the immersion procedure. This technique is recommended when the treatment area does not permit direct contact of the sound head. This can occur in areas of bony prominence or excessive curvature, or in the presence of open wounds. The coupling agent in this case is water, which is regarded as the ultimate medium for ultrasound energy transmission. Avoid air bubbles in the water and on the sound head to prevent the reflection of sound waves and reduction of transmission.

The following procedures are required for the underwater technique. The body part is submerged in clean water at about 80° F. The sound head is held half an inch to an inch from the treatment area. The intensity should be increased gradually, and the sound head should remain in motion. Hold the sound head flat against the skin surface to maximize energy penetration and absorption. Should air bubbles collect on the treatment area or the transducer, brush

them away using a piece of gauze attached to a tongue depressor. Applying alcohol to the treatment area and the sound head before therapy will reduce air bubbles.

Although all clinical decision-making about frequency, intensity, and wave-form

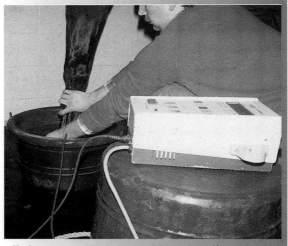

Underwater treatment combines the effects of hot soaking with ultrasound.

should remain constant with either direct contact or underwater techniques, the latter requires several precautions. The ultrasound unit must be plugged into a receptacle equipped with a ground fault interrupter. This will protect both the horse and the therapist from the risk of shock associated with the leakage of low-level currents. Also, be careful to inspect the lead connecting the transducer to the ultrasound unit for breaks. The presence of cracks, breaks, or imperfections in the insulated lead wire presents a serious risk of injury to both the therapist and patient.

Fluid-Filled Bag Technique

The fluid-filled bag technique, though rarely used, presents an alternative to underwater ultrasound application. Like underwater ultrasound, this technique is useful in the presence of irregular contours and skin sensitivity in the treatment area. This technique also helps in the treatment of more proximal extremities such as the shoulder or hip, where submersion in water is impractical. A thin-membraned bag, such as a surgical glove, can be used for this procedure. The coupling agent inside the bag can be water, mineral oil, or glycerin.(26) Using degassed water rather than tap water will eliminate air bubbles inside the bag.

Use the following procedures when applying ultrasound through a fluid-filled bag. Avoid air between the sound head and the bag by firmly pushing the sound head into the bag throughout the treatment. Remember that any air between the sound head and the bag will reduce transmission of energy. Applying the medium inside the bag to the sound head and to the treatment area further increases the transmission of ultrasound energy to the target tissues. Move the sound head "within the bag" just as you would during the direct contact application. Maintain an appropriate amount of pressure against the bag to prevent air from interfering with transmission. Keep the sound head at a 90-degree angle to the bag and avoid moving the bag on the skin. All movement should occur between the sound head and the bag. One drawback to this technique is the additional interfaces formed between the sound head and bag and the bag and the skin, which increase the likelihood that energy will be diluted.

Draper's Top 10 Ultrasound Errors

Renowned ultrasound researcher David Draper recently compiled a list of the 10 most common errors clinicians make using therapeutic ultrasound.(27) The following list illustrates the list compiled by Draper and recommendations to equine therapists to avoid these pitfalls.

Common Ultrasound Application Errors and Correction

1) Treatment area too large. Do not treat area larger than two times ERA.

2) Treatment time too brief. Five minutes treatment time for two times ERA.

3) Using preset intensities. Choose intensity based on therapeutic goals.

4) Incorrect frequency. Use 1 MHz for deeper target tissue and 3 MHz for superficial target tissue.

5) Failure to observe the stretching window. Tissues must be stretched during or within two to three minutes of completing

ultrasound therapy.

6) Use of ice before therapy. Do not pre-cool tissue before applying ultrasound.

7) Misuse of couplants. Choose a couplant with transmission greater than 80% of water for most effective results.

8) Applying only sub-sensory ultrasound. Patient may feel a slight warmth during treatment.

9) Speedy sound head. Move sound head at a rate of four inches per second.

10) Failure to understand laws governing therapeutic ultrasound usage. Become familiar with local and state regulations.

Phonophoresis

Phonophoresis is transcutaneous drug delivery supplemented by the use of ultrasound waves. At one time it was thought that ultrasound waves drove the medication through the skin and into deeper target tissues in much the same way deep heating is delivered to target tissues. Recent studies suggest that ultrasound has a chemical and thermal effect on the skin that allows the topical medication to be absorbed more readily. This can occur through dermal capillary vasodilation associated with the heating of the skin and via an increase in cell membrane permeability.

Animal studies have demonstrated the delivery of medications to tissues at a depth of 5 to 6 centimeters.(28) One study demon-strated increased absorption of topical medication with the use of ultrasound compared with topical application alone.(29) The value of phonophoresis versus ultrasound alone continues to be debated. When applying phonophoresis, the coupling agent used is extremely important. A study by Cameron and Monroe in 1992 identified ultrasound transmission of various popular phonophoresis media in comparison to water. (30)

The study concluded that the effectiveness of phonophoresis in drug delivery depended greatly on the product used for transmission. Phonophoresis can be useful to deliver medications locally in a painless and non-invasive way. Byl, however, cautions clinicians to consider the appropriateness of the medication used during phonophoresis and recommends using a coupling agent with a transmission rate of at least 80% water.(31)

To carry out phonophoresis, the drug is placed on the skin with ultrasound transmission gel over it. The goal is to enhance trans-dermal penetration of the drug while providing the therapeutic benefits of ultrasound. Not only is the selection of coupling agent important, but it is important to select a drug that transmits ultrasound well. Many topical drug preparations would not be effective.

This procedure tests the transmission quality of a desired drug:

First, form a two-inch rim above the face of the transducer by placing a strip of wide tape around it. Place a layer of the drug medium on the transducer surface and fill the remainder of the well with water. Turn on the unit to 1 W/cm2 and 100% duty cycle. If the medium transmits ultrasound at all, the water will be agitated. If the medium transmits ultrasound poorly, the water will remain still.(32)

To increase the success of phonophoresis treatments, it is recommended that the treatment area be hydrated before treatment to increase cell permeability. It also might be useful to shave the treatment area to increase tissue permeability.

Maximizing circulation to the area by using heat before ultrasound might help the medication penetrate the skin farther. Finally, a dressing that seals the treatment area and prevents moisture escape should be applied for several hours after phonophoresis treatment is completed.(33) This occlusive dressing is thought to increase the amount of drug delivered to target tissues.

Precautions

While therapeutic ultrasound often proves valuable in the treatment of musculoskeletal dysfunctions, the therapist must use caution to avoid injury to the patient. This chapter has discussed the risks of overheating

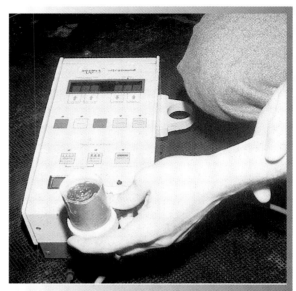

Form a two-inch rim above the face of the transducer by placing a strip of wide tape around it.

the periosteum, unstable cavitation, and superficial tissue burns. The clinical decision-making regarding ultrasound frequency, intensity, wave-form, pulse rate, coupling medium, treatment time, and treatment area all contribute to the safe and effective application of therapeutic ultrasound.

The following is a list of precautions to protect the clinician and the patient;

• Maintain a moving sound head when applying ultrasound treatments. This allows uniform heating of all tissues in the treatment area and greatly decreases the risk of tissue burns caused by "hot spots."

• Maintain a constant pressure on the sound head during the treatment. Avoid breaking contact with the skin while the ultrasound unit is on. Decreasing the interface between air and the sound head reduces the amount of energy attenuation and protects the transducer's crystal from becoming overheated.

• Replace the crystal before using the ultrasound unit to administer future treatments if a humming sound is heard. This could indicate a cracked crystal.

• Using ultrasound on the following conditions — unhealed fractures, surgically repaired tendons and ligaments, metal implants, and areas of decreased sensation — requires caution.

• The use of ultrasound over unhealed fractures can be painful and might cause alterations in tissue healing. In cases of fracture, the ultrasound energy often will increase the horse's resting pain level.

• The use of ultrasound over newly repaired ligament and tendon requires close communication with the veterinarian to avoid disruption of tissue healing.

• Metal implants will reflect the ultrasound energy, causing overheating of more superficial tissues.

• Finally, ultrasound can be administered over areas of decreased sensation but only with extreme caution with regard to intensity and coupling techniques to prevent tissue burns.

Contraindications

Avoid the use of ultrasound on or around the eyes; in the presence of cardiac pacemakers; over reproductive organs; over the spinal cord; and over the pregnant abdomen, pelvis, or lumbar spine. Ultrasound also should be avoided in the presence of malignant tumors, thrombophlebitis, cardiac disease, and infection. The effects of ultrasound might cause exacerbation of all these conditions. Lastly, the use of ultrasound over the epiphysis (growth regions) of long bones is contraindicated. Ultrasound has been shown to cause bone growth disturbances in experimental situations.(34)

Conclusion

Ultrasound's high-frequency acoustical energy can be used to deliver deep heating to target tissues at depths of 5 centimeters. The physiologic effects of ultrasound include both thermal and mechanical phenomena. These effects include decreasing pain, increasing collagen tissue extensibility, decreasing muscle spasm, and facilitating tissue healing. Ultrasound, when used in conjunction with therapeutic exercise, is a valuable therapeutic modality. To use ultrasound effectively and safely, the therapist must be aware of the physiological effects, application techniques, precautions, contraindications, and clinical decision-making associated with the modality. The Arndt-Schultz principle applies to therapeutic ultrasound application; that is, too small an amount of energy produces no useful effect, too much energy destroys tissue, but the appropriate amount of energy provides the desired therapeutic effect.

(James R. Scifers, MPT, ATC, contributed to this chapter.)

Definitions

Acoustical streaming — Unidirectional flow of tissue components in an ultrasound field.

Adhesions — Abnormal adherence of collagen fibers to surrounding structures. Restricts normal elasticity of structures.

Beam non-uniformity ratio (BNR) — Value indicating the uniformity of the ultrasound beam.

Bursitis — Inflammation of a bursa due to trauma or chronic irritation. Can lead to thickening of bursa wall, degeneration of epithelial lining, adhesions, and calcific deposits.

Cavitation — the vibrational effect on gas bubbles by an ultrasound beam, may be stable or unstable.

Compression — The process of increasing density and weight.

Duty cycle — the percentage of time that ultrasound energy is being transmitted, "on time."

Effective radiating area (ERA) — The area of the faceplate of the ultrasound head described in centimeters.

Frequency — A measurement used to calculate and predict the depth of penetration of ultrasound waves, measured in megahertz (MHz).

Hot spots — The summation of ultrasound energy in one area, causing increased risk of tissue damage.

Micromassage — Oscillation of tissues and cells in pulsed ultrasound fields.

Periosteum — The outermost layer of bone.

Piezoelectric crystal — A transducer that converts electrical energy into sound energy.

Phonophoresis — Transcutaneous drug delivery supplemented by the use of ultrasound.

Range of motion — Normal amount of movement between two bony levers.

Rarefaction — the process of decreasing density and weight.

Reflection — The rebounding of radiant energy from a surface not penetrated.

Refraction — Deflection from a straight path as a ray passes from one medium to another.

Spatial average intensity — The average intensity of ultrasound as measured by dividing total power by ERA.

Spatial peak intensity — The greatest intensity found anywhere within an ultrasound beam.

Transducer — A device used to convert

energy from one form to another.

Temporal average intensity — The intensity of pulsed ultrasound calculated by averaging the intensity during both "on" and "off" times.

Temporal peak intensity — The maximal intensity of the pulsed ultrasound wave during the "on" phase.

References

1. Steward, HF. et al. 1980. Considerations in ultrasound therapy and equipment performance. *Phys. Ther.* 60:425.

2. *Sound Advice: Thermal Ultrasound.* 1995. Topeka, KS.:PTI, Inc.

3. Ibid.

4. Draper, DO. and Ricard, MD. 1995. Rate of temperature decay in human muscle following 3-MHz ultrasound: The stretching window revealed. *J Athl Train.* 30:304-7.

5. Rose S. et al. 1996. The stretching window part two: Rate of thermal decay in deep muscle following 1-MHz ultrasound. *J Athl Train.* 31:139-43.

6. Kisner, C. and Colby, LA. 1996. Therapeutic Exercise: Foundations and Techniques. 3rd ed. Philadelphia: FA Davis Company.

7. Adams, OR. 1987. *Lameness in Horses.* 3rd ed. Philadelphia: Lea and Febiger.

8. Griffin, J and Karselis, T. 1982. *Physical Agents for Physical Therapists.* Springfield, IL.: Charles C. Thomas.

9. Bierman, W. 1954. Ultrasound in the treatment of scars. *Arch. Phys. Med. Rehabil.* 38:209-13.

10. Szumski, AJ. 1960. Mechanisms of pain relief as a result of therapeutic application of ultrasound. *Phys Ther Rev.* 40:117.

11. Michlovitz, SL. 1996. *Thermal Agents in Rehabilitation.* 3rd ed. Philadelphia: FA Davis.

12. Middlemast, S. and Chatterjee, DC. 1978. Comparison of ultrasound and thermotherapy for soft tissue injuries. *Physiotherapy.* 64:331-32.

13. Turner, T. et al. 1991. Effects of heat, cold, biomagnets and ultrasound on skin circulation in the horse. Proceedings American Assocation of Equine Practitioners. San Francisco, CA. 249-57.

14. Falconer, J. et al. 1990. Therapeutic ultrasound in the treatment of musculoskeletal conditions. *Arthritis Care Res.* 3:85.

15. Reid, PC. et al. 1972. *Training: Scientific Basis and Application.* Springfield, IL: Charles C. Thomas.

16. Herra-Lasso, I. et al. 1993. Comparative effectiveness of packages of treatment including ultrasound or transcutaneous electrical nerve stimulation in painful shoulder syndrome. *Physiotherapy.* 79:251-53.

17. Morcos, MB. and Aswad, A. 1978. Histological studies of the effects of ultrasonic therapy on surgically split flexor tendons. *Equine Vet J.* 10:267-8.

18. Enwemeka, CS. 1989. The effects of therapeutic ultrasound on tendon healing: A biomechanical study. *Am J Phys Med Rehabil.* 68:283-7.

19. Enwemeka, CS. et al. 1990. The biomechanical effects of low-intensity ultrasound on healing tendons. *Ultrasound Med Biol.* 16:801-7.

20. Jackson, BA. et al. 1991. Effect of ultrasound therapy on the repair of Achilles tendon injuries in rats. *Med Sci Sports Exerc.* 23:171-6.

21. Byl, N. et al. 1993. Incisional wound healing: a controlled study of low and high dose ultrasound. *JOSPT.* 18:619.

22. Roberts, M. et al. 1982. The effects of ultrasound on flexor tendon repairs in the rabbit. *Hand.* 14:17.

23. Behrens, BJ. and Michlovitz, SL. 1996. *Physical Agents: Theory and Practice for the Physical Therapist Assistant.* Philadelphia: FA Davis Company:

24. Docker, MF. et al. 1982. Ultrasound couplants for physiotherapy. *Physiotherapy.* 68:124.

25. Hayes, KW. 1993. *Manual for Physical Agents.* 4th ed. Norwalk, CT: Appleton & Lange.

26. Hecox, B. et al. 1994. *Physical Agents: A Comprehensive Text for Physical Therapists.* Norwalk, CT: Appleton & Lange.

27. Draper, DO. 1996. Ten mistakes commonly made with ultrasound use: Current research sheds light on myths. Athletic Training: *Sports Health Care Perspectives.* 2:95107.

28. Griffin, JE. et al. 1965. Ultrasonic movement of cortisol into pig tissues. II. Peripheral nerve. *Am J Phys Med.* 44:20.

29. Novak, EJ. 1964. Experimental transmission of lidocaine through intact skin by ultrasound. *Arch Phys Med Rehabil.* 45:231.

30. Cameron, MH. and Monroe, LG. 1992. Relative transmission of ultrasound by media customarily used for phonophoresis. *Phys Ther.* 72:145.

31. Ibid.

32. Byl, N. 1995. The use of ultrasound as an enhancer for transcutaneous drug delivery: Phonophoresis. *Phys Ther.* 75:539-53.

33. Ibid.

34. DeForest, RE. 1953. Effects of ultrasound on growing bone: experimental study. *Arch Phys Med Rehabil.* 34:21.

Recommended Readings

Behrens, BJ. and Michlovitz, SL. 1996. *Physical Agents: Theory and Practice for the Physical Therapist Assistant.* Philadelphia: FA Davis Company.

Downer, AH. 1978. *Physical Therapy for Animals.* Springfield, IL.: Charles C Thomas Company.

Hayes, KW. 1993. *Manual for Physical Agents,* ed. 4. Norwalk, CT.: Appleton & Lange.

Hecox, B., Mehreteab, TA., and Weisberg, J. 1994. *Physical Agents: A Comprehensive Text for Physical Therapists.* Norwalk, CT.:Appleton & Lange.

Levenson JL. 1983. Weissberg MP: Ultrasound abuse: case report. *Arch Phys Med Rehabil.* 64:90-91.

Michlovitz, SL. 1996. *Thermal Agents in Rehabilitation,* ed. 3. Philadelphia: FA Davis

Company.Prentice, WE. 1990. *Therapeutic Modalities in Sports Medicine,* ed. 2. St. Louis, MO.: Times Mirror/Mosby College Publishing.

Starkey, C. 1993. *Therapeutic Modalities for Athletic Training.* Philadelphia: FA Davis Company.

Photon Therapy —
Therapeutic Laser

It isn't the instrument, but the music that matters...
Leonard Bernstein

HUMANS have always recognized that light has natural healing powers. In scientific terms, light refers to a broad band of wavelengths of radiation. Color, on the other hand, refers to a very narrow band of radiation that our eyes can detect. We intellectualize the different wavelengths as soothing or energizing, pleasant or unappealing. Color affects how we feel mentally and physically.

The visible light spectrum, our rainbow of red, orange, yellow, green, blue, indigo, and violet, are different wavelengths of energy. Red, yellow, and orange are wavelengths that stimulate, while blues and greens are sedating or soothing. With the discovery of single wavelength light devices, such as the ultraviolet light for dermatology and now lasers, a new frontier of light therapy became possible.

Surgical lasers and therapeu-

tic photon emitters are not the first therapeutic tools to make use of light. In the early

Drawing of Sir Isaac Newton separating the solar spectrum into its visible components.

20th Century, artificial ultraviolet radiation devices were developed to treat skin diseases. Ultraviolet light is still used to treat psoriasis. At wavelengths of 150 to 390 nanometers, ultraviolet (found beyond the violet end of the spectrum) light waves are too short for the human eye to perceive. Their existence was discovered in 1801 by Johann Ritter, who noted the chemical changes that this light wavelength could create.

The previous year, Sir William Hershell found radiation with wavelengths that were too long to be visible, yet caused an elevation in temperature registered by a thermometer. These heat-producing waves were called infrared because they were beyond the end of the red spectrum. Light-emitting therapy systems produce energy in the infrared or near infrared portion of the light spectrum. Depending upon the wavelength produced, the light either will be invisible to the human eye or a brilliant red. Wavelengths that produce a blue or green light also are being studied for therapeutic effects.

Light-emitting therapeutic devices often are called lasers. The term laser, an acronym for Light Amplification by Stimulated Emission of Radiation, is applied generally to many light-emitting devices used in medicine, industry, and everyday life. It indicates that the emitted light's power is greatly increased, or amplified, by emissions from substances contained in the apparatus. The concept of stimulated emissions was developed by Albert Einstein in 1917. His theory suggests that when the molecular arrangement of an atom is altered, light of a particular frequency will be given off. This physical phenomenon can be provoked by the arrival of another particle of light, or photon, vibrating at the same frequency. This phenomenon continues to repeat, and the stimulated emission of radiation occurs.(1)

As a therapist, I am fascinated by what happens when this specialized light encounters living cells. When a photon is absorbed by a biological molecule, the electrons in that molecule are raised to a higher energy state. This excited molecule then must lose its extra energy. This energy can be used to initiate chemical changes in the way the molecule operates or interacts with neighboring molecules. Photobiological responses are the result of chemical changes produced when a cell absorbs electromagnetic radiation.(2)

Light, magnetic fields, and electricity are forms of electromagnetic energy that can be absorbed by cells and used as energy for cellular function, called biostimulation. The tools that will be discussed in this chapter are photon energy delivery devices. They are popularly called lasers, although many are not lasers in the strict definition of the term. Words become embedded like fossils in our everyday language, and although a word can be used incorrectly, it is used continuously, out of habit.

Because helium-neon (HeNe) lasers were used in early research and are the best documented of all the therapeutic lasers, we see names such as low-level laser, infrared laser, cold laser, and low-power laser attached to all light-therapy devices. There is no consensus on the proper name for these tools.

HeNe lasers produce a brilliant, visible red light. They are not commonly used in equine therapy because they require a gaseous medium and a sensitive glass tube for light production. They are large and expensive. One such laser was recently priced for the veterinary market at $22,000. The more popular tools available today do not require this type of light-emitting mechanism, but use semiconductor diodes. These light-emitting diodes are less expensive and tiny by comparison. Some manufacturers of photon energy devices call their light-emitting diode a laser diode; some call them superluminous diodes. The energy packet, the entity of change in the tissues, is the photon. The appropriate name for this therapy is photon therapy because it is the interaction between the photon and the cell components that initiates biological changes. In this text photon therapy will be used to describe all therapeutic use of light.

True laser light is different from all other light in the following ways: It is always mono-chromatic, or light of one wavelength; and it is always coherent and tightly collimated. I came to this understanding after many conversations with Dale Bertwell, developer of Equi-Light Photon Therapy Systems. Bertwell has pioneered our understanding of photon therapy through research support and tenacious scrutiny of the modality. He realized that the energy produced, rather than the device, creates the biological effect.

Before we plunge into this challenging arena of information, pause for a moment to ponder the notion of an external energy source — light — affecting cellular processes beneath the skin surface. What organisms in the cells below the skin are affected by light? The idea that there are molecules receptive to light, below the protective covering of our skin or the horse's hair coat, is intriguing. As it turns out, our bodies give off infrared radiation, and radiation of other wavelengths, in the visible light portion of the electromagnetic spectrum. We give off light, we absorb light, and biological processes are stimulated when we do.

Light-absorbing molecules are found in enzymes and proteins in the tissues and blood. Proteins are complex organic compounds made of amino acids. They are essential to the cell's structure and ability to function. Enzymes are catalysts, meaning that when an enzyme is activated, it in turn activates many more reactions, causing a "cascade" or chain reaction of biological events. This is a relatively large series of events compared with the rather small amount of light energy that triggered them.

Photon therapy is an ideal tool to use in the acute situation because photo-biostimulation does not increase tissue temperature. There is no danger of aggravating the inflammatory phase or increasing intertissue bleeding. More impressive are the effects on non-responsive wounds or slow-to-heal injuries. When an injury has failed to respond to medical treatment, photon therapy can stimulate natural body processes, activating waste removal and increasing repair activity. The beneficial effects of this process include pain relief and blood and lymphatic stimulation.

Light is Energy

Light is energy in the form of radiation that is characterized by its wavelength. A wavelength is the distance between one peak of electromagnetic energy and the next. They are expressed in nanometers (nm), one-billionth of a meter. Our eyes perceive light between 393 nm and 759 nm.

Light forms a small part of the continuous spectrum we call the electromagnetic spectrum. Other wavelengths in this spectrum include radio and TV waves, X-rays, gamma rays, and cosmic rays.

Photon therapy uses wavelengths found just outside the visible red portion of the light spectrum, in the infrared region. Infrared wavelengths are longer than visible red waves and shorter than microwaves. They are considered therapeutic because they are absorbed by protein molecules in tissue and blood cells, stimulating cell activity that has been disturbed by injury. It is the photon, the energy particle of the light wave, that is the catalyst for increased cell activity.

There are perhaps thousands of types of lasers and light-emitting devices in medicine, in industry, and in our everyday lives. The lasing, or the light-emitting medium, determines the light's wavelength. The wavelength determines the effect of the device. In surgery, where lasers have virtually replaced the scalpel, or industry, where

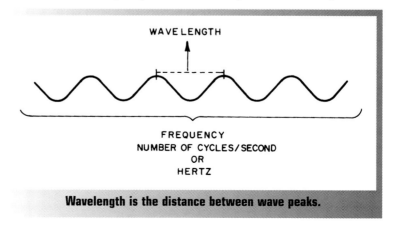

Wavelength is the distance between wave peaks.

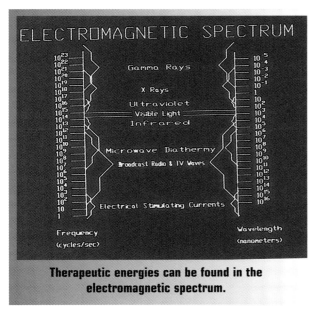

Therapeutic energies can be found in the electromagnetic spectrum.

radiation with a target site." Photon therapy devices have an output power lower than 100 milliwatts (mW) and power densities of less than 50 $mW/cm2(3)$

Characteristics of Therapeutic Light Monochromaticity

Lasers and photon therapy devices produce light that is monochromatic, or of one specific wavelength or "color." Ordinary light is made up of many different wavelengths, which register individually on our brain as a certain color and collectively as white. The spot of light from a flashlight, which gives off many wavelengths, is white. The HeNe laser produces a pure, brilliant, red light, as no other colors, or wavelengths, are included.

Manufacturers can use filters or colored lenses to make a multi-wavelength light source more monochromatic. A filter simply blocks out some wavelengths, so the loss of light energy with this technique of "lasing" is considerable. Diode devices emit light in a small range of wavelengths and are not as tightly monochromatic as true lasers. This actually could prove to be a valuable feature as different cells require different wavelengths for absorption. A small range of wavelengths, rather than a single wavelength, could make these tools more versatile.

The light's wavelength determines its

lasers are used to carry information, make measurements, and perform various other functions, different lasers produce different effects. Carbon dioxide produces the CO_2 laser emissions used for cutting in surgery. The argon laser is used for blood vessel coagulation. Surgical lasers evaporate tissue in what is called "bloodless surgery" because tissue is cut and coagulated in a single stroke of the extremely high energy beam of light.

By contrast, therapeutic photon energy does not raise tissue temperature above 36.5° C, or normal human body temperature. The effects are due to light-tissue interaction, or photo-chemical changes, and not to heating. In 1994, the American Society for Laser Medicine and Surgery announced a definition for photon therapy, saying it was the "nonthermal interaction of monochromatic suitability for absorption by the molecule. Atoms making up the biological tissues of skin, blood, nerve, etc., have a specific absorption spectra, or range of wavelengths, that they will absorb. This wavelength specificity determines whether photon therapy can have an effect on a given tissue.

Collimation

Collimation refers to the extreme parallelism of laser radiation, which is emitted in a well focused beam. All of the photons are traveling in exactly the same direction. By contrast, the sun's radiation or light from a light bulb is emitted in all directions. Although photon therapy devices produce only a small fraction of a light bulb's output, this output is "bundled" into a tight, parallel beam, increasing the amount of energy.(4) This allows true lasers to be held at a dis-

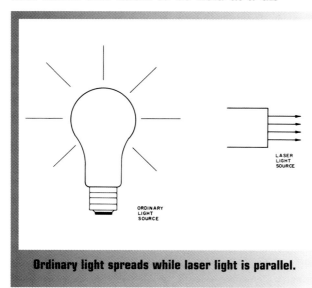

Ordinary light spreads while laser light is parallel.

tance from the skin without losing significant energy in the spot of light. Diode devices produce a beam with some divergence and must be held in contact with the skin surface to avoid losing energy from beam spread.

A non-divergent beam produces an extremely small focal spot, resulting in very dense local radiation. Diode devices produce a somewhat divergent beam with fewer photons per unit area. Imagine a flashlight pointed toward and held very close to the wall. The spot of light is bright and forms a well-defined circle. Move the flashlight away from the wall and observe how the brightness fades and the spot grows in size. The lack of collimation in a flashlight beam allows the light to spread, decreasing photon density where the light contacts the wall.

Ideally, photon therapy is applied with the treatment head in contact with the skin to reduce scatter as much as possible. When the injury to be treated is an open wound, placing a sheet of thin, clear plastic (such as a baggie or plastic food wrap) over it can block contamination but allow entry of the photons.

Coherence

In a coherent light beam, all the photons in the light waves travel in a recurring sequence (in phase). The peaks and valleys of the waves line up and travel that way over a long distance. Wavelengths and wave frequencies vary in ordinary light, resulting in much canceling out of energy production as waves bounce into other waves, scattering the photon energy. When the photons travel with a high degree of order and in a fixed phase relationship, energy in each wave is reinforced and the power of the radiation amplified. This characteristic can be found only in what are called "true lasers." The HeNe laser was the first commercially available source for coherent light.

Photon therapy devices used on horses contain diodes that produce non-coherent light. The clinical significance of coherence is being debated in the scientific literature on therapeutic laser application. According to researchers, coherence is lost as the beam passes through the first millimeter of tissue.(5) When therapeutic lasers are used, the coherency factor of tissue itself is higher than the coherency factor of the light wave, resulting in scattering of the photons and a disruption of this feature. If coherence is lost by the time the beam has passed through the first 1 mm of tissue, this property has no therapeutic significance.(6) Because light reaching the target tissue is no longer coherent, even when true lasers are used, most researchers agree that photo-biostimulation does not depend on coherence. Depth of energy penetration and absorption are determined by the strength of the light energy source (its power) and the light's wavelength.

The Gas Laser

Gas serves as the medium in most medical and HeNe lasers. This gas is contained in the laser tube, which has a fully reflective mirror at one end and a partially reflective mirror at the other. Electricity excites the lasing medium. An excited gas molecule will release a photon, a quantum of radiant energy, creating the stimulated emission. The fully reflective mirror reflects the released photons back into the lasing medium, creating a buildup of photons inside the tube. When sufficient energy is built up, the light is emitted through the partially reflective mirror.(7)

Light from this type of laser often is called true laser light because it is coherent. It is an intense beam of pure, essentially monochromatic light, which does not diverge. The beam is a highly concentrated source of radiant energy.

The Semiconductor Diode

In the semiconductor diode, a solid, semiconducting material is used to convert electrical energy into light, a process called electro-luminescence. The material is called semiconducting because electricity can flow

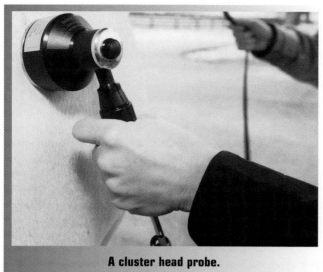

A cluster head probe.

easily in one direction, but meets total resistance in the other. Electrical current flowing across a junction between a positive (p-type) and a negative (n-type) material, the p-n junction, produces extra electrons in this band of semiconducting material. Alloy compositions, such as gallium aluminum arsenide (GaAlAs) or silicone and germanium, give sufficient p-n junction energy to emit light energy as the by-product of resistance. This total composition is called a light-emitting diode, or LED. An infrared emitter based on GaAs has a higher emitting efficiency than an LED in the visible wave band. Infrared emitters can be from 10% to 40% efficient light emitters, with the rest of the energy given off as heat. Visible light LEDs are found in laser pointers, price scanners at supermarkets, and stereo components.

The first diodes used for photon therapy were introduced in the early 1980s. Semiconducting light-emitting diodes have gone through a growth spurt in terms of power output and have increased in brilliance over the past 15 years. The term superluminous is now used for diodes that produce a high level of energy for the amount of current flowing through them. These diodes produce light that is monochromatic, but not coherent.

Gallium arsenide crystals, a man-made substance, emit light when stimulated by an electrical current. GaAs lasers produce wavelengths of 904 nm. There is no color associated with this wavelength because it is too long for our eyes to detect. GaAs systems often were found in early models of therapeutic lasers, but are not widely used today because of advances in technology. Gallium aluminum arsenide (GaAlAs) lasers recently have appeared on the market with wavelengths ranging from the visible red to the near infrared, depending on how much aluminum is used in the diode.(8)

Pulsed and Continuous Output devices and User Controlled Frequencies

Photon therapy can be applied in the continuous or pulsed modes. In the continuous mode, radiation is constant while the unit is turned on. Some diodes produce too much heat when run continuously and therefore must be used in the pulsed mode. In the pulsed mode, output is interrupted, switching on with a very brief burst of radiation and switching off just as briefly, in a cyclic pattern. Each pulse duration can range from several nanoseconds to several milliseconds, depending on the pulse width or duration set by the manufacturer. A pulse of about 200 nanoseconds often is used in photon therapy tools.

Research has shown that tissues can be pulse-rate specific. Pulsing the output from any equine therapy modality, whether it is photon therapy, electricity, ultrasound, or magnetic fields, appears to make the energy more acceptable to the cells. Is it the resonance of the cycling that appeals to the cell molecules? Or, is it the inter-pulse interval giving the molecules the chance to absorb the energy that makes the pulsed mode effective? In all the rhythms of life there are bursts of energy alternating with empty spaces, the spaces being as important as the energy. Music is a series of notes and quiet spaces. I have read that laughter is a pattern of staccato bursts of sounds at a 3:1 ratio of sound and rest. Physical exercise has the greatest benefits when interspersed with periods of rest.

Useful therapeutic tools reflect the natural rhythms of life and use life's natural energies. Only recently has science moved from studying the macro effects of therapeutics, such as vasodilation and temperature change, to the micro effects of activity inside the cell. Although molecular biology is a new field, Hippocrates, a physician who lived in 400 BC, said, "Honor the healing power of nature." This statement reflects an innate understanding of effects beyond our ability to see with the eye.

Some units have user-controlled frequency parameters. The frequencies are controlled by the amount of electricity flowing across the diode. These duty cycles produce a range of pulsing frequencies. The lower pulse rates effectively reduce the total energy output. The theory is that certain tissues will absorb specific frequencies. Dr. Marvin Cain, a renowned veterinary acupuncturist, thinks these specific frequencies will prove to be appropriate to specific tissue types. Although this is not scientifically proven, it is best to follow manufacturers' guidelines on frequency settings.

Calculating the Treatment Dose

The therapist must be able to calculate the time necessary to deliver a consistent treatment dose. Information needed to make this decision includes:

- average power output of the unit in watts.
- size of the spot of light in cm2.
- energy density in W/cm2.
- size of the area to be treated in cm2.

Begin by calculating the unit's power or energy density with the following formula:

power density (W/cm2) = average power (W)/spot size (cm2).

If using a cluster head, calculate the unit's total power density by multiplying the power density by the number of diodes.

Recommended energy dosages found in the literature are given in joules/cm2. Watts and joules are related by time. You can compute the time necessary to deliver the dose with this formula:

Time (seconds) = joules /total power density.

The recommended energy delivery for therapy ranges from one to four joules for effective treatment. More research is needed to establish actual energy requirements for photon therapy. Some manufacturers provide treatment recommendations based on experience. Until scientific results are established, follow the manufacturers' recommended treatment times.

Many units give only the peak power, so the user must calculate the average power to begin to use the formulas above. Peak power is the amount of energy per burst and does not take into account the off time. When the inter-pulse interval is factored in, the amount of actual power is much lower.

For example, supposed a unit is advertised as having a peak power of 30 W. This could sound like a lot of output power. But if

Elephant being treated with photon therapy.

the pulse width, or time the photons flow, is 0.000000115 seconds, (115 nanoseconds), and the frequency is 73 Hz, the average power is only .25 mW. (9)

When only peak power is given, one can compute the average power with the following formula:

**average power (W) = peak power (W) X
pulse width (seconds) X frequency (Hz).**

Pulse width is the actual time the burst of photon energy is on. The frequency is the number of bursts per second. Although the peak power is often the only pulse characteristic given by the manufacturer, it is not the only piece of information needed to understand the unit's treatment capabilities. Power density, sometimes called energy density, is more important than peak power in arriving at the appropriate amount of time needed to deliver a therapeutic dosage.

A question often asked about photon therapy is, "Does the energy penetrate sufficiently to reach the target tissues?" If the incident dose is sufficient and the wavelength appropriate, it does reach the target tissues. The case of the arthritic elephant lends credence to this statement. Ginny, a 57-year-old elephant at the Denver Zoo, had experienced chronic arthritis in her left carpal joint since 1984. Her right carpus started to become stiff in 1989. By 1995, both carpal joints had worsened progressively and she was using her trunk as a cane. She began to shift much of her weight to her rear legs, where some instability was evident. Oral and injectable anti-inflammatory drugs offered little help. After

using the Equi-Light, a photon therapy device available for use on horses, Ginny had significantly greater range of motion in her ankle and once again could bear full weight comfortably. Using this therapy for 40 minutes a day proved successful where an array of balms and painkillers had failed. Because of the success of photon therapy the elephant was taken off all pain medication. Her mood brightened—no small consideration for zoo keepers. Subsequently, several other zoo animals were treated with photon therapy.

Delivering the Photon Dose

Once the dosage has been calculated, there are a few other points to remember to optimize treatment. Several factors can

Single diode held perpendicularly and next to the skin.

affect the amount of light that enters the tissue. To optimize photon penetration, the operator must keep the treatment head in contact with the tissue, and the light beam must strike the tissue perpendicularly. Photon energy can be scattered and reflected to a greater extent when the emitting surface is not held in contact with the skin surface or is held at an angle. When using a single diode probe, place the diode next to the skin, rather than on the hair. Hair is made of protein, which will absorb and scatter the photon energy to some extent. As the treatment head moves farther from the treatment tissue, scatter, reflection, absorption, and beam spread reduce the density of light energy. According to the Inverse Square law, the beam intensity is reduced by the square of the distance from the treatment tissue.

The effects of photon energy are cumulative, with repeated doses having more impact than a single, extended application. Depth of penetration is not determined by the length of treatment time. To illustrate this important point, let's go back to our flashlight analogy. If you direct the light beam to the wall you can continue to aim at the wall for hours or days, (although you surely have something better to do), and the photons will not penetrate the paint or plaster or reach the insulation beneath the plaster board. The characteristics of the light beam and the power output of the flashlight do not provide sufficient energy to drive the photons past the surface.(10) Depth of penetration is not determined by time, but by wavelength and power.

As the beam of light energy travels through space or tissue, it can be reflected, scattered, refracted, or absorbed by molecules it encounters. Visible light on the skin surface is merely reflected light that is not penetrating. To have therapeutic value it must penetrate to the target tissue and be absorbed there. The term penetration refers to passing through something and suggests a driving force. The driving force in photon therapy is the unit's power output. Output power must be sufficient to push the photons past the barrier of the skin.

Absorption is the process of taking up and holding. For photon therapy to have therapeutic effects, it must be absorbed by the target tissue. Tissues that absorb photons take on their energy. The near infrared wavelengths, from 700 nm to 1600 nm, are primarily absorbed in protein. Protein molecules are found throughout the tissues, providing a widespread absorption pattern.(11)

Biological Effects

This versatile therapy can be used for both acute and chronic injuries and for a variety of problems. Photon therapy can address pain, blood circulatory and lymph system stagnation, and surface and deep wounds. When treating an injury, we look at it from a "macro level" perspective. But before the injury's visible manifestation, a "cascade" of events preceded it. This cascade occurs on the molecular level, making it all the more fascinating and challenging to understand.

The "Biological Field Theory" provides the theoretical basis for the effects of photon therapy. This theory purports that a biological energy field exists around every cell, and certain resonant frequencies exist in the field. Energy levels in larger structures, such as the organ and the organism, exert influence on cells' energy levels. Photon resonance can restore the normal energetic status of the cells when they are out of phase with the organ's frequency.(12)

The first law of photobiology states that radiant energy must be absorbed to cause an effect. For an atom to absorb light, the energy carried by each of the photons must equal exactly the energy required by one of the atom's electrons to move it to a higher energy state. A photon's energy is dictated by its wavelength. Molecules are said to be wavelength specific because they will absorb energy that matches exactly the energy needed by the electrons they contain. When the cell molecule absorbs photon energy, its own energy level is increased. This can change chemical bonding or excite chemical activity in the cell structure. Researchers have found that the wavelength specificity of absorption is one of the single most important concepts in photobiostimulation and that it represents the reason results obtained with a unit operating at one wavelength cannot necessarily be expected when another wavelength is used.(13)

Photons are absorbed by the mitochondria in the cell. The mitochondria are molecules that contain many enzymes important in metabolism. They produce most of the energy required by the cell through production of adenosine triphosphate, or ATP. The removal of phosphate releases large amounts of energy used for biological reactions. The mitochondria are stimulated to produce enzymes or neurotransmitters such as serotonin and endorphins. As one cell responds to the arrival of photon energy, a "cascade" effect takes place, which causes other cells to respond until even those cells outside the area of stimulation have increased their function.

Skin cells will absorb light of shorter wavelengths, in the 632 nm range. Infrared waves are longer, around 810 nm, and will penetrate to deeper tissues. Acupuncture point stimulation has been done with longer wavelengths. As we learn more about the nature of these points, we might learn the exact wavelength for optimal stimulation.

We are standing at the threshold of a new frontier, a frontier so tiny it cannot be seen with an ordinary microscope.

Photon therapy is used primarily for its analgesic effects and to stimulate wound healing. Other uses include scar tissue reduction and bone healing. The mechanism of influence on nerve conduction and cell metabolism is becoming clearer as research explores the effect of photon energy.

As with all equine therapy tools, the treatment's success depends on the correct diagnosis. Always have a complete veterinary evaluation before beginning any photon energy treatment.

Pain Relief

Both acute and chronic pain respond to photon therapy. When acute pain results from sports trauma, inflammation produces pain signals that travel in the brain via neurotransmitters. Nerves that carry pain messages quickly send the message to the cerebral cortex, where pain is felt. Pain serves as the body's request for a rest and chance to repair. But an athlete involved in competition or training might not have the opportunity or desire to quit entirely. A combination of equine therapy and judicious rest can control minor acute pain. This cannot be said, however, without

emphasizing that pain signifies injury. An acute injury becomes a chronic one if the body is not given sufficient time to repair. Fortunately, equine therapy can shorten this time period, allowing the injured part to return more rapidly to full function.

Conventional treatment of chronic conditions often requires larger and larger doses of pain-relieving medications. The dosage of photon therapy and other forms of equine therapy, however, tends to decrease as the treatment continues. Treatment frequency decreases as well over the course of therapy. I often begin a therapy regimen with daily treatments, reducing to every other day, then to once or twice a week as the injury improves.

Photon therapy suppresses conduction in sensory nerves, thereby reducing pain.

Photon therapy decreases nerve conduction speed, reducing the number of pain message impulses that travel to the brain's recognition centers. Interfering with sensory nerve transmission can affect pain perception. Studies using various cooling and heating techniques have shown that prolonged cooling of a nerve will slow impulse transmission. Warming the tissues around a nerve will cause an increase in nerve transmission velocity.

Two contrasting reports investigated the effects of photon therapy on nerve conduction velocity. One human study used infrared radiation at doses of 20 seconds and 120 seconds per cm2 over the radial nerve. The results showed no effect on the nerve's conduction rate or on the temperature beneath the area.(14) Another report discussed the use of a HeNe laser over the radial nerve at a dose duration of 20 seconds per cm2. The results indicate that sensory nerve conduction is significantly slower following HeNe radiation, resulting in the same effects as cooling the nerve.(15)

Photon therapy was compared with an ice pack application. The authors found a 14% decrease in nerve conduction rate with photon therapy compared with a 24% decrease following 20 minutes of ice pack application directly over the nerve.(16) Although perhaps not as effective as ice in slowing nerve conduction velocity, altering the speed of nerve message transmission is thought to be one way photon therapy relieves pain.

A study using rabbits found photon therapy suppressed conduction in unmyelinated A delta afferent sensory nerves (nerves that rapidly transmit pain). This study provides evidence to indicate that therapeutic levels of photon energy suppress impulse conduction within a peripheral nerve.(17)

To make the most effective use of photon therapy for pain relief, specific acupuncture points, trigger points, and nerves are treatment targets. This requires accuracy on the therapist's part and knowledge of the location of these structures. If photon therapy is not applied accurately, it won't relieve the pain.

Acupuncture and Trigger Points

This book will not describe in detail acupuncture technique or the location of acupuncture points. This has been done authoritatively in Veterinary Acupuncture and in other texts on the subject.(18) The brief description here and the reference list at the end of this chapter should stimulate a captivating journey of investigation.

Veterinary acupuncture is an ancient practice in China, dating from 3,000- 2,000 BC. The first mention of acupuncture in an American medical text was in 1895. Awareness of this technique did not reach this country until the 1970s. Physical therapists in America have identified and made use of trigger points since the 1940s.

Determining the differences and similarities between trigger points and acupuncture points has been a subject of debate. These specialized areas of tissue are similar in many respects. Although the locations of acupuncture and trigger points are not in exactly the same place in all individuals, they occur in areas or zones that are the same in all patients. Looking at acupuncture and trigger points charts will give an idea of their location.

An active acupuncture point or trigger point will twitch when stimulated. Stimulation irritates the nerve arrangement beneath the skin. Often it is the nervous system structures of the muscle, the motor point, the muscle spindles, the Golgi tendon organ, and the free nerve endings. The skin over these points has lower electrical resistance, making it easy to locate with a point finder.

Both trigger and acupuncture points can be found in muscle, fascia, skin, and ligaments. They are thought to "arise" as a result of strain, sprain, decreased circulation, increased metabolism, or some change in organ function. Stimulating these sites will relieve pain and elevate the endorphin level in the blood. Because these points produce a continuous low level of noxious input into the central nervous system, inactivating them eliminates a source of pain. Finding these points and subjecting them to stimulation is central to equine therapy for pain. Photon therapy dosage for these points is one to eight joules per point. This broad range reflects the lack of consensus on dosage information in the scientific literature.

A study on the effects of photon therapy was recently and enthusiastically reported. Three different devices were applied to trigger points in 243 human patients: an HeNe 632.8 nm laser, an 820-830 nm continuous emission device, and a 904 pulsed emission device. The author states that the results were better than expected when such conditions as headaches, tenosynovitis, low back pain, radicular pain, and Achilles tendinitis were treated by stimulating associated trigger points. It was theorized that the reduction in trigger point pain results from increased oxygen to hypoxic cells in the trigger point areas and removal of waste products through circulation increases. The author observed less use of analgesic drugs or a complete exclusion of drug use with the photon energy treatments.(19)

I have found an effective approach to injury therapy includes addressing the injury site directly as well as the associated acupuncture and trigger points. Veterinary acupuncture diagnosis will locate appropriate points for treatment with photon therapy. Sensitive and careful palpation will enable you to assess progress. When electrical stimulation, ultrasound, magnets, or photon therapy is used on the primary injury site, photon therapy applied to the associated trigger or acupuncture points can complete the treatment. If the therapist is unsure of the exact point location, a cluster head probe helps reduce the margin of error because it covers a larger area of skin.

Photon therapy can be the treatment of choice for reducing the sensitivity in these specialized tissue areas because it is painless. Ear points and points on the horse's lower leg can be treated safely, as can young or nervous horses. Photon therapy evokes a calming response in nervous horses, if applied with sensitivity.

Reducing the sensitivity of these points helps to restore normal muscular balance and makes the horse feel more comfortable. If an amperage meter could be used on these points, it would show that they exhibit lowered resistance to electricity compared to the surrounding skin. The effect of the HeNe laser on skin resistance overlying trigger points has been reported favorably.[20] The resistance of skin over trigger points increased following a 15 second delivery of laser at a continuous output of .95mW. Increased skin resistance could indicate reduction in tenderness and muscle spasm associated with the trigger point.

An interesting but unpublished study measured the tissue temperature using liquid crystal thermography at the injury site before and after laser stimulation. Heat production remained unchanged during and after the application of photon therapy. However, when photon therapy was applied to associated acupuncture points far from the sight and to auricular points (acupuncture points in the ear), a thermogram showed decreased temperature, indicating decreased inflammation.

The placebo effect can confound the results of treatment sessions and scientific studies when humans are used as subjects. With this in mind, a study using laboratory mice compared laser analgesia with analgesia from acupuncture or morphine.[21] Both GaAs and HeNe lasers were used, but neither was found to produce an analgesic effect on the same level of analgesic drugs. Both the morphine and acupuncture treatments produced marked delays in response time to painful stimulus. In my view, this is a desirable effect of photon therapy. It does not obliterate nature's protective pain response. Pain is decreased in most instances, but not completely blocked, as it can be with more aggressive approaches. The pain response will be there when it is needed to protect the body from overuse or injury.

To quiet the response in active trigger points, a single diode device is applied directly to the point for one or two minutes. Skilled manual palpation is more accurate than a point finder to locate the points. After all the points have been addressed, they can be re-checked with manual palpation. They should be non-responsive or significantly reduced. This approach is combined with application of the appropriate therapy directly to the site of the primary lesion.

Chronic Pain

The problem of chronic pain was addressed in a study using a 1mW HeNe laser to treat subjects with pain lasting more than six months.(22) Photon therapy was applied three times a week for 10 weeks to specific sites over the radial, median, ulnar, and saphenous nerves in humans. The control subjects received radiation to sites near but not over these nerves. Subjects who received photon therapy over the nerves experienced pain relief after four to eight treatments. After 12 to 30 treatments, pain relief lasted longer. The control subjects experienced no pain relief, a testimony to the precision with which photon therapy must be applied to get results. The subjects who eventually became pain-free demonstrated an increase in serotonin metabolism as measured by urinary excretion of a serotonin metabolite. Serotonin is a nerve-sensitizing substance coupled with endogenous opioids that provide pain relief. If its reduction can be measured and linked to relief from chronic pain, perhaps this opens avenues for the study of pain relief in the horse.

Photon therapy can be used to treat chronic pain.

Lymphatic and Circulatory Effects

Two important targets for photon therapy are the lymphatic system and the blood capillaries. The lymph system consists of small vessels resembling blood vessels and lymph nodes or glands. This system plays a vital role in defending the body against infection. Lymph is derived from parts of the blood that have filtered through blood capillary walls. The lymph vessels carry wastes, cell debris, and fats to the lymph glands, where bacteria and other harmful microorganisms are filtered out. The lymph cells — lymphocytes — play a role in immunity by producing antibodies and substances that destroy viruses. We read more and more these days about the scavenger "B" and "T" cells as our knowledge of immunity increases. These cells are lymphocytes, the "B" cells being bone marrow-derived and the "T" cells coming from the thymus, two organs of this system.(23) Stimulating the activity of these scavenger cells reduces edema and shortens the inflammatory phase.

The blood circulatory system is the oxygen and nutrient transport system for all the body tissues. Edema reduction and tissue repair rely on local capillary vasodilation to bring oxygen and nutrients to the cells and to carry away waste products of injury. Nitric oxide, a gas molecule identified in the 1980s, has been called one of the body's most potent vasodilators. Nitric oxide is attached to the hemoglobin molecule in the blood, the protein molecule that transports oxygen to the tissues. Proteins in the blood absorb photon energy very effectively, as shown by the photo below.

Lymphatic treatment

The lymphatic system's importance is often overlooked in the repair of equine injuries. Trauma results in local swelling. Ice and compression wraps should alleviate this symptom in the first few days after injury. If edema remains as thick, doughy tissue, it is called chronic lymphedema. The term pit-

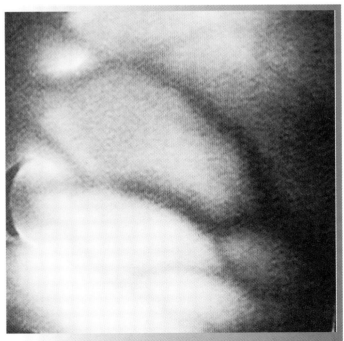

Blood vessels in a human hand absorb nearly all photon energy and appear black.

ting edema is sometimes applied because of the dent that can be left with finger pressure. This edema represents a lymph flow blockage and buildup of protein-rich fluid. If lymphedema is caught early, it can be treated successfully. The most effective treatment includes controlled exercise, manual massage, compression wraps, and photon therapy. Unfortunately, equine therapy often does not begin early in the process, but instead is used as a last, desperate effort. Once the edema has stagnated, scar tissue forms. Often the lymph nodes are damaged, making it unlikely that the limb will return to normal. Photon therapy can encourage drainage if begun early enough. The following discussion of the benefits to damaged lymphatic vessels comes from Ohshiro in his book, *Low Level Laser Therapy*. (24)

The lymph system is a closed system with the blood circulation. Lymph passes through several sets of nodes, then returns to the blood circulatory system through the thoracic duct and the right lymphatic duct. The nodes act as filters but can become overworked and succumb to the infection they are trying to combat. When tissues are injured, lymph and blood vessels are damaged and leak their contents into the surrounding tissue. This edema causes swelling and pain as nerves are damaged or pressured. Because the body's natural drainage system is damaged, the waste removal and healing processes are slowed down.

Photon therapy helps reduce the edema and prevents a recurrence of swelling. Applying a compression wrap will reduce local edema, but the swelling will return soon after the wrap is removed. Photon therapy stimulates the lymphatic system, its ducts, and nodes to help the body assimilate nutrients and remove toxins from the bloodstream. Photons are well absorbed by the lymph and aid in dispersing congestion in these vessels. Our clinical experiences with horses are confirmed by Ohshiro as he describes the increase in lymphatic flow and corresponding increase in blood flow rate following photon therapy. The large vessels close to the skin surface actually enlarge with photon therapy.

The therapist must find the appropriate lymph channels and their proximal and distal nodes to stimulate lymph movement. The approach I prefer, and the one recommended by Ohshiro, is to begin stimulating the nodes closest to the center of the body and work toward the distal nodes. Beginning closer to the center of the body opens the channels "downstream," allowing lymph flow toward the center of the body where it is more easily resorbed. All sites along the lymph tract must be addressed to open the whole system for improved circulation. Using a cluster head will make treating these sites easy and efficient. One device, pictured in this chapter, offers cluster pads that can be wrapped in place, which frees the hands for massage. Long, stroking massage aids photon therapy in moving lymph from the limbs toward the center of the body.

Cellulitis, an inflammation of the tissues around an infected bone, joint, or tendon sheath, can be treated with photon therapy. As with any injury, the sooner cellulitis can be addressed, the greater the chances for success. This condition begins with swelling at the infection site, but soon the area of edema spreads as the lymph vessels become blocked. The lymph vessels of the horse's leg do not have valves to combat gravity's downward pull on the fluid. Muscular action keeps the circulation flowing. If left untreated, the connective tissue becomes denser and scar tissue forms. What started as a liquid becomes a mass of dense scar tissue. Early application of photon energy stimulates the phagocytes (white blood cells that can absorb and destroy waste or harmful bacteria) in the lymph. If the condition is allowed to persist, scar tissue becomes an irritant in itself and inhibits reduction of swelling.

Ulcerative lymphangitis is an inflammatory condition of the lymph vessels resulting from a bacterial infection. A lower leg injury allows bacteria to enter that overwhelms the immune system. The lymph channels back up until the leg is severely swollen. Abscesses often break out, giving the appearance that the skin has burst. This condition is difficult to control. The appropriate medical care, along with early application of photon energy to the lymph nodes, electrical stimulation to the entire limb, and controlled exercise, provide a chance for recovery.

Relieving edema reduces pain, enabling the horse to use the limbs fully so that natural circulatory and lymph pumps can activate and maintain the reduction of swelling.

Blood Circulation

A common use for photon therapy involves treating open wounds and wounds to subcutaneous tissue, such as muscles and tendons. Photon therapy is most impressive when it is used to treat wounds that either have failed to heal or worsened during conventional medical treatment. In our clinical observation, it helps stop infection and closes the wound quickly without an accumulation of proud flesh. Photon therapy apparently fights bacteria and also appears to enhance the horse's "host response" by controlling infection through the immune system.

Proud flesh is the overproduction of collagen from cells that have changed because of injury. These cells normalize and become healthy skin cells, no longer forming a barrier to wound closure. We have treated many dermal wounds, and they have all responded well to photon therapy. Many of the wounds had persisted for months and were infected. Even such severe cases readily respond to photon therapy, healing with strength and little scar tissue. Photon therapy has the advantage over electrical stimulation, another effective way to stimulate wound closure, in that it cannot be felt by the horse. This makes wound treatment on foals or fractious horses safe.

Because nitric oxide is considered such a potent vasodilator, a study using human subjects sought to determine whether nitric oxide levels in the blood could be raised by applying photon energy.(25) A 60 diode cluster pad, delivering 810 nm, monochromatic infrared light, was applied to the arm for 30 minutes. In blood drawn from the experimental area, nitric oxide was elevated 16% to 25% on the treated limb compared to 8% to 18% on the control limb.

To study the systemic effects of monochromatic infrared light, the researchers placed photon therapy pads over the subjects' jugular veins. Blood again was drawn from the arm. After 30 minutes of treatment, blood and plasma levels of nitric oxide had increased in both forearms, sampling sites that were remote from the site of light application. The researchers proposed that photon energy releases nitric oxide from hemoglobin, resulting in better tissue nutrition and less ischemia.

Pressure sores and open surface wounds

Body surface wounds fail to heal for many reasons, the most common being poor circulation, infection, recurring injury, and poor responsiveness of the body's own stimuli to promote healing. These wounds respond successfully to photon therapy, which triggers the repair response and reduces recovery time. An approach considered progressive in human medicine

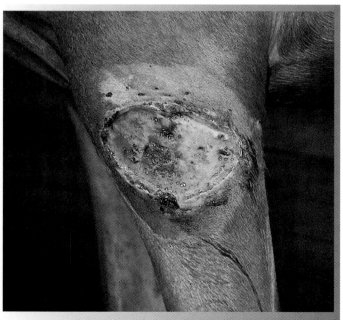

The right half of this scrape wound has been treated with photon therapy.

involves giving the patient growth factor therapy extracted form the patient's blood. Non-healing wounds have healed in 12 to 16 weeks with this costly therapy. Photon therapy stimulates non-healing wounds immediately; evidence of healing is seen with the first treatment. Several studies are under way to validate the use of photon energy on wound healing and to determine the optimal doses.

When HeNe laser therapy was used on wounds in cattle, it was found to minimize inflammation and edema formation as well as to improve skin regeneration and collagen synthesis. In a comparison of photon therapy at $3.64 \, j/cm2$ to suture closure, the sutures produced greater skin thickness at the closure site. Blood flow and the morphology of the epidermis in the photon-treated group was more like normal tissue, with collagen fibers more normally arranged. Tensile strength was significantly greater in the photon therapy group, meaning that the wound closure had more strength in withstanding stress.(26)

Pressure sores, or decubitus ulcers, occur when a horse spends an unusual amount of time lying down. Ill-fitting bandages or splints left on too long cause pressure sores. Pressure on bony prominence causes the skin to become ischemic and eventually to break down because the constant pressure occludes blood vessels and deprives the tissues of nutrition. Deep sores begin in the subcutaneous tissues where muscle and fat have less resistance to pressure than the skin. Destruction can occur in these tissues while the skin covering them shows only a slight redness. Eventually the skin breaks down and the deeper necrosed tissues are exposed. These wounds can be very deep, even exposing bone in extreme cases.

Preventing pressure sores includes regular turning of a foal and careful padding of an older horse. Real sheepskin pads offer the benefit of natural oils for the dry skin that results from lack of circulation. Splints should contour to the body and be carefully padded so there are no rough edges or folds. PVC pipe splints must be removed several times a day and the leg checked for hot spots. If you feel a hot spot on a bony prominence, apply ice cup massage and then photon therapy immediately.

Photon therapy is applied directly to the wound to stimulate epithelial regrowth and to stimulate microcirculation. In our observation, these wounds begin to close up, even if the horse continues to spend considerable time lying down. Conversely, these wounds will not heal and will worsen if they are not treated with photon therapy or with electrical stimulation.

A remarkable case involving severe, bone-depth pressure sores on a foal was treated using photon therapy. This foal developed numerous health complications at birth and was in a coma for several weeks. During this time, deep dicubital sores developed on every bony prominence of the body. Several of these sores became infected and persisted without healing for several weeks. Photon therapy was applied to the sores every other day for two months. The shallow, non-infected sores closed steadily with no complication. The deep, infected sores presented a challenge that was met with a combination of medications and photon therapy. The photon therapy stimulated the expulsion of pus from the wounds, debriding the wounds naturally. Because these wounds could not be bandaged easily, this natural debridement was an important part of keeping the wounds free of debris. It was rewarding to see very little dense connective tissue adhesion to the bone in the deepest wounds. Scars that adhere to the underlying bone can cause great discomfort and restricted movement. Photon therapy softens scar tissue, making it more elastic so that natural movement can elongate the tissue.

Photon therapy is easily tolerated by a newborn foal. A caring therapist who delivers a treatment that leaves the foal more comfortable can provide a beneficial imprinting experience. When medication and bandaging experiences are traumatic, a calming experience with equine therapy can leave the foal with a more cooperative attitude.

Skin surface wounds respond quickly to photon therapy. The first sign of healing is at the wound edges, as epithelial regrowth begins as a white line. The width of this line expands, and it develops the coloration of normal tissue as epithelial cells migrate to the wound. The next indicator is decreased wound depth. Wounds naturally debride with photon therapy, more productively sloughing off the waste. The photo below shows a scrape wound that was treated on the right side with photon therapy. The left side was not treated. An increase in lymph vessel and capillary vasodilation rids the wound of waste. Allowing the waste to stagnate around the wound increases scar tissue and slows healing.

Open wounds can present a problem because of the difficulty in keeping a bandage in place, the attraction of flies carrying bacteria, and the frequent inability of stitches to hold in an area that moves. Any tool or procedure that would aid in rapid wound closure would help. Photon therapy may be such a tool.

Many scientific investigations have been devoted to determining how photons affect tissue repair. Stimulation of DNA and RNA synthesis as well as improvement in the wound's micro circulation have improved with photon treatment.(27)

Collagen, the cells from which tissue is formed, is produced by fibroblasts. Fibroblasts increase in number under the influence of photon therapy.(28) Collagen provides the healing tissue with increased tensile strength and resilience, enabling it to withstand the stress of movement. Wounds treated with photon therapy do not break down over time and have less scar tissue to weaken them. Studies have measured the tensile strength of wounds stimulated by photon therapy, finding that they resisted breaking more than untreated incisions.(29,30)

Laminitis

Laminitis is defined by the American Association of Equine Practitioners as an inflammation of the sensitive laminae of the foot. The definition also states that there are many factors involved, including changes in blood flow through the capillaries of the foot. Capillaries make up the bed of microscopic vessels that supply nutrition to the sensitive laminae overlying the coffin bone. The capillaries carry nutrition to the hoof tissues and remove waste. During the acute phase of laminitis, these vessels shut down. Dr. Doug Allen, laminitis researcher at the University of Georgia, found that within 16 hours the hoof's blood supply is cut by at

least half. According to Dr. Prabin Mishran of Cornell University, it could be due to the circulating toxins (endotoxins) from the decayed bodies of millions of bacteria in the large bowel, or an overabundance of circulating histamine released as part of a widespread inflammatory process, or perhaps both. The blood is apparently bypassing the capillary bed via the arterio-venous (AV) shunts. Mishran reports observing severe damage in the walls of these vessels, making them unreliable conduits of blood.

Horsemen have recognized the syndrome for 150 years, but it remains a leading cause of disability or death in horses. A handbook of veterinary homeopathy published in 1854 lists overeating and intestinal

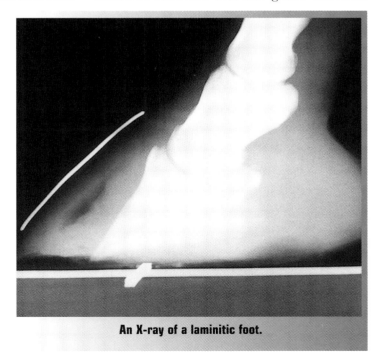

An X-ray of a laminitic foot.

insults as causative factors. A recent list from the AAEP includes toxic levels of grain, eating lush grass, systemic disease problems, high temperature, toxemia, retained placentas, supporting limb breakdown, excessive exercise, improper hoof care, and reaction to drugs. Laminitis can cause severe pain and sometimes be fatal, as it was to the great racehorse Secretariat.

Tissue deprived of oxygen eventually dies. If the horse is not treated soon enough or effectively, the laminae suffer irreversible damage. As the laminae die, the coffin bone (the third phalanx) starts to rotates downward in response to pull from the deep flexor tendon attached to the base of the coffin bone. The laminae and connective tissues are torn from the inside of the hoof wall.

Mild cases of laminitis can leave the horse with some athletic ability, but at the price of muscle and foot soreness. The classic grades of laminitis are:

Stage 1) The horse shifts its weight and moves stiffly. No lameness at the walk, but has lameness at the trot.

Stage 2) The horse is willing to move but is lame at the walk. The horse allows its feet to be handled.

Stage 3) The horse will not allow its foot to be picked up and resists moving.

Stage 4) The horse refuses to move and is in obvious pain.

Lateral radiographs of the third phalanx will help in determining the extent of damage. If the coffin bone is displaced, the horse is said to have chronic founder. Symptoms of previous bouts of laminitis include displacement of the coffin bone in relationship to the hoof wall and the sole, elevated hoof temperature, digital pulse, a dish or concave shape to the front of the hoof, and grooved hoof walls. The horse might move in a heel to toe manner.

In my experience, laminitis responds well to photon therapy. When the acute stage of laminitis has subsided, enhancing circulation in the foot can help limit damage, experts say. Once again, the nitric oxide (NO) molecule comes into play. Nitric oxide is an inorganic free radical gas that was discovered only 10 years ago. Vascular endothelial cells are able to synthesize NO from the enzyme L-arginine for its use as a transcellular signal.(31) Stimulating the release of nitric oxide activates the horse's own vasodilating mechanism.

Nitric oxide might be the molecule responsible for the effects of nitroglycerin in treating post-traumatic laminitis. Dr. Chris Pollitt makes the relationship clear by explaining that nitric oxide is now known to be the most potent of the body's natural vasodilators. It is manufactured from argenine, a simple amino acid, by cells lining all blood vessels. Nitroglycerin creams or patches act as an external source of nitric oxide with the effect of rapid vasodilation. After the metabolic crisis of laminitis is over, nitroglycerin is used to aid healing.

But administering the patches or creams poses human risk. Dr. Ric Redden reports that despite wearing two pairs of rubber gloves, he felt an immediate, severe headache and increased heart rate while working on a horse which had been treated with nitroglycerin cream. Using photon therapy to release nitric oxide from hemoglobin avoids this risk.

Our approach is to place a cluster pad over the coronary band in front and over the digital artery and vein on the lateral and the medial sides of the lower leg. The coronary band is dense with capillaries that nourish hoof tissue. The digital artery is the main vessel that serves the foot. This arrangement allows these structures to receive photon energy directly. Treatment is given for 30 minutes once or twice a day. After the discomfort has subsided, which could be in as few as three or four treatments, treatment can be reduced to every other day. Photon therapy also is used on acupuncture points in the musculature of the hips and back, which often are sore from shifting weight off the front feet.

In our experience, photon therapy helps the digital pulse subside and reduces the horse's discomfort when standing. The horse spends less time lying down and might require less pain medication. One stallion could not tolerate walking on the asphalt barn aisle before we began treatment. He willingly did this after two weeks of photon therapy; in addition, he trotted along his fence line, something he had not done for years.

Often our patient is a mare with a history of increased discomfort from laminitis as pregnancy advances. With photon therapy to the coronary band for 30 minutes three times a week, we see a gratifying increase in comfort level. Patients often need less therapy as treatment progresses to maintain the same comfort level. This therapy has benefited these mares greatly, enabling them to complete their pregnancies with no distress. Although equine therapy does not offer a cure for laminitis, it can certainly bring blessed relief to the suffering horse.

Arthritis

Osteoarthritis is the most common human and equine joint disease. It stems from the cumulative effects of wear and tear on the joints and causes damage to the cartilage on the joint surface. Free radicals and enzymes that are released undermine the collagen matrix and lead to degeneration. The time for effective treatment is in the very early stages, which can be identified with thermography if done routinely on young horses in training. Once the joints have begun to deteriorate to the point of X-ray detection, it is probably too late for physical therapy.

Bone Healing

Our experience in bone healing is limited to sesamoid fractures in young horses. This is relatively common in Kentucky when foals, turned out with their mothers, sustain fractures from leaping and running. To treat the condition, cluster pads are wrapped on the medial and lateral sesamoid of each fetlock. The foal usually stands quietly throughout the treatment. X-rays indicate a shortened healing time and reduction in swelling. Our experience is supported by research using doses of 2.4 joules (J) applied with an HeNe laser to experimental tibial fractures in mice. The treated group displayed an increase in the number of blood vessels and faster formation of osseous tissue compared to the control group.(32)

GaAlAs semiconductor photon therapy was applied to bone and cartilage during joint immobilization using the rat knee as a model. X-ray absorptiometry was used to analyze bone mineral density after six treatments at 3.9 W/cm2 and 5.8 W/cm 2. Both treatment doses resulted in preventing the biomechanical changes normally associated with immobilization.(33)

Contraindications for Photon Therapy

Photon therapy has few contraindications. Because photon therapy devices are easy to use and obtain, many treatments no doubt are given at an incorrect dosage and to undiagnosed conditions. For effective use of these valuable tools, obtain a complete veterinary evaluation and diagnosis before therapy begins. Perhaps the biggest

A photon therapy device with cluster pads that can be wrapped in place.

danger in using these devices is mistaking symptom relief as a cure for the problem. Unfortunately, it is all too common to see a trainer resume the horse's training before the tissues have healed sufficiently. Pain is nature's warning sign that a problem exists. The problem could worsen and become untreatable or more difficult to treat successfully if this signal is ignored or covered up through pain reduction techniques. Insufficient knowledge can hamper optimal use of photon energy. Photon energy quickly reduces pain and tissue swelling, but time is still needed for complete cell repair and tissue maturation. The tensile strength that comes from full repair allows the structure to be stretched without tearing.

Use caution when treating a pregnant mare, avoiding acupuncture points associated with disruption of pregnancy (LI4, SP6). Discuss this with a veterinarian who specializes in acupuncture.

Cancer lesions should not be treated with photon therapy. There has been no link established between cancer and photon energy, but the effects on existing cancer have not been studied enough.

Avoid looking into the beam of light as corneal damage can occur. Although equine therapists use a less intense beam than those used for humans, caution is advised.

Before using photon energy devices, discuss possible drug interactions with your veterinarian. Iodine or other topical applications that leave a film of color on the skin should be washed off because they will alter the wavelength or block the transmission of light.

Conclusion

In the first edition of this book published in 1990, I quoted some thoughts expressed to me at that time by Donald E. Hudson, president of the Respond Company. These thoughts remain pertinent.

"Laser therapy has come a long way in the past five years. This is particularly true in Europe, where the majority of the scientific studies are conducted and 75% of all lasers, cold and hot, are sold. New studies emerge continuously. Awareness of their results will help the user to develop skill in laser use so more consistent clinical results will be possible.

" 'Laser' systems were introduced to the racetrack in the '70s by salesmen selling the units. Exaggerated claims for the products elevated our expectations beyond what could be reasonably expected. Many of these units were underpowered and lacked an adequate treatment guide. Many of these companies are out of business now. The companies that have endured produce a laser with more power, make reasonable claims for their machines, and include a treatment guide honed from field work over the years. The laser industry in America today has achieved a level of maturity and credibility in 1990."

This level of credibility has grown over the nine years since Hudson made these statements. The legacy of determined effort to understand the mechanism of action of this therapeutic modality has been seized by Dale Bertwell of Equi-Light, Inc.

Equine therapists owe a debt of gratitude to manufacturers who endeavor to increase our knowledge base. It is time that honesty prevails concerning output characteristics, so the equine therapist can deliver the most effective dose of photon energy.

Definitions

Diode — A semiconducting device that allows electrical current to flow only in one direction. One that is widely used is the p-n junction diode.

Endogenous opioids — Narcotic-like compounds produced within the body.

Epithelium — Layer of cells forming the epidermis of the skin.

Joule — Energy produced by one watt of power operated for one second.

Mitochondria — The source of energy in the cell.

Nanometer — One billionth of a meter.

Nanosecond — One billionth of a second.

Placebo — An inactive substance given to satisfy the patient's need for medication or used in controlled studies to provide a comparison for a substance being tested.

Radiant energy — Emission of energy from a central source.

Refraction — Bending of a ray of light as it passes from one medium to another of different density.

RNA — Abbreviation for ribonucleic acid. Initiates and participates in the manufacture of a protein molecule.

Semiconductor — A material of intermediate conductivity. Semiconductor devices often use silicon when they are made as part of diodes.

Spectrum — Chartered band of wavelengths of electromagnetic vibrations.

Watt — Unit of electrical power, equal to a current of one amp under one volt of pressure.

Wavelength — The distance measured from any given point to the next point characterized by the same phase.

References

1. Colov, HC. 1988. *Biostimulation by Low Power Laser.* Proceedings of the conference Low Power Laser, Uniondale, NY. 18-21.

2. Smith, KC. 1991. *The Photobiological Basis of Low Level Laser Radiation Therapy.* Department of Radiation Oncology at Stanford University School of Medicine.

3. Dameya, T., Wang, L., and Yamada, H. 1990. A review of clinical applications of low level laser therapy in veterinary medicine. International Laser Therapy Assoc. Naha City, Okinawa. 162-171.

4. Baxter, D. 1994. New York, NY.: Churchill Livingstone. 39.

5. Ibid. p38.

6. Karu, T. 1987. Photobiological fundamentals of low-power laser therapy. *IEEE J Quant Elect.* 23:1703.

7. Ben-Hur, E. and Rosenthal, I. 1987. vol III. CRC Press. 20.

8. Baxter. 27.

9. Atkins, P. 1997. *Thor Laser Therapy Systems.* personal communications

10. Kerte, J. and Rose, L. 1989. *Clinical Laser Therapy.* Scandinavian Medical Laser Technology. Copenhagen, Denmark: p. 25.

11. Ohshiro, T. and Calderhead, RG. 1990. *Low Level Laser Therapy: A Practical Introduction.* New York, NY.: John Wiley. 16.

12. Seitz, L. and Kleinkort, J. 1986. *Low Power Laser: Its Application in Physical Therapy. Thermal Agents in Rehabilitation.* SL. Michlovitz, ed. Philadelphia: FA Davis Company. 217-38.

13. Baxter, DG. 1994. *Therapeutic Lasers.* New York, NY.: Churchill Livingstone. 34-35.

14. Greathouse, DG., Currier, D., and Gilmore, R. 1985. Effects of clinical infrared laser on superficial radial nerve latency. *Phys Ther.* 65:1184-87.

15. Snyder-Mackler, L. and Bork, CE. 1988. Effect of helium-neon laser irradiation on peripheral sensory nerve latency. *Phys Ther.* 68:223-25.

16. Lee, JM. et al. 1978. Effects of ice on nerve conduction velocity. *Phys Ther.* 64:2-6.

17. Kasai, S. et al. Effect of low-power laser irradiation on impulse conduction in anesthetized rabbits. 1996. *J Clin Laser Med Surg.* 14:107-09.

18. Shoen, A., ed. 1994. *Veterinary Acupuncture, Ancient Art to Modern Medicine.* Goleta, CA.: American Veterinary Publications.

19. Simunovic, Z. 1966. Low level laser therapy with trigger points technique: a clinical study on 243 patients. *J Clin Laser Med Surg.* 14:163-67.

20. Snyder-Mackler, L., Bork, CB. Burbon B., and Trumbore, D. 1986. Effects of helium-neon laser on musculoskeletal trigger points. *Phys Ther.* 66:1087-90.

21. Lundberg, T. et al. 1987. A comparative study of the pain relieving effect of laser treatment and acupuncture. *Acta Physiologica Scandinavica.* 131:161-62.

22. Walker, J. 1983. Relief from chronic pain by low power laser irradiation. *Neuroscience Letters.* 43:339-44.

23. Ohshiro, T. and R. G. Calderhead. 1990. *Low Level Laser Therapy: A Practical Introduction.* New York, NY.: Wiley & Sons. 55.

24. Ohshiro, T. 1991. *Low Reactive- Level Laser Therapy: Practical Application.* New York, NY.: Wiley and Sons. 60-62.

25. Horowitz, LR. and Burke, TJ. Accelerated Wound Healing with Monochromatic Infrared Light: Possible Mechanism of Action. Under peer review.

26. Ghamsari, SM. et al. 1977. Evaluation of low level laser therapy on primary healing of experimentally induced full thickness teat wounds in dairy cattle. *Vet Surg.* 26:114-20.

27. Enwemeka, CS. 1988. Laser biostimulation of healing wounds: specific effects and mechanisms of action. *J Ortho Sports Phys Ther.* 9:333-37.

28. Mester, AF. and Mester, A. 1989. Wound Healing. *Laser Therapy.* 1:7-15.

29. Surinchak, JS. et al. 1983. Effects of low-level energy lasers on the healing of full-thickness skin defects. *Lasers in Surg and Med.* 2:267-74.

30. Kovacs, IB., Mester, E., and Gorog, P. 1974. Stimulation of wound healing with laser beam in rat. *Experientia.* 30:1275-76.

31. Knowles, R. G. and Moncada, S. 1994. Nitric oxide synthesis in mammals. *Biochemical J Reviews.* AE. Pegg ed. Portland Press:1-10.

32. Trelles, MA. and Mayayo, E. 1989. Bone Fracture Consolidates Faster with Low-power Laser. *Lasers in Surg Med.* 7:36-45.

33. Akai, M. et al. 1997. Laser's effect on bone and cartilage change induced by joint immobilization: an experiment with animal model. *Lasers Surg Med.* 21:480-84.

Magnetic Field Therapy

*I believe that there is a subtle magnetism in Nature, which if we unconsciously yield to it, will direct us aright…*Thoreau

WHEREVER there are moving electrical currents, a surrounding magnetic field exists. Because of the moving ions in our cytoplasm, humans and horses are electrical beings. Weak electrical currents are associated with wounds and can have either a positive or negative effect on healing. Cells oscillate at frequencies from the hertz (Hz) to the Megahertz (MHZ) range, creating alternating current fields thought to form an intercellular communication system.

Research shows that magnetic fields extend in all directions from all living organisms. Some life forms, including humans, are capable of detecting these fields. Birds use them to guide their north-south migratory routes. Whales use them for their sense of direction. And people who practice "energy healing" believe the process is based on interaction between the therapist and patient's electrical and magnetic fields.

An electrical field is created by voltage, or electrical pressure, in a wire. When an electrical device is plugged in, the wire carries voltage and emits an electrical field. The strength of the field is measured in volts per meter. (1) A magnetic field is produced by the flow of electricity through the wire when the device is turned on. The strength of magnetic fields is measured in gauss (G), named after Karl Friedrich Gauss, the German mathematician and astronomer

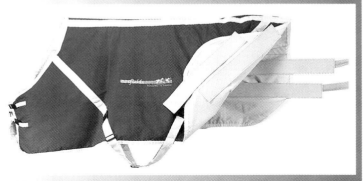

Magnets are used for many sports injuries. A magnetic blanket.

who discovered this method of measurement. The strength of the Earth's magnetic field (around 1 G) can be used as a reference for understanding the strength of therapeutic magnets (300 to 1,000 G).

Safety of Electromagnetic Fields

Over the past decade, public fears about the hazards of electrical and magnetic fields have risen, despite increased demand for electrical power and increased usage of computers and other electronic equipment. Millions of dollars have been spent studying the safety of these fields. Research from around the world, however, seems to conclude there is no concrete evidence that electromagnetic fields pose a health hazard. Indeed, there is a growing body of evidence linking them to health benefits.

Because therapists are exposed to electromagnetic fields emitted from equipment, a study sought to measure the field strength emitted from the Megapulse unit.(2) The Megapulse, manufactured in England, produces electromagnetic radiation at 27.12 MHZ. Like the units popular in America, it delivers patient adjustable short pulses. This study looked at the unit's power output when there was no patient. With the unit at full power, the field strength was well within the safety limits set by the government. The authors point out that these units are usually operated at lower output settings with the field directed at the patient. They concluded that there appeared to be no health hazard to the staff.

Effects of Magnetic Fields

Should we separate permanent magnets from pulsed electromagnets in terms of effect? Much research still needs to be done to determine whether the body differentiates energy from different sources. When a permanent magnet is applied to living tissue, the magnetic field is then in motion because of the inherent movement of the cells. Perhaps the body acts as a transducer for all incoming energy. If the energy is within the window of usable strength, wavelength, or frequency, the tissues can make use of it.

In the studies cited below, both magnetic modalities have been found to provide a safe, non-invasive therapy.

Blood Flow

Equine therapy often seeks to increase metabolism and tissue repair because these things are associated with increased blood flow. In a study to determine whether static magnets alter flow characteristics, a saline solution and distilled water were exposed to a static magnetic pad. The saline flow increased to a statistically significant level, but the flow of distilled water was not affected.(3) In my opinion, this study has little to do with the body, since it is non-dynamic, but it does point out a magnetic field's influence over ionic particles.

When magnetic pads are worn for an hour or more, the tissue under the pad can become quite warm, indicating an increase in local blood flow. The blood is composed of ions, which could be affected by the magnetic field. But there might be an even more interesting phenomenon going on here.

A 1981 report proposed a link between magnetic fields and infrared wavelengths. A magnetic or electrical field has a wavelength and frequency that determine the field's energy density. The scientists determined that a magnetic field of 0.1 to 1 G could have effects on the body equivalent to infrared wavelengths of 7.9 and 2.6 microns. The molecules in the body that detect this energy are the mitochondria, melanin, and retinal rods, those same molecules that detect infrared light.(4) Recently the use of magnetic fields has expanded to include nerve regeneration, wound healing, skin graft integrity, and other conditions that are thought of as appropriate to photon therapy. Data on these uses is preliminary but intriguing.

One study looked into using magnetic fields to heal soft tissue wounds. The authors applied pulsed electromagnetic fields (PEMFs) to the wounds using the wave-form parameters used for bone healing. They then analyzed the wounds for differences in contracture and epithelialization and the number of fibroblasts present. The authors determined that parameters used for nonunion bone repair did not affect soft tissue healing and that different wave-form characteristics were needed to activate soft tissue.(5) Since this study was done in 1986, PEMFs of 100 Hz with a 16 hour on/eight hour off cycle have been found to strengthen surgical wounds.(6)

Neurotransmitter Function

I recently have become interested in how magnetic fields affect mood, behavior, and memory. Like other energetic modalities, magnetic fields apparently affect the activity of neurotransmitters, which are chemicals produced in the brain that determine sleep patterns, pain perception, healing rate, and mood.

One recent study looked at using magnetic fields to treat depression. Twelve adults whose depression did not respond to other forms of treatment received two weeks of transcranial magnetic stimulation at 20 Hz. A small but powerful electromagnet was placed on the scalp, causing cortical neurons just below the skull to depolarize. After five daily

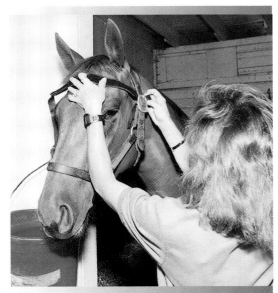

Magnets used on the browband can have a calming influence on a horse.

treatment sessions, 11 of the 17 patients showed a marked improvement that lasted for two weeks, and no one reported significant adverse effects. All the subjects eventually responded positively to the therapy.(7) This study opens the door to serious thought about using magnetic stimulation for mood improvement. Related studies are exploring the treatment of neurologic disorders including epilepsy, Parkinson's disease, and learning disabilities.

My experience with horses is supported by the study just described. While wearing a magnet attached to a brow band, most horses experience profound mental quieting. The breathing and heart rate slow, and muscle tension eases.

Place a 600 G magnet on the center of the horse's forehead, between the two supraorbital foramina, over the cerebrum. Magnetic field stimulation of glands or other structures in the brain might convey messages such as "increased production of melatonin." Melatonin is a hormone that regulates sleep and mood. The magnetic field modifies the local environment of the cells, changing transmembrane fluxes of molecules such as calcium or other substances important in cell function. Calcium movement through cell membranes affects the cells' metabolic activity and ATP production.

When placed on the horse, the magnetic brow band sits between two acupuncture sites used for tranquilizing. This area of the forehead is called the "third eye" in Eastern spiritual traditions, and is considered a gateway to the inner self. According to Ayervedic tradition, adjusting the resonance of the third eye increases intuitive abilities and has a grounding effect. It is interesting that humans everywhere touch this area of the forehead when trying to concentrate. Using the magnetic brow band does not make a horse sluggish or unpredictable as tranquilizers do. They are simply calmer and more in control.

The effects of the brow band magnet are illustrated in the following case report. A Thoroughbred mare required two long-acting tranquilizers, reserpine and prolixin, as well as ½ to ¾ cc of acepromazine before she would train. Using the brow band magnet immediately calmed her behavior, so the use of tranquilizers was cut back. After the mare had worn the magnet for three days, she trained willingly with no tranquilizers.

Horses using magnets cope well in many situations:

• When confined to a stall, these horses are calm and do not resort to vices such as stall walking or fretful behavior.

• After a training session, they are able to relax, which is vital to recovery from strenuous exertion.

• They have less pre-show anxiety.

• They aren't as afraid of frightening

obstacles, such as introduction to a trailer, starting gate, or wash stall.

• They behave well around the veterinarian or blacksmith.

• Yearling colts have less biting and mouthy behavior around the vet or blacksmith.

• Mares and foals have less weaning stress.

• They learn new skills more easily.

• Horses which must be tranquilized will not require chemical restraint when the magnet is applied before the stressful activity.

Pain Relief

Studies on the therapeutic effects of magnets date back to 1938, when an electromagnet suppressed or removed pain from the skin of human patients.(8)

The use of magnets to relieve pain has become popular among athletes, especially golfers and football players. Professional golfers have been forced to quit playing because of chronic back pain. Magnets allowed these athletes to return to their sport and in some instances even improved their game. Professional athletic trainers have observed that athletes recover from football injuries or from surgeries faster when magnets are worn. Chronic disabilities such as fibromyalgia, bursitis, and arthritis are relieved by wearing magnetic pads or sleeping on a magnetic mattress.

Magnets are available in wraps that fit various body parts of both the human and the

A magnetic wrap for tendons.

horse. Back support wraps can relieve chronic back pain, and magnetic blankets can relieve muscle discomfort in horses.

A double-blind study was designed to test the effects of magnets on 50 patients suffering from pain associated with post-polio syndrome.(9) Trigger point pain is associated with joint pain as well as muscle tightness. The syndrome is characterized by both myofascial pain and joint pain. Those who suffer from post-polio syndrome have increased sensitivity to painful stimuli and find little relief from conventional therapies such as aspirin or non-steroidal anti-inflammatory drugs.

The participants in this study had experienced post-polio syndrome for at least four weeks and had not taken analgesic medications. Static magnets with strengths of 300 and 500 G were taped on the skin over painful trigger points and directly on pain sites for 45 minutes. The control group was given inactive magnets. After the magnets were removed, 75% of the patients with active magnets reported significant pain reduction.

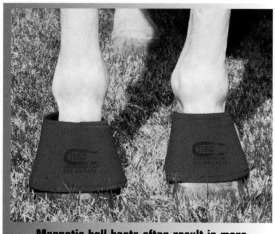

Magnetic bell boots often result in more flexibility in the horse's back.

Only 19% of the patients in the control group experienced even a small decrease in pain. No side effects were reported.

This study showed that static magnetic fields can effectively control pain in patients with post-polio syndrome. The authors found that myofascial and arthritic pain responded equally well to the treatment. Not only did the pain in the area immediately under the magnet respond, some

patients felt pain relief in areas far from that site. The study also found that the benefits lasted days and weeks after the magnets were removed.

When magnets are used to relieve pain, there are no side effects and relief comes quickly. In addition to helping the specific problem, magnets can benefit the entire body. For example, when a horse wears magnetic hock wraps, back muscle tightness is reduced. Also, the use of magnetic bell boots often results in more flexibility in the horse's back. This effect probably is a relaxation response resulting from pain relief in the hock or foot. In an effort to protect the uncomfortable area, the horse maintains chronic muscle tension, which eventually becomes muscle contractures and spasm. When the area is no longer uncomfortable, the muscles can relax.

A study published in 1988 sought to determine the effects of a magnetic necklace on neck and shoulder pain.(10) This study was an attempt to substantiate a Japanese report from 1975. In the earlier study, a necklace with a magnetic flux density of 700 or 1,300 G relieved chronic pain and stiffness. The scientist proposed that sufferers had "magnetic field deficiency syndrome," a concept still heard today. In the more recent report, which used necklaces of 1,300 G, it is interesting that both the subjects wearing the magnetized necklaces and those wearing the placebo necklaces said they experienced pain relief. Almost all the subjects thought their necklaces were magnetized. The new study also found that large nerve fiber conductivity in the arm increased in those wearing the magnetized necklace.

An unpublished study at the University of Kentucky's Gluck Equine Research Center tested pain relief in the horse. Permanent magnets were applied to the pastern and held in place with a wrap. Non-magnetized discs were applied to the control horses in the same manner. After the magnets had been in place for 12 hours, a pain reflex test was conducted to measure the amount of time between the onset of stimulus and hoof withdrawal. The limbs treated with magnets were slower to respond to the stimulus.(11) The results of these two studies indicate that magnetic fields influence nerve conduction rate.

Arthritis

A human study examined the effects of magnetic fields on osteoarthritis. Patients with knee and cervical spine pain received half-hour treatments with a pulsed electromagnetic field device. Both sets of patients showed highly improved comfort level that in some cases lasted a month after completion of therapy. Comparing their findings to studies using non-steroidal, anti-inflammatory medications, the authors found that acetaminophen brought a 22%

Magnetic hock wraps can reduce back muscle tightness.

improvement; ibuprofen, 30%; and pulsed electromagnetic fields, 37%. With the two drugs, relief lasted only as long as the medication was administered. The effects of the PEMFs lasted well beyond the duration of the study.(12)

Soft Tissue Repair

Magnetic field stimulation apparently dilates capillary beds, thereby increasing circulation and aiding soft tissue repair. Scintigraphy was used to demonstrate increased blood flow resulting from applying a permanent magnet on the equine third metacarpus. The majority of equine limbs tested showed increased circulatory and metabolic activity. Scintigraphy uses bone-seeking radiopharmaceuticals to detect changes in bone metabolism. It is used diagnostically to detect stress fractures, infections, and the cause of certain lamenesses. In this study scintigraphy was used to quantify the metabolic activity in the soft tissue and bone after a permanent magnet had been applied for 24 hours.(13)

Although it is uncertain how much information from laboratory animal studies can be applied to horses, such studies form the basis of our understanding of the effects of both therapeutic and medical tools and procedures. One study used 80 rabbits to observe the effects of PEMFs on ligament healing. Different magnetic intensities were used, including 0 for the controls, and 2, 10, and 50 G for the experimental groups. The frequency and pulse widths were 10 Hz and 25 microseconds, respectively. Stimulation doses were daily for one, two, three, four, and five weeks.

The PEMF-treated tissue showed an earlier increase in capillaries and fibroblasts and more matured, prominent, longitudinal orientation of collagen fibers than the control group. These changes were most significant in the group receiving the 50 G stimulation. All the stimulated groups showed increased tensile strength at one and two weeks after the operation; no strength advantage over the controls was shown at three and four weeks, however. The authors concluded that PEMFs enhanced the early stage of ligament healing, and that 50 G seemed to be the most effective intensity. Therefore, applying PEMFs to ligament injuries might promote early recovery.(14)

The same investigators repeated this study to observe the effects of PEMFs on collagen production and maturation. The same treatment parameters were used and, again, the 50 G group showed the most significant increases in blood flow. The collagen content in the PEMFs groups increased significantly compared to that of the control group. The authors observed increased fibroblast activity at two weeks in the 50 G group, with increased collagen production indicating an accelerated healing process.(15)

Bone Repair

The use of magnetic fields for bone repair originates in the concept of the "current of injury," which holds that stress on a bone (as well as soft tissue) causes tiny electrical currents — piezoelectric potentials — to signal cells to send bone nutrients to the distressed area. The pulsed electromagnetic fields are thought to mimic the natural piezoelectric potentials that signal osteoblasts to begin the repair process.(16) Apparently these signals can be detectable, as seems to be the case when people with injuries swim with dolphins. The dolphins unfailingly hover around the patients with their noses toward the injury site. Apparently sensing the current of injury, the dolphins sometimes contact the site for extended periods. Further, these people report a significant relief of what had been intractable pain.

The literature on magnetic field effects is filled with anecdotal evidence, causing much criticism that magnets used for therapy are based on little scientific evidence. This situation is changing, and an increasing number of studies are being done to clarify the effects. At the risk of adding to the pile of unsubstantiated reports, I cannot resist passing along a discussion that came to me through e-mail:

A Standardbred pacer sustained a coffin bone fracture in 1976 that did not heal for four months. The therapy originally prescribed consisted only of stall rest. Hearing of his plight, a group involved in human research on nonunions — failures of bones to heal — made a device to try on the horse. A resistance coil and battery pack device was constructed for the horse's foot and he was treated daily with a pulsating 60 cycle current. The fracture soon healed, and the horse resumed training. That was 20 years ago. Many such clinical examples are now on record, yet we still have doubts about the use of magnetic fields for bone healing.

Horses have been used as subjects in studies examining how pulsed low frequency electromagnetic fields influence bone formation. In one recent study, holes were bored into the diaphyseal region of the metacarpal bones of six adult horses. The treated horses received PEMF therapy at 28 G, 75 Hz for 30 days. The amount of bone formed and the mineral deposition in the treated horses significantly exceeded that of the controls. The low frequency PEMFs were found to stimulate bone repair and improve the osteogenic phase of the healing process.[17]

One of the earliest studies designed to gather controlled data on PEMFs and acute bone healing in the horse was reported in 1984 by veterinary surgeon Larry Bramlage. A 1 millimeter (mm) defect was created in the mid-shaft dorsal cortex of the metacarpus or metatarsus of six adult horses. PEMF therapy was applied for two hours daily. Radiographic and histologic comparisons of the repair found no significant difference in the healing rates between treated and non-treated horses. These authors did not find PEMFs to be of value in acute bone healing.[18]

The results of studies carried out 10 years later reach the opposite conclusion. Bramlage acknowledges that the exact mechanism of bone electrostimulation had not been worked out in 1984 and that a clear definition of osteogenesis and of bone healing was still needed. Because the effect of electromagnetic stimulation on osteogenesis greatly depends on the intensity and pulse duration, a study to determine the optimum settings was conducted in 1996. Eight different intensity levels and frequencies were used with five different pulse durations. Significant elevation in enzyme activity in bone marrow and osteogenesis were observed at intensities of 0.4, 1, and 2 G. Frequency settings proved to be insignificant to the outcome. Pulse durations of 25 and 50 microseconds produced more significant results than the other pulse durations.(19).

The scientist who has perhaps contributed the most to our understanding of the healing potential of magnetic fields is C. A. Bassett. He has conducted research and reported on the development and application of pulsed electromagnetic fields for nonunion fractures and other osseous conditions for 25 years. He has found PEMFs to be more than 90% effective in adult patients when used in conjunction with good management techniques. Bassett contends that bone unions occur because the weak electrical currents induced in tissues by the pulsed fields promote calcification of the fibrocartilage in the fracture gap. He says it is clear that different pulses affect different biologic processes. Selecting the proper pulse for a given pathologic entity is similar to the specific selection of pharmacologic agents.(20) This therapy deserves more careful study in the horse. Its efficacy, safety, and simplicity has prompted its use by the majority of orthopedic surgeons in this country.

A study examined the effect of PEMFs on bone loss associated with disuse by applying 1.5 Hz at 30 microsecond bursts to bones deprived of their normal functional load. After 12 weeks of stimulation at one hour a day, five days a week, the PEMF-treated bones had decreased by 9% in a cross-sectional area, compared to 23% for the untreated bones. The authors concluded that PEMFs reduced bone resorption on the bone surface.(21) Such an application could help in the treatment of osteoporosis.

To test this hypothesis, a 72 Hz PEMF was applied to the radii of osteoporosis-prone women for 10 hours a day for 12 weeks. Bone minerals were analyzed before, during, and after exposure. The bone mineral densities of the treated radii increased significantly in the immediate area of the field but decreased during the following 36 weeks. Studies such as this could lead to a method for treating the whole body in preventing or treating osteoporosis.(22)

Magnetic Field Devices

Devices that produce a magnetic field generally are divided into two groups: those made from a permanently magnetized material and those produced by a pulsing direct current.

Pulsing Electromagnetic Fields

Pulsed electromagnetic fields are time-varying magnetic fields with characteristics that induce voltage wave-form patterns in bone and soft tissue similar to those resulting from physical activity. (23) The biological effects are not caused by heating and have been the subject of extensive scientific study since the early 1970s.

PEMFs are produced when an intermittent direct current is passed through resistance wire. The wire is formed into coils; the more turns of the coil, the greater the strength of the magnetic field. These coils are enclosed in leather or plastic housing and placed directly on the treatment area. When the lower limb is treated, the injury can be placed between two coils, strengthening the magnetic field. Specific frequencies have been found to stimulate the healing of nonunion fractures, and PEMFs have FDA approval for this use.

Pulse frequency should be selected based on the nature of the injury. An acute injury is generally treated with lower frequencies, while chronic injury is treated with higher frequencies. Mid-range frequencies are used to relax the muscles and mind. Treatments generally range from 30 min-

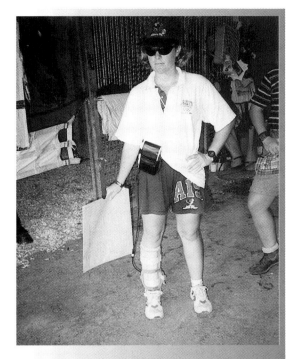

A rider who missed the Olympic Games in Atlanta due to a fracture that is being treated by pulsed magnetic therapy.

utes to an hour once or twice a day. When using PEMF devices, allow the horse to go into what I like to call meditative sleep and end the treatment when he wakes up.

Static magnets

Permanently magnetized material includes neodymium, ceramic, aluminum, nickel, iron, and cobalt.(24) The magnetized material is embedded in a flexible rubber or plastic pad. These pads come in shapes designed for wear on specific areas of the body for up to eight hours at a time.

Several companies offer wraps designed to conform to specific parts of the horse's leg.

Magnetic Pellets

Small ferrite magnetic pellets can be used on active acupuncture and trigger points. These pellets are available in sizes from 0.08 mm to 1.3 mm in diameter and strengths from 800 to 9,000 G. They are held in place with adhesive plasters or skin-safe glue. As Peggy Flemming, DVM, explains it, the injury current flows along acupuncture meridians and is perpetuated at acupuncture points, which, acting as semiconductors, amplify the signal along the meridian.(25) Overly strong magnetic pellets placed on an active acupuncture point or trigger point can cause discomfort. The most popular gauss level seems to be around 600.

Contraindications

Magnetic fields provide a safe, non-invasive form of therapy and have few contraindications. Perhaps the only danger would come from using magnets without a complete veterinary diagnosis. Do not leave magnetic wraps on for extended periods of time, especially during hot weather, as the wrap can rub a sore on the skin. Any wrap should be checked after an hour for hot spots or areas of pressure that could cause a sore. Acute injuries should be treated with ice and compression rather than with magnets.

Definitions

Electrical field — Force of electrical origin is exerted on a charged body placed at that point.

Electromagnet — A piece of metal that becomes a strong magnet when an electric current is passed through wire coiled around it.

Gauss — Unit of magnetic flux density.

Magnetic field — the space around a magnet in which its power of attraction is effective.

Magnetic flux — The total number of magnetic lines of force passing through a specified area

Permanent magnet — A magnet that retains its magneticism after the magnetizing force has been removed.

Tesla — Unit for measuring magnetic flux density. 1T = 1 Weber per meter squared.

Weber — Unit of magnetic flux (no accounting for area.)

References

1. Hudson, D. and Hudson, D. 1998. *Magnetic Field Therapy in Complementary and Alternative Veterinary Medicine.* AM. Schoen and SG. Wynn, eds. St. Louis, MO.:Mosby. 274-96.

2. McDowell, AD. and Lunt, MJ. 1991. Electromagnetic field strength measurements on megapulse units.

Physiotherapy. 77:805-09.

3. Pratt, G. 1998. The effect of the BIOflex magnet pad on flow rate of 5% aqueous saline solution. International Symposium on Biomagnetics, Magnetotherapy, and Postural Activity as described by Hudson and Hudson in *Complementary and Alternative Veterinary Medicine, Principles and Practice.* St. Louis, MO:Mosby. 280.

4. Cope, FW. 1981. On the relativity and uncertainty of electromagnetic energy measurement at a superconductive boundary, application to perception of weak magnetic fields by living systems. *Physiol, Chem, & Physics.* 13:231-38.

5. Glassman, LS. et al. 1986. Effect of external pulsing electromagnetic fields on the healing of soft tissue. *Ann Plast Surg.* 16:287-96.

6. Mentes, BB. et al. 1996. Influence of pulsed electromagnetic fields on healing of experimental colonic anastomosis. *Dis Colon Rectum.* 39:1031-38.

7. George, MS. et al. 1997. Mood improvement following daily left prefrontal repetitive transcranial magnetic stimulation in patients with depression: A placebo-controlled crossover trial. *Am J Psychiatry.* 154:1752-54.

8. Hansen, KM. 1983. Some observations with view to possible influence of magnetism upon human organism. *Acta Med Scand.* 97:339-64.

9. Vallbona, C. et al. 1997. Response of pain to static magnetic fields in post-polio patients: A double-blind pilot study. *Arch Phys Med Rehabil.* 78:1200-03.

10. Hong, CZ. et al. 1988. Magnetic Necklace: Its Therapeutic Effectiveness on Neck and Shoulder Pain. *Arch Phys Med Rehabil.* 63:462-66.

11. Thompson, K. unpublished study on magnetic pads and reflex pain. Gluck Equine Research Center. University of Kentucky.

12. Trock, DH. et al. 1994. The effect of pulsed electromagnetic fields in the treatment of osteoarthritis of the knee and cervical spine. Report of Randomized, Double Blind, Placebo Controlled Trials. *J of Rheum.* 21:1903-11.

13. Kobluk, CN. et al. 1994. A scintigraphic investigation of magnetic field therapy on the equine third metacarpus. *Vet Comparative Ortho Trauma.* 7:9-13.

13. Lin, Y. et al. 1992. Effects of pulsing electromagnetic fields on the ligament healing in rabbits. *J Vet Med Sci.* 54:1017-22.

15. Lin, Y. et al. 1993. Collagen production and maturation at the experimental ligament defect stimulated by pulsing electromagnetic fields in rabbits. *J Vet Med Sci.* 55:527-31.

16. Bassett, CA. et al. 1977. A non-operative salvage of surgically resistant pseudoarthrosis and nonunions by pulsing electromagnetic fields. *Clin Orthop.*124:128-43.

17. Cane, V. et al. 1993. Pulsed magnetic fields improve osteoblast activity during the repair of an experimental osseous defect. *J Orthop Res.* 11:664-70.

18. Bramlage, LR. et al. 1984. The effect of a pulsating electromagnetic field on the acute healing of equine cortical bone. Proceedings American Assocation of Equine Practitioners. 30:43-48.

19. Matsunaga, S. et al. 1966. Osteogenesis by pulsing electromagnetic fields (PEMFs): Optimum stimulation setting. *In Vivo.* 10:351-56.

20. Bassett, CA. 1985. The development and application of pulsed electromagnetic fields (PEMFs) for un-united fractures and arthrodeses. *Clin Plas Surg.* 12:259-77.

21. Skerry, TM. et al. 1991. Modulation of bone loss during disuse by pulsed electromagnetic fields. *J Orthop Res.* 9:600-08.

22. Tabrah, F. et al. 1990. Bone density changes in osteoporosis-prone women exposed to pulsed electromagnetic fields (PEMFs). *J Bone Miner Res.* 5:437-42.

23. Bassett, CA. 1989. Fundamental and practical aspects of therapeutic uses of pulsed electromagnetic fields (PEMFs). *Crit Rev Biomed Eng.* 17:451-529.

24. Hudson, D. and Hudson, D. 1998. Magnetic Field Therapy in *Complementary and Alternative Medicine.* Schoen and Wynn eds. St. Louis, MO:Mosby. 275.

25. Flemming, P. 1994. Acupuncture for Musculoskeletal and Neurologic Conditions in Horses in *Veterinary Acupuncture, Ancient Art to Modern Medicine.* AM. Shoen, ed. Goleta, CA:*American Veterinary Pub.* 506.

PHOTO CREDITS

CHAPTER 1
Mimi Porter, 11, 12, 24, 26; Anne M. Eberhardt, 17, 18, 22-23; The Blood-Horse, 27; courtesy of Tracy A. Turner, DVM, 28.

CHAPTER 2
Mimi Porter, 31, 39-41; Anne M. Eberhardt, 34, 39-41; Nanette T. Rawlins, 35.

CHAPTER 3
courtesy of Ronald J. Riegel, DVM, 43; Anne M. Eberhardt, 46.

CHAPTER 4
Mimi Porter, 52-54; Tempra Technology, 55; EBI,Inc. 56, Anne M. Eberhardt, 57.

CHAPTER 5
Mimi Porter, 61-62, 66, 70, 73, 74, 75; Robert Altman, 65; Anne M. Eberhardt, 74, 76, 79.

CHAPTER 6
Anne M. Eberhardt, 83-84, 88, 98, 100, 105, 108; Mimi Porter, 89, 91-92, 94, 96, 103, 111-112, 115, 119.

CHAPTER 7
Anne M. Eberhardt, 125, 128, 133; Mimi Porter, 131, 134, 136, 143-144, 147.

CHAPTER 8
Mimi Porter, 153, 156, 158, 163, 174. 180; John Porter, 157; Anne M. Eberhardt, 160, 166, 170; Equi-Light, 162, 171; Ric Redden, DVM, 177.

CHAPTER 9
Norfields, 185, 189, 191; Anne M. Eberhardt, 187; NRG, 190; Mimi Porter, 195.

Editor — Jacqueline Duke
Book design — Brian Turner
Cover photos — Anne M. Eberhardt, Barbara D. Livingston
Back cover photo — CliX Photography

MIMI PORTER, a pioneer in equine therapy, has drawn on her experience in human sports medicine to develop her concepts for rehabilitating injured horses. Porter, who has had a lifelong association with horses, began considering the possibilities of applying her therapeutic skills to horses during her 10-year tenure as an athletic trainer at the University of Kentucky.

In 1982, an equine veterinarian came to her for help in recovering from an ankle sprain. That encounter prompted Porter to found Equine Therapy Inc. the next year as it became clear that there was a need for physical therapy skills in equine medicine.

Porter, who lives in Lexington, Ky., earned a master's degree in physical education from the University of Kentucky in 1975 and became a nationally licensed athletic trainer in 1976. In 1990, she published the first edition of *Equine Sports Therapy*, and in 1996, served as staff equine therapist at the Olympic Games in Atlanta.

In addition to *The New Equine Sports Therapy*, Porter is a regular contributor to *The Horse: Your Guide to Equine Health* and has written for a number of veterinary publications.

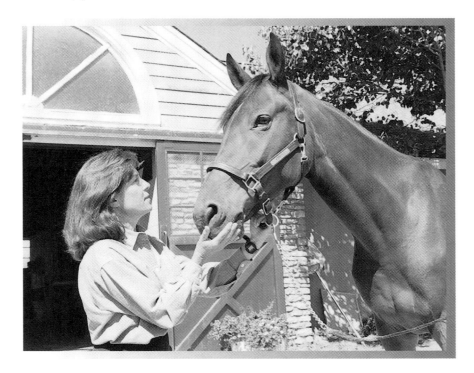